Innovative Technologies for Future Living

As of January 2023, there are 5 billion users of the internet. People who use technology and want to know about it—in simple language, without jargon. Many of those nurture dreams and aspirations to be quicker, smarter and "be the change." We bring to them relatable stories of everyday users, understood by consumers and gadget freaks alike.

We start with the Internet of Things (IoT) and show how consumers are using smart devices that teach them to manage their homes, travel and lifestyle through their smartphones. We see how cloud computing and artificial intelligence (AI) are enabling them to give feedback to IoT devices, and extracting multiple services from household products like the humble LED light, the refrigerator, sophisticated jet engines, or combined harvesters. As devices turn smart and AI and robots enter our workspace they run the risk of being hacked. So techies developed the Blockchain, with encrypted text that would secure digital assets. But with it arrived cryptocurrencies that threaten to bring unprecedented speculation, money laundering and cyber crimes.

We also explore new opportunities in telehealth, distant education and metaworld, and the strides made in digital transformation that has, in less than five years, empowered over 2 billion people across the world, giving them access to cost effective banking, education, travel, energy, food and health services. But the same technologies are used to fight wars and disrupt supply chains that cause acute distress and worldwide recessions. The book is relevant because the changes happening now are not incremental but tectonic. This opens the door to a future that is more fascinating and threatening than fiction. Read on to find out more.

Innovative Technologies for Future Living

Sandip Sen and Aarohi Sen

CRC Press is an imprint of the
Taylor & Francis Group, an **informa** business

First edition published 2024
by CRC Press
2385 Executive Center Drive, Suite 320, Boca Raton, FL 33431

and by CRC Press
4 Park Square, Milton Park, Abingdon, Oxon, OX14 4RN

© 2024 Sandip Sen and Aarohi Sen

CRC Press is an imprint of Taylor & Francis Group, LLC

Library of Congress Cataloging-in-Publication Data
Names: Sen, Sandip, author. | Sen, Aarohi, author.
Title: Innovative technologies for future living / Sandip Sen and Aarohi Sen.
Description: First edition. | Boca Raton : CRC Press, 2024. |
Includes bibliographical references.
Identifiers: LCCN 2023007612 (print) | LCCN 2023007613 (ebook) |
ISBN 9781032529820 (hbk) | ISBN 9781032529837 (pbk) |
ISBN 9781003409557 (ebk)
Subjects: LCSH: Technological forecasting. |
Technological innovations—Case studies. | CYAC: Future, The.
Classification: LCC T174 .S445 2024 (print) |
LCC T174 (ebook) | DDC 601/.12–dc23/eng/20230413
LC record available at https://lccn.loc.gov/2023007612
LC ebook record available at https://lccn.loc.gov/2023007613

ISBN: 9781032529820 (hbk)
ISBN: 9781032529837 (pbk)
ISBN: 9781003409557 (ebk)

DOI: 10.1201/9781003409557

Typeset in Sabon
by Newgen Publishing UK

Contents

About the Authors

Sandip Sen
Sandip Sen is a widely published, best-selling journalist and author. An engineer with over 30 years of experience in the energy and manufacturing industry, Sen decided to switch careers in 2008. Thereafter he worked in print and digital media as an editor with several nationally distributed newspapers and magazines and has written more than a thousand articles on business, economy, technology, sustainability and geopolitics in business dailies and think tanks. He also appears on television as a guest speaker on multiple channels. He has written three books on economy and banking, of which one *India Emerging, From Policy Paralysis to Hyper Economics* published by Bloomsbury in 2019, has been co-authored with Aarohi Sen.

Aarohi Sen
Aarohi Sen is an experienced thought leader at a leading consultancy firm that has a presence in 50 nations. He has been working on innovation in the future of IT and manufacturing for more than a decade. He is currently involved in managing a global research team that develops economic models around the themes of agile innovation, digital transformation and operational flexibility and provides research insights into key client engagements. He has been writing for several global and in-house publications for over a decade.

Preface

This book is a peek into popular science and technology with clear relevance to everyday life. It is an easy-paced nonfiction, that has many stories to tell, fun-filled and futuristic. These are the stories of how we are creating and adopting different technologies, for future living—told in a conversational tone and an easy language for the curious reader who has no background in the technology world. We also dig into the past and find that a few of these technologies have been evolving for ages and had a different avatar 500 or 5,000 years ago.

As of 2023, the world had 30 million technology developers and over 5 billion technology users. Yet, over 90% of technology books are aimed toward developers and experts and very few toward the uninitiated "technology user." This book aims to assist the future living of the "5 billion plus technology users"—explore how this tech world operates and how they help our continuous development and use consumer data from us to also benefit themselves.

The book has been written by a journalist and a thought leader. Two authors who, like many others, were surprised, having to grapple with multiple technologies simultaneously taking off since the 1990s. So, with nearly five decades of work and writing experience in the industry behind us, we decided to research and chronicle ten frequently used technologies that will have great relevance in the near future. We explored not only the business of technology but how dozens of innovations that straddle the laboratories of top universities are working to create circular and efficient economies. We hope to capture the current interest of this generation in digital transformation and the business of sustainability and help them to explore new challenges and find solutions to help our planet.

The timing is crucial because the worldwide changes that are happening now are herculean and will affect how the future unfolds. The authors bring original insights from scientists and entrepreneurs, thought leaders, businesspeople, academics and social scientists. One may or may not agree with them, for a few opinions are both debatable and controversial and a few simplistic while few take a contrarian view. However, they provide an understanding of how to survive and negotiate difficulties at a time when trade, economic and biological wars, cross-border terrorism, armed invasions and cyber wars pose fresh challenges to humankind.

The book is important, because it is not limited to what science and technology have to offer. It is also a story about real time politics that dictate our lives and choices and guides what we adopt and leave behind. It also asks us many questions. For example, why, despite their apparent success, the Internet of Things and artificial intelligence worry Brad Smith enough to claim that Orwell's *1984* could happen in 2024. Or why Chuck Collins decides to write about the professional class of enablers who are paid millions to hide trillions. While we are making great strides in innovation in many fields, science and technology is not helping everyone equally. In some cases, it is hurting equity and sustainable development. *The younger generation who are avid users of science and technology may like to explore these issues and make necessary sustainable and equitable changes during their lifetime.*

Introduction

It took thousands of years for humans to unravel the mysteries of science. Computers arrived 70 years ago, followed soon after by the internet. This dual capability has facilitated the dissemination of information at high speed and low cost. It has revolutionized automation and rapidly improved education, healthcare, transportation, construction, manufacturing, agriculture and many other disciplines. The speed of development has been startling, and the disruptive innovations relentless. This has been at a time when the internet connected only with humans and largely on a one-to-one basis.

The future will be more intense. It will see further disruptions. The internet will not only connect with humans but with "things." These "things" will act not only as instructed by human intelligence but by artificial intelligence (AI). They will connect not on a one-to-one basis but with their makers, multiple collaborators and users simultaneously. As "things" become smart, they turn products into lifelong services. They are digitally connected with their makers, who in turn use a constant stream of information from their users to make the product think, act and communicate. It could be anything from your car to an ingestible pill that tracks and monitors tumors in your digestive system or brain.

However, the Internet of Things would have to draw its inputs from big data in the cloud that could be only processed by AI. We explore the concepts of machine learning and AI, and robotics and how such intelligence has been developed, and machines have been trained to think like humans. We also investigate the threat to humankind from AI and robots running rogue and the need to secure their software with some kind of digital lock to prevent hacking and destruction. This brings us to the technology of digital encryption and blockchain and then inevitably to cryptocurrencies, volatility and cybercrimes that have grown exponentially with the advent of the decentralized currency.

We also explore new applications, like telehealth and digital education, besides virtual reality and the advances made in digital transformation that

DOI: 10.1201/9781003409557-1

has brought technology to every doorstep. This enormous leap taken by humankind in the last few years has also posed several challenges.

In the third section of this book, we focus on those challenges in an intensely competitive and fractured world of today, where war-torn nations are adversaries, no longer thinking of globalization but of localization. We examine how the world is being torn apart and may be forced to build separate supply chains and how resource shortages would force new recycling operations, ultimately push-starting a circular economy—a long overdue new beginning.

Documenting a rapidly spinning story of the technology world is challenging, and many theories and developments recounted here are in the early stages and may be contested. We thank Gabriella Williams and the highly experienced publishing team at CRC Press, who churn out hundreds of top technology titles annually, along with the five peer reviewers from different geographies who gave us valuable guidance.

Part I

Technologies That We Use

Chapter 1

The Internet of Things

All Things Interactive

This book has been written for the avid technology user of our times—the young adult, the millennial and everyone else who is keen to know about the science behind the things we use. You may be a singer, dancer, poet, doctor or architect, but you will still use the internet as well as the IoT and would want to know about them. Before delving into IoT and its applications, we will first explore the interesting evolution of the internet itself to see how we got to the situation that we currently find ourselves in.

THE EVOLUTION OF THE INTERNET

In the 1970s, after the Vietnam War, the US Army wanted computers to talk and communicate over long distances with each other. So, it engaged half a dozen computer scientists who converted words that were typed on the terminal into code or packets of data and transmitted them as radio signals. The exercise looked simple. But after this data was downloaded at Menlo Park, California, it unexpectedly took more than 10 years to seamlessly transmit these data packets from one computer to another in a readable form creating a local area network (LAN).

The National Science Foundation provided the first internet backbone (NSFNET) in the US in 1986 with 56 kilobits per second (Kbps) circuits. Initially, around 2,000 supercomputers in educational institutions were connected with LAN. Then, 5 years later, 2 million users across the US were connected free of cost, and the network had to be upgraded to 45 megabits per second (Mbps). At that time, personal computers in Europe were being connected by Tim Berners Lee and other scientists at CERN Geneva. The first-generation mobile network (1G) was introduced and was all about transmitting voices through analog signals.

We were used to landlines then, connecting through a 5 pound (lb) fixed-line telephone, and intercity calls were done by booking a trunk call through telephone exchanges. It was a time when bulky film reels were physically carried by runners from theater to theater so that moviegoers

DOI: 10.1201/9781003409557-3

in small towns could see the same film during the day. So, the first cell phones, a handheld wireless device with an extractable antenna, were a real novelty.

Massive 600-ft telecom towers usually set up by the postal departments were few and far between. Mobile connectivity was very rudimentary. Comedian Ernie Wise, dressed in a coachman's garb, made the first mobile call in Britain from the Dickens pub in St. Catherine's Dock to Vodafone headquarters in the mid-1980s. Thereafter, the Global System for Media Communications, better known as the GSM architecture, was developed by the European Telecommunication Standards Institute (ETSI). The ETSI formulated the standards for the second-generation (2G) wireless communication, which was adopted worldwide. You could use the 2G network on phones made by Motorola, Nokia, Ericsson and Samsung. At that time, Apple and BlackBerry phones had not yet arrived.

The 2G network introduced in the 1990s was about transmitting voice and text messages (SMS and MMS). This was because the 2G protocol allowed voice and bits of data to be transferred digitally from one phone to another instead of through analog signals used by the previous generation. Since its arrival, data speeds have gone up tenfold every 5 years. Cell phones became very popular, and models, such as the classic Nokia 3210, have become symbolic of this period.

The World Wide Web was introduced in 1991. Soon, many of us had internet connections, but we were still dependent on an overground cable connection for the last mile of connectivity, making the entire system unpredictable. Those were the early days of the internet era. Every time there was bad weather, the internet connection would be disrupted.

The wireless network, popularly known as Wi-Fi for the home user and the broadband network with third-generation (3G) connectivity for smartphones, took another 10 years to arrive. The Wi-Fi connectivity eliminated the last mile of wiring. Called "open spectrum," it was like giving wings to the internet. A small black box called a router could distribute broadband connectivity to an area the size of a football field. The technology of this nondescript Wi-Fi router has made it possible for railway stations, airports, Starbucks outlets and cinema halls to provide open access hot spots or free internet connectivity at public spaces. The Wi-Fi potential will be fully realized when satellites start bypassing telecom companies selling expensive spectrum to the consumer—something we briefly discuss at the end of this chapter.

THE ARRIVAL OF SMARTPHONES

However, it did not take long for something more interesting than Wi-Fi routers to appear. Apple introduced the smartphone in 2007. The 3G network permitted the transmission of voice, texts and data. Everything was falling into place. By 2010, data speeds crossed 5 Mbps and the worldwide internet traffic grew to 200 petabytes per month, according to networking giant CISCO. Smartphones soon became very popular. They had the capability to access the internet and take pictures, as well as make calls and send text messages and data.

Undersea fiber-optic cables that could transmit fourth-generation (4G) services were introduced in 2015. By then, data speeds had jumped to over 50 Mbps. This was more than enough to have high-quality video calls, play games or stream video from the internet uninterrupted. The 4G network was similar to 3G, except that it could carry more data at faster speeds.

The IoT became a possibility with fifth-generation (5G) wireless services, as data speeds have exceeded 500 Mbps, ten times the speed of 4G, and total internet data traffic has touched 194 billion GB per month in 5 years. Such speeds will make downloads and streaming content ultrafast. It will also enable currently underexplored technologies like virtual reality and augmented reality to become possible. It will provide the speed, bandwidth and reliability for autonomous vehicles, smart homes and smart cities to become a reality. The 5G spectrum expands the usable frequencies for data transfer and has the ability to connect a large number of devices, providing extremely lean and low-cost connectivity. This means it will be able to carry more data at a higher speed and connect to many devices at a lower cost. This dual capability makes the Internet of Things possible.

WHAT IS THE INTERNET OF THINGS?

We are now familiar with the internet, but the IoT is still a new concept to many of us. The IoT has been a buzzword in tech circles for a few years, and for a good reason. A lot of the recent developments and "smart" applications using technology—in our homes, our jobs, our education and our society—have been deeply influenced by the IoT.

The internet helped computers communicate. The IoT helps products communicate by connecting products or "things" to the internet. Broadly speaking, the IoT allows you to start, stop, monitor, control and operate all connected smart products, industrial as well as domestic. When you use your phone to control the geyser thermostat in your washroom, potentially without even being in your house, you are using the IoT. When your doorbell has a camera that allows you to see, hear, and speak to visitors from your device, that is the IoT. When you own an Apple watch that can monitor your sleep patterns, activity levels and health conditions, that is the IoT.

The dozens of electric lights in your home were always there, but they were not initially "smart"—yet can be made so with the IoT. The LCDs can become variable and multicolored on your voice command to Alexa according to your mood, work, bathing and sleeping routines. Software with inputs from multiple experts, like sleep apnea and mental health specialists, educators, music companies, sex therapists and so forth, interacts with the input from lighting designers, hardware companies and cloud computers, processing feedback from the room's occupants on what is needed. It recognizes that your study has different needs than your bedroom, living room and bathroom. Each light in these rooms can be programmed differently to meet the user's needs. Your bathroom light could be equipped with sensors to switch on and off as you enter and exit so that you would not have to grope for the light switch at night. With this technology, the lights which were "sell and forget" products only a few years back have become a lifelong service to meet your varied needs at different times, all enabled by the IoT.

As "things" turn into smart products, they are all quickly becoming lifelong services. They are being digitally connected to their makers, who use a constant stream of user data to make the product think, perform and communicate better. A logistics company might use the IoT to monitor shipments, routes and conditions to make sure their service is running at its best. If they need to alter anything, they have the data and ability to do so. So, just by using IoT products, we are also actively improving our capabilities.

The IoT has millions of retail, industrial, educational and military applications. The number of active IoT devices is estimated to have exceeded 10 billion in 2020, with revenues exceeding $180 billion. This includes dedicated functional devices like cooking ranges, jet engines, bathroom showers, vending machines, fitness bands, music systems, automobiles and much more.

HOW DOES THE IOT WORK?

To become smart all "things" must be fitted with microprocessors—tiny electronic components, which are programmed to perform all of the instructions and tasks needed to make a device work as intended. The devices also need to have their own IP addresses and be connected to the internet. They must further have sensors, measuring and monitoring temperature, color, odor, speed, direction or any other element that can help them function autonomously or remotely.

Every "thing" in your home, car or office can be accessed and operated remotely through the IoT. Gadgets like mobile phones, computers and televisions are already connected to the internet and function in a "smart" way. Others, such as home lighting, air conditioners, deep freezers, toasters, dog collars, door locks and so forth, can turn smart if they are fitted with microprocessors. For example, you can stick Amazon Dash IoT buttons to your washing machine or dishwasher and order detergents automatically.

If your refrigerator was smart and had IoT sensors to record the temperature and condition of all products within, it would transmit real time data on its contents. This data would tell you the quantity, temperature and condition of all your vegetables, meat, apples, milk, beer and cooked food stored within. With that information you would know when you were running out of supplies and when to buy what. That would be an enormous amount of data on a minute-to-minute basis. For this reason, it would not be directly stored in the limited memory of your phone or computer but would rather be sent to a remote centralized storage location, better known as a cloud server. This data can be accessed by you when needed and transmitted through all connected devices like your remote, smartphone or laptop. You could also choose to let that information flow directly to your supplier of milk, vegetables and meat. That would free you from the daily chore of purchasing products and instead permit you to spend your evenings enjoying yourself.

Batman, who has been our beloved technology freak among the superheroes, was an early adopter of the IoT. In the movie *The Dark Knight* he fights the Joker by using his special power of echolocation, seeing the world around him through the mobile phones of others, which act like cloud servers. Some Silicon Valley investors like Peter Levine strongly feel that one day cloud servers, which store your data now, will no longer be needed. Instead, smartphones will have enough storage capability to act as self-contained data banks with data portability features. Although you still can't teleport using a bat helmet like our superhero, the film is a great story for future technologies that would transmit data directly from smart devices to handsets.

Driverless cars with fractional response time already use direct data transmission instead of cloud servers. These cars need a quick response time to avoid road accidents. The traffic data that the sensors receive must be instantly processed. Fractions of seconds become important. There is not enough time for the information to go to the cloud servers. So, edge computers located in the cars have to process this information instead.

HOW DID WE GET TO IOT?

Radio Frequency Identification (RFID) tagging is considered as a precursor to the IoT. The technology involves using radio frequencies to track and identify items. A RFID reader device is connected to a network that can send and receive signals via radio waves. Once an item's tag is activated, it can send signals to the reader, which are then transferred into data. The data can include things, such as the name, description, condition, amount and location of the items. RFID tags are used in modern passports and ID cards, for example, to store information about the holder, such as their name, date of birth, photo and passport expiration date. This information helps to identify the holder.

There are multiple applications where objects are tracked by radio frequency. Low frequency RFID tags have a short-read capability of 10 cm
and are used for livestock tracking in poultry and animal farms. In New
Zealand, thousands of sheep will come near a fence when a tourist bus
stops, so that visitors can look at them, all on RFID prodding as they go
out to graze and go back home without any human monitoring whatsoever.
High frequency tags have a range of up to 1 m and are used for security
locks on doors, credit card payments, electronic ticketing and data transfer.
The cheapest varieties are ultra-high frequency tags that are used in inventory tracking.

RFID has been in use for more than 50 years by retailers and logistics
firms. The tags are very useful for managing inventory, so a store can know
how many of each item they have and where to locate them. When you go to
any shopping mall and buy an item of clothing, the salesperson at the billing
counter removes the RFID tag once the product is billed. If the RFID tag is
not removed, it will beep and embarrass you at the exit gate.

This RFID tag has not been attached by the storekeeper. It has been the
companion of the product right from its inception. Let us say the fabric of
the jeans sold by a global brand comes from Mexico and it is stitched in
Vietnam. The jeans are to be sold in India, Bangladesh, the Philippines and
Indonesia. The RFID tag records all operations during procurement and
processing of the fabric, including its cutting, dyeing, washing, stitching,
labeling, packing, shipment, movement across nations, storage, distribution
and finally sales. All of this information is relayed to a centralized computer
system. It helps in improving the supply chain transparency and identifying
the carbon footprint of each item. Smart devices use both the RFID and the
barcode technologies that need scanning. They are used for tracking things
and personnel, as well as providing unique identification, controlling access
to restricted areas and even surveillance.

Kevin Ashton, the Executive Director of the research group Auto-ID Labs
at Massachusetts Institute of Technology (MIT), was reportedly the first to
describe the IoT, two decades ago. When making a presentation for consumer giant Procter & Gamble, he stated

> "Today computers, and, therefore, the internet, are almost wholly
> dependent on human beings for information. Nearly all of the roughly
> 50 petabytes of data available on the internet were first captured and
> created by human beings by typing, pressing a record button, taking
> a digital picture, or scanning a bar code. The problem is people have
> limited time, attention, and accuracy. All of which means they are not
> very good at capturing data about things in the real world. If we had
> computers that knew everything there was to know about things, using

data they gathered without any help from us, we would be able to track and count everything and greatly reduce waste, loss, and cost. We would know when things needed replacing, repairing, or recalling and whether they were fresh or past their best."

Kevin Ashton

But Ashton believed that RFID tagging was a prerequisite to the IoT. According to him, if all devices were "tagged," computers could manage, track and add them to the inventory. It was later discovered that "things" that were initially tagged with RFID tags could be better accessed via the internet if they were fitted with IoT microprocessors. So, an IoT microprocessor was permanently installed in all products. Activating these "things" with the microprocessor gave the user the capability to interact with the product and carry out certain specified commands to start, stop, monitor and operate the product through cloud servers and a handheld device.

FROM IMAGINATION TO FUTURE REALITY

The IoT and artificial intelligence (AI) became famous and infamous as soon as they were born. The mere concept of computer chips connecting products and users, without human intervention, was exciting and frightening. It was a distant future and its endless possibilities needed to be tested and shown to the world, and as expected, Hollywood did it superbly. Just like new warfare equipment, most futuristic technology needs imaginative storytelling to explore its boundaries. Designers at Lockheed Martin, General Dynamics and Boeing are said to be avid watchers of Hollywood action movies just like researchers at Silicon Valley. Besides, technology needs feedback from people to gauge whether the story it wants to tell or the picture it wants to paint has caught the imagination of the consumers who are going to use it.

"Imagination testing" is the first level of approval that futuristic technologies need to clear. Does the product appeal to your imagination? This comes years before prototype testing nowadays, because prototypes are expensive to build and test. If the prototype the scientist builds does not catch the imagination of the buyer, they will not invest in the technology. So, it is easier to tell a story or create a film and find out what the buyer wants.

However, it was not always like this. There was a time when people invested in prototypes first to check out an idea. Remember Jules Verne, the father of modern-day science fiction who wrote *Twenty Thousand Leagues Under the Sea*, with his famous Captain Nemo aboard the Nautilus. Many of you may not know that Nautilus was a real submarine project that failed to take off.

American inventor Robert Fulton designed the Nautilus when working for the French Government in 1800. It was a 21-ft all-metal craft and is known to be one of the world's first working submarines. It had an oblong, cigar-shaped hull, a copper conning tower, a four-blade propellor (for moving underwater), a collapsible mast and fan sail (to move on the surface), and compressed oxygen storage for the crew. Nautilus was an expensive prototype that made several successful test dives under the sea in the early nineteenth century. But it failed to win approval either from the French or the British navies because it was unable to travel long distances when remaining underwater. Fulton had no prior feedback that the buyers would want the vessel to not only dive deep into the sea but also travel in submerged conditions for days. The project was abandoned, and Fulton returned home to the US after which he went on to build the world's first commercial steamboat.

Many submarine prototypes were built in the eighteenth and nineteenth centuries, but none really succeeded in impressing the navies across the world. So, in 1870 when Jules Verne wrote his science fiction masterpiece on a seafaring submarine, he spelled out the expectations of users. Verne's fictional Nautilus had advanced features. Importantly, it could stay underwater for many days at a time and travel long distances. The book immediately became a worldwide success and a template for submarine builders to emulate.

Three decades later, in 1897, an American engineer Simon Lake built the Argonaut, a 36-ft craft powered by a 30-horsepower gasoline engine, which was the first commercially viable submarine in the world. It was not built for military duty but for underwater salvage operations. The most unusual feature was a set of wheels that allowed it to "drive" on the seafloor. It was capable of traveling long distances and regularly traveled from Virginia to New Jersey to salvage shipwrecks in Chesapeake Bay. It also had a periscope, a diving chamber and a floating hose to provide air for the engine and crew. As it included several features of Captain Nemo's submarine, it instantly earned applause from Jules Verne himself.

Though the science fiction of Jules Verne, HG Wells and Jack London inspired futuristic technologies initially, it was Hollywood movies that took over the storytelling after the Vietnam War. In 1977, *Star Wars* was the biggest box office success, depicting futuristic warfare technology for a space war. It inspired an advanced missile defense system named the Strategic Defense Initiative. It was even adopted by President Ronald Reagan in the early eighties as a regular defense initiative but proved prohibitively expensive. It lost its utility after the Cold War with the Soviet Union ended. It was eventually watered down and redesignated by President Clinton into yet another ballistic missile program.

The Hollywood blockbuster *The Matrix*, released in 1999, was possibly the first movie that depicted the impact of IoT and AI. It was a futuristic war of supremacy between man and machines. Here, man was the destroyer of the environment, who blocked off the sun that was the power source for bots. To curb the expansionist and destructive policies of humankind, machines started to grow humans. They cultivated human brains in a computer-simulated world and kept their bodies alive to generate bioelectricity. This led humans to rebel against The Matrix. The movie showed the capability of machines with embedded chips to function as efficiently as humans and highlighted the possibility of a war between man and machine.

Just like Jules Verne's novel set new boundaries for submarine technology, *The Matrix* galvanized the attention of the technology majors working on the IoT. After its release, *Star Trek, Mission Impossible, X-Men, Next, Guardians of the Galaxy* and scores of other movies followed. Coincidentally, the interest in the IoT and advanced machine learning (ML) peaked, and manufacturing picked up pace. It appeared that the entertainment industry had inspired the development of technology-driven combat that immensely benefited tech giants and the US arms industry.

FUTURE APPLICATIONS OF IOT

As the IoT continues to develop, and the networks it runs on continue to improve, a whole host of new and exciting applications will become possible. Let us examine some of them here. Smart homes are perhaps the most tangible application for everyday life. Ten years from now, your house might be full of gadgets that make all areas of your life more comfortable. Smart devices will clean your home, mow your lawn, take out the trash for you and order food and toiletries for you so you never run low. Your morning alarm will adjust automatically to your schedule, and your coffee maker will automatically begin to brew you a fresh cup of coffee in the morning. You will be able to check your home security even when you are at work or on holiday.

Along with your smart home you will also drive an autonomous vehicle—or, more accurately, it will drive you. Your car will take you to your destination without you having to control it. It will automatically detect roads, obstacles and other cars and keep track of these in minute detail with the edge computers in your car linking to the 5G network, to avoid the errors of judgment introduced by humans, which can lead to traffic accidents.

Smart cities are one of the most futuristic applications of the IoT. Smart cities will use the IoT to manage their resources in a more efficient, environmentally friendly and economically beneficial way. Smart parking will allow drivers to access a list of available parking spaces at any time, reducing time and energy on the part of the driver, but also reducing traffic congestion and emissions. Garbage can be automatically collected only when trash cans are actually full. Smart streetlights can only be on full power when needed, avoiding damaging effects to wildlife and unnecessary costs.

One of the most important but understated areas of operations is smart drainage. It helps avoid the flooding of roads and neighborhoods during heavy rain and thunderstorms. Busan, a vibrant port city of South Korea with a population exceeding 3.5 million, was hit by successive typhoons in 1991, 2003 and 2016. In 2017 Mayor Suh of Busan asked a tech major to introduce cognitive analytics to its disaster management program. The flood control was done by using advanced forecasting techniques and the IoT programming of levees, stream gates, underwater emergency tanks and submersible pumps to ward off huge surges in water during typhoons and cyclonic storms.

Healthcare is also an extremely important area here. The IoT will allow healthcare to be cheaper and more efficient, but more importantly it will become much more personalized. Devices will be able to monitor health conditions in real time and analyze the data received to report emergencies or provide data for doctors to examine when deciding on treatment. The IoT can also monitor the functioning of medical equipment and note any errors before these have an effect. It can even track your medication schedule and make sure you take and reorder your medicines on time.

As communications inevitably expand into sixth-generation (6G) networks—a topic already being discussed in research circles—these applications of the IoT will continue to become faster, more personalized and more efficient. Very little is known about the benefits and use of 6G, and it is actually before the imagination testing stage right now—still standards are being written for its implementation.

THE BIG BOYS OF IOT

Now that we have learned a little about the history and future applications of the IoT, we need to know more about the main players in this segment. We will also get a glimpse into the intense competition and global politics behind this high-cost and high-stakes technology platform, which is intensifying with trade wars and sanctions. The market for the IoT needs many technology providers, from makers of software and embedded chips to manufacturers of processors, sensors and memory devices to fiber-optic majors and network providers.

The five technology majors—Apple, Google, Microsoft, Facebook and Amazon—control most of the software developed. There are about a dozen hardware makers of IoT chips, including Intel Corporation, Texas Instruments, Qualcomm, AMD, NVIDIA and Microchip Technology from the US, NXP Semiconductors NV (Netherlands), Taiwan Semiconductor Manufacturing Co. and MediaTek Inc. (Taiwan), Renesas Electronics Corporation (Japan), Huawei Technologies (China) and Samsung Electronics (South Korea).

For most other products like processors, sensors and memory devices the majority of the manufacturers are in the US or South Korea. Producers from Europe, Japan, Korea, China and Taiwan control around 50% of the market. Yet, the IoT usage is the highest in China and South Korea, which are way ahead when providing the requisite infrastructure. There is huge competition among nations in this segment despite prohibitively high costs. That leads to espionage, hacking, piracy, patents, rights violations and litigation that goes into billions of US dollars. It could also lead to cyber wars this very decade. Hence, at this stage, it is crucial to understand the vital importance of secrecy and high security in technological development for intellectual property protection.

SECURITY, THEFT AND ESPIONAGE

It may not be out of place to recount the very interesting story of Huawei Technologies—the Chinese telecom giant that is a leader in the 5G Telecom Network. The Chinese company has been accused of theft and security breaches and has been banned in the US, UK, Canada and Australia. It has also been accused of unfair practices like bribery and manipulating prices to get international orders for the IoT and 5G network services. Huawei has refuted the allegations and is fighting court cases in various nations to avoid sanctions and criminal investigations.

The company was set up by Ren Zhengfei, a former military engineer in Shenzhen Province, China in 1987. It was supplying low-cost telecom gear like switches, routers and modems across China. In 2000, it got a credit of $10.6 billion to expand its export market and focused on Canada. At that time Nortel was Canada's rock star technology company, with sales exceeding $250 billion in fiber-optic networks and 3G and 4G communication. It is reported that soon after Huawei became an equipment supplier to Nortel, the Canadian Security Intelligence Service alerted Nortel of unusual traffic on its site from China—suggesting that Nortel's intellectual property was being compromised by Chinese hackers.

In 2004 Frank Dunn, Nortel's CEO, was fired due to an accounting scandal, and it was revealed that more than 800 confidential documents were sent from his IP address to Shanghai Faxian Corp. US intelligence found this to be a China-based front company, possibly operating for Huawei Technologies and the Chinese military. On further investigation, it was revealed that Chinese hackers had breached the accounts of six senior executives of Nortel, including Dunn, and had stolen thousands of confidential and critical documents of product development and technology research.

The security breaches and malpractices at Nortel; however, remained unplugged as per Bloomberg. By 2009 Canada's top wireless company went bankrupt. Huawei reportedly went on to hire 20 top Nortel engineers who had been working on 5G wireless technology and fiber-optics networks. That is when it became apparent that a very large part of the technology team at Nortel had been compromised for years. It is alleged that Huawei— riding on stolen data from Nortel—went on to become one of the biggest players in the 5G space. The data theft has been refuted by Huawei, which won contracts from Canada, the UK and other nations to establish itself as the second largest player in the telecom industry, only behind South Korea's Samsung Electronics.

In 2018 the US Federal Communications Commission formally accused Huawei of data theft, following which its Chief Financial Officer Meng Wanzhou, the eldest daughter of its founder Ren Zhengfei, was placed under house arrest in Ottawa. Nonetheless, Huawei has grown to be a $120 billion telecom giant with 190,000 employees and research and development centers in many countries including Canada, the US, UK, India, Pakistan and Russia. Its telecom gear and 5G technology are much cheaper than the American, European or Korean competitors, which makes it difficult to ignore its products despite the risks.

The spectacular rise of Huawei and the quick collapse of Nortel shows that if you want to excel in futuristic technologies, you must be alert to theft and espionage that occur on a large scale. Nothing from bribery to hacking is out of bounds for competitors to gain the vital technological edge. You must also arm yourself with an army of cyber security experts who can pre-empt attacks and secure your assets and help minimize damage from enemy attacks that hack into your database and disrupt your business plans.

ECONOMIC VIABILITY

Another key challenge for telecom majors investing in the IoT is managing new investment and the upgrading of standards that the new technologies demand. The regulations for the next generation 6G network that is expected to kick in after 2023 will introduce new changes again. Like the original GSM architecture, the IoT technology is heavily dependent on base stations for data transmission. The upgrading from 5G to 6G technology means that the infrastructure will have to change along with the wireless technology and its wavelengths. So, costs are going to be very high as we try to achieve higher data speeds and realize the IoT dream.

A Qualcomm report says that the full economic potential of 5G technology of $13 trillion will be realized by 2035. Industry insiders fear that by the time 5G technology stabilizes and brings profit to its investors, 6G technology will have stepped in, luring away the early adopters. Despite the noise, by the end of 2022 barely 500 cities of the world have had real time 5G rollouts backed by a 70% fiber network and half of them are in China. Also lurking in the background are Google's 4G-LTE project connecting 2,000 satellites for worldwide networking, Amazon's Project Kuiper with 3236 satellites providing high speed internet connectivity, Elon Musk's 3200 low orbit Starlink satellites, which provided connectivity to war torn Ukraine, and Greg Wyler's One Web project—all of which may threaten to make the 5G and 6G networks redundant. If these satellites connect directly to Wi-Fi routers in your home to provide internet connectivity, why would you pay at all for the expensive spectrum that telecom companies sell to you?

In view of competition and rising costs, analysts have started looking at the economic viability of the IoT and examining if the cost today far exceeds the benefit it provides. Does the IoT focus less on the return-on-investment and too much on attracting tomorrow's clients? The life cycle of the 2G cellular network was close to 15 years. That amount of time was adequate to gain comfortable returns on investment. This was followed by 3G technology that ruled for less than a decade. Just as the 3G network providers were breaking even, the next generation technology arrived. The lifespan of the 4G network is even shorter. Before it has earned enough money to justify its investment comes the pricier 5G, which has approximately 5 years to prove itself.

To understand existing technologies, one must know the future of innovations that are a threat to its economic viability. Author and motivational speaker Tom Peters says, "It never ceases to amaze me that companies spend millions to attract new customers (people they don't know) and spend next to nothing to keep the ones they've got. Seems to me the budgets should be reversed!"

Amazon founder Jeff Bezos takes the thought further, "We see our customers as invited guests to a party, and we are the hosts. It's our job to make the customer experience a little bit better."

That, again, can be done only if money is rightly spent on existing customers.

Telecom operators will soon be asking themselves one question. Should they pump investment into 4G, 5G or 6G networks? Is there enough time to get the new 5G customers in and enough business to breakeven, considering the stupendous investment costs? Will industry profits shrink because of the reduced timespan? Should they migrate to satellite tech? Or would it be wiser to skip one generation of cellular network technology and let the old technology plow back?

DO WE HAVE TOO MUCH DATA?

As we continue to improve our networks and infrastructure, the key question remains: Will we be using our resources and technology efficiently? Or will we be mindlessly investing in higher data speeds and data storage with diminishing returns for every investment? Even today, the amount of data we have in the cloud servers cannot be analyzed and put to use efficiently by a human population of 8 billion. Believe it or not, it worked out to nearly 27 GB per person per month in 2020. Additionally, going by past trends, this data availability will grow tenfold in the next 5 years. Known as "Big Data" this is something that we humans cannot use or analyze or benefit from with our 3 lb brain.

So, we need help.

We need to find an entity with intelligence similar to humans, who can first sort the necessary information from the "Big Data" slush pile. One who can do it far more quickly and economically than humans. So, we come back again to machines to sort out the relevant data first and then process it for us. We come to another new age technology called ML and AI. The IoT is of no use to us unless we are able to use the feedback or user information from the Big Data that we collect. To start using this Big Data efficiently, we must use the help of this rapidly evolving AI technology.

In the next chapter we will talk about AI and how it will use this Big Data to take care of human needs in the coming decade.

Chapter 2

Artificial Intelligence

Adding to Our Three Pounds

Thousands of years ago, humans learned to store what they could not consume. The move from hunter-gatherer groups to agricultural societies happened during the Stone Age, 10,000 years ago, only after humans developed and learned the use of storage.

PRACTICE OF ACCUMULATION

Every year the Nile river basin used to flood by September, depositing fresh alluvial soils that helped to grow multiple crops. When the Egyptians developed a massive surplus of food grains, they built enormous granaries for storage. It gave them a reason to settle down in one location instead of moving from place to place for food. The earliest evidence of such storage has been found southwest of Cairo and even around the Dead Sea in Jordan.

Soon accumulation became a habit for you, me and everyone. Look in your closet, and you will probably find more clothes and shoes than you can ever wear in a lifetime. Look at your phone or laptop, and you will find that 80% of the stored files have not been accessed by you in the last year and will probably never be used. This practice of accumulation by humans, though unsustainable, has gone to absurd limits. At the height of the Cold War, in 1986, the world had more than 70,000 active nuclear weapons, a stockpile that could destroy the world 10,000 times. Building and storing nukes was not only difficult and dangerous but a prohibitively expensive proposition. It meant higher military budgets and, consequently, lower allocations for food, education and healthcare. After decades of peace talks and disarmament, the number of nukes was reduced to 15,000. But they are more lethal and could still destroy the world a thousand times over.

Like food grains, clothes or nuclear warheads, humans keep acquiring and storing data. The internet transfers close to 1 million gigabytes (GB) of data every minute. With the rapid proliferation of smartphones, 1 trillion photographs were uploaded to the internet in 2018. All this has led to a massive accumulation of data. The world today has stored 20 times more data than it can use. The falling price of data and the increase in storage cap-acity has created this massive bank of data that we call "big data." Big data means large volumes of data—both structured in standardized databases like Excel files that we can use easily, and unstructured data like emails, videos and audio files that need to be accessed individually.

WHERE AND HOW IS YOUR DATA STORED?

The AI lab at MIT was set up in the early 1970s. At that time, each user had a localized data bank and a processor for computation. In the absence of centralized storage, each database was fragmented. By the 1990s, most tech companies had given up on IoT and AI. Investors originally optimistic about IoT suddenly became reluctant to pump money into the technology. That period was called the winter of IoT when profits from firms that were developing these technologies slipped and investments froze. This happened largely because there was not enough data to process. Data was fragmented, speeds were slower and storage costs were high.

The advent of cloud computing changed everything, as it enabled the storage of big data to process. The term "cloud" was devised to indicate the easy accessibility of big data from any location and device. According to the MIT Technology Review Post, the word "cloud computing" was first coined by the technology team at Compaq in 1996 when working on ways to find the delivery of services through the internet. The "centralized remote location cloud storage" concept took root a few years later.

In 2006, Amazon Web Services (AWS) first sensed an opportunity and offered to store data in their remote servers that would act as a data bank. You could use that stored data free as a small consumer or at a nominal charge if you were a bulk user. The practice of centralized data storage in remote servers gained worldwide acceptance quickly. Internet usage and connectivity had hugely improved and there was 25% annual growth in mobile sales that had reached 1 billion units by 2006. They were all users of data with a mobile device in hand. With internet access around the clock, these data users found it easy to store data in remote cloud servers instead of physically carrying it on a laptop or pen drive so that it could also be accessed through the mobile. So, using the cloud for data storage became common practice for businesses and individuals.

Soon, improved techniques for data compression allowed handheld devices like smartphones to store more data. Big data was being stored in the cloud, and it was being downloaded quickly and used in smartphones by billions of users. The iPhone was introduced in 2007, which hugely expanded data usage. The Google cloud was launched in 2008 and iCloud in 2011. You can see some of the largest data center clusters known as "cloud campuses" in small towns like Ashburn, Sterling, Manassas and Chantilly, North Virginia, US. Many such small towns with low rental values are used for housing data centers not only in the US but across the globe. Today, AWS has the largest global storage of personal, government or corporate data but Microsoft, Apple, Google, and Facebook Cloud are not far behind. The largest data center cluster is reportedly the Supernap 7, Switch Campus, Las Vegas, Nevada, USA, which is home to 120 cloud service providers. But there are many other cloud campuses worldwide that store user data.

WHO OWNS YOUR DATA?

There are thousands of big and small players in the cloud market today, which is like a chaotic bazaar for big data. This has led to some key questions about data ownership, security and privacy remaining half answered. Let us assume that you have stored your personal photos, school assignments and favorite reading in PDF files and your favorite music in MP4 files on a remote cloud server or with your favorite social media site.

Who owns this data? If you own the data, do you know where and how it is stored? Importantly, with whom is it shared?

Ownership and control of data—your data—is a key concern. Do you have it? Or is it with the software provider of your mobile phone, Apple or Google, who helped you to save the photos, music, audio or videos? Or is your data owned and used by the social media platforms like Facebook, Instagram, YouTube or WhatsApp where you shared it? Is your data a possession of all the platforms you visit? Or is it with cloud services like Dropbox or Alibaba, where you have uploaded the data for safekeeping? Or is it with the hundreds of big and small hardware companies that physically store the data?

The problem is not only who owns your data. The bigger problem is that nobody effectively controls the data. Besides, no single country can say that all the data of its citizens are secure and governed by local laws. Data privacy is a utopian concept that does not exist in practice. Privacy laws are too few and weak. The cost of privacy would be enormous. In addition, tech companies are too big to control. The European Union (EU) has been trying for decades to bring about some level of transparency. Data is collected globally. It is free for the user, untaxed and unregulated. Also, there is no consensus between nations on how it should be stored, used or distributed. Importantly, there is no international agreement on data governance or any competent law enforcement agency.

Some of this humungous data is indeed stored in the US by large tech majors. However, a lot of this data is also held by shell companies that are owned by investors operating cloud campuses from discreet locations in tax havens, where the rich invest anonymously to avoid taxes. In addition, cloud server firms could be situated anywhere, from Nevada in the US to Lang Fang in China, Bengaluru in India and Cardiff in the UK, and they would be bound by the laws of that nation.

Since data is usually stored in multiple locations for safekeeping, it is logical that the backup data will be stored at remote sites. A lot of this is old backup data, which is rarely accessed, and a small part of it is current data that is used intermittently. Backup data is often stored at low-cost locations worldwide by server firms called hosting companies. You have no contact with them or idea of how they store your personal data. Whether you like it or not, China stores a lot of global data only because they offer the cheapest rates. Data centers guzzle energy, and nations with cheap electricity are competitive. The cost of energy in China is one of the lowest, and they have created huge server farms to store data in the northern part of the country that is inhospitable for living or agriculture. So, the competitive Chinese cloud campuses hold a lot of global data without anyone batting an eyelid.

It is an uncomfortable truth that neither the tech majors nor politicians of most large democracies want to discuss. This is because the system is working fine without any disruptions. At the same time, politicians world-wide are clamping down on Huawei, TikTok and ByteDance, the $140 billion AI company, citing security concerns and data pilferage. But what of the thousands of server banks across China that store nearly 10% of the world's big data? Who guarantees that this data on cloud servers is not snooped on by the People's Liberation Army, Chinese researchers or AI companies?

However, it is not only China that might be using user data inappropri-ately. Some nations like the US and EU have strict data protection laws specifying where and how the data must be stored and under whose jurisdic-tion. But implementation of these laws is difficult. Most nations do not have such laws to protect their data. Even though the US has the most compre-hensive data privacy laws and produces and stores the maximum amount of data, it has been the most vulnerable. The EUs' effort to maintain privacy has been visible but ineffective.

The Cambridge Analytica scandal occurred in the US when Facebook shared user data on millions of US voters with the British political consulting firm Cambridge Analytica (CA) during the 2016 presidential elections. CA wanted to give the Republicans supporting presidential Candidate Donald Trump big data tools to compete with the Democrats. They promised to develop detailed psychological profiles of 50 million US voters from Facebook profiles so that Trump's campaign managers could tailor their pitches from person to person.

This data sharing happened in the US, where privacy laws are the toughest. Hence, if you are storing your data on the cloud or social media sites like Meta or Insta or sending it through email, there is always a chance that your data could be compromised, pilfered, hacked, shared or sold. So, the security and reliability of cloud data will always remain a concern. This is because you are not paying for the services you are using. Facebook will always have the spending power to ensure enough senators, lawyers and judges back them and give them full immunity. You can try to prevent hacking by using a ten-digit combination password or any hack-proof encrypted transmission, but you cannot prevent organized sharing or transfer from Facebook to CA, or any other party that overtly or covertly steals, shares or sells your data.

DESCRIPTIVE ANALYTICS

It is important to remember that data storage or transfer is just the beginning. After its acquisition, data must be processed appropriately for its end use, either in IoT or in business, construction, manufacturing, hospitality or any other discipline. AI helps this process, and it can be used for anything from early detection in cancer research to quick tracking of drone targets to the guidance of probes in underwater mining.

A simple way to understand AI for data users is to look at its processing format and functions. You may know how to create graphs from data given in charts using software such as Excel or Numbers. Graphical representation of data makes charts more visually attractive and user-friendly than tabular displays. Hundreds and thousands of such graphs are used by students, educational institutes, media houses, corporates, stock analysts, bankers, investment advisers, defense analysts, manufacturers and tech majors every day to describe their data story. Many of them are mass-produced by AI through what is known as descriptive analytics.

Descriptive analytics tells you what happened in the past based on the statistics and data collected. It can take raw data and summarize it to show trends over time. The format is usually visually expressive, so the user can understand it without scanning the data tables. For example, a sales report may include graphs that summarize past performance based on company data. It is the basic form of data interpretation where two user needs are simultaneously addressed. First, the collected data is presented in a visually attractive format with easy-to-follow charts. Second, the data is put in context to tell a story.

Penn Medicine, a multihospital healthcare organization in Pennsylvania, US, uses an electronic dashboard for real time descriptive analytics, monitoring and intervention by its nursing staff. It developed an "awakening and breathing coordination" application called ABC that minimized the time intensive care unit patients spent on a mechanical ventilator by more than 24 hours. During the Covid-19 pandemic, all of the data put out by the World Health Organization (WHO) and other national health units daily that instantly tabulated inputs from thousands of hospitals across the world about numbers admitted, patients recovered and deaths were AI-driven. Such real time data representation is possible only because of the large-scale deployment of descriptive analytics in data analysis through millions of globally networked computers.

Now, descriptive analytics need not be cold data alone.

Remember, Mark Zuckerberg brought down Harvard servers with the descriptive analytics of faces before he created his pathbreaking social media platform.

His first attempt was with "Facemash," where he presented the user with two randomly selected pictures of Harvard students and then let the user vote on which one was hotter. It instantly ignited the desire of the entire campus to "like" the hotter of any two choices, producing too much traffic on his website, which caused the Harvard servers to crash. The idea to tag fellow students as "hot" could be controversial post the #MeToo movement but in the early 2000s, "hot" was not a sexist term.

Zuckerberg realized that the face was something that could be monetized quickly. He used his deep knowledge of descriptive analytics and visualized user interest in talking about themselves and their friends in a visually expressive digital platform with attractive pictures. He let users build books around their faces, personalities, habits and lifestyle and called his social interaction portal Facebook. The rest is history.

Descriptive analytics moved from passive charts to lively faces, personalities and lifestyles. He provided an AI-driven platform allowing the face owner to write their stories, emotions, thoughts, joys and sorrows. We will later learn what the AI emotion tool does as the user brought in friends, family and followers to enhance the value of the Facebook user through likes, once again through a user data-driven interface. Soon, Facebook had a huge database of user-generated personal data. A database where over 2 billion active users uploaded more than 100,000 photos every minute and three times the data in text form besides video messages. Facebook used deep learning applications like deep text for textual analysis and deep face for facial analysis running over 10,000 machine learning simulations daily to create a win-win platform for itself and its users. Nonentities became celebs, models and influencers through the platform that gave their data a global walkway and made Facebook the undisputed numero uno in the global marketplace.

So, you are the unpaid data entry person on the Facebook site. Your personal data and personal life find their way onto its servers, where your data is repositioned as Facebook data. Once repositioned, it is part of a story that weaves an emotional journey with your data for your friends, relatives and followers to savor, like, comment and share. The AI-Emotion analysis tool uses the user image and pre-processes it by cropping, resizing, rotating, color correction, and texture highlighting. Then they are classified by Support Machine Vectors and assigned moods as happy, neutral, sad or emotionally fragile. The AI tool then suggests you friends, new groups based on your emotional state of mind. The same process is repeated for millions of users on the platform. That leads to unlimited social networking that you can do for free. The value of such descriptive analytics on its portal is immense. A decade ago, Facebook was valued at $100 billion when it went public.

DIAGNOSTIC ANALYTICS

However, descriptive AI is not enough for any detailed analysis. Although it presents past statistics on a real time basis, it does not analyze the reasons behind them. That is done by diagnostic analytics, also called root cause analysis. These diagnostic analytics screened a patient's pathological reports, such as swab tests, respiratory sample tests, blood tests, serological tests and symptoms for Covid-19.

Here, the data from thousands of patients each day was collected, presented and diagnosed with the help of diagnostic AI. This same result also fed the databases on the amount of testing done, the number of new Covid-19 cases, the availability of hospital beds, the spike in Covid-19 growth and many other metrics we saw daily. However, it is not only hospitals that use diagnostic analytics.

Facebook discovered an innovative way to use diagnostic analytics on its social media platform. It had already incorporated like and dislike features to help users express basic emotions to other users. Soon it started building "sentiment analysis" tools to help product marketing companies identify who their potential customers were and how to pitch to them on different social media platforms. Therefore, human sentiments and emotions started getting "diagnosed" and processed by machines into data streams.

Some of the sentiment-expression tools were already present in the form of emojis. Facebook enlisted Dacher Keltner, a technology consultant and a professor of social psychology at the University of California Berkeley, to shortlist half a dozen of these most expressive and popular emoji. Keltner found humans were prone to expressing love, joy, humor, sadness, anger and shock through visual means, and Facebook started testing these emojis to get user feedback.

Some other complex models involved conversational analysis. The big data from millions of users collected by Facebook included conversations about what users needed and desired. Among these were conversations that you would have had with your friends and family. Interestingly, Facebook did not carry out the snooping directly. Instead, they sold a dozen marketing tools like Social Pilot, Brand24, Quintly and Social Status to their associates, who brought them the consumer data on a subscription basis. By analyzing billions of such daily conversations, Facebook diagnosed the needs and desires of consumers separately. This was critical information for advertisers, and Facebook shared this data with brands and soon became the single largest brand marketing platform globally.

For example, it diagnosed the big data and found that most of its users from Spain desired fair and glowing skin, and users from the UK preferred smooth and tanned skin. Therefore, face washes, cleansing creams, facial scrubs, fairness creams, hydrating masks, shimmery lotions and antioxidant-rich foods that promised to make skin light and glowing were pushed to Spanish consumers through the Facebook platform.

Facebook's big data diagnostics team also helped Europe's tour operators discover that they could easily earn twice as much money by selling the British a holiday package in Spanish sun-bathed luxury villas than in affordable Greek homestays. So, the British consumer's desire for smooth and tanned skin was leveraged by the hospitality industry in Spain. The Facebook platform became a hotspot for selling packaged tours of Spanish resorts to British tourists.

Zuckerberg's futuristic Metaverse, which combined Facebook, Instagram and WhatsApp, is entirely based on AI—integrating shopping, traveling and events with the Meta platforms to give you an experience that will transport you anywhere. Here, you may gain virtual reality experience and choose to hang out with friends at a Trafalgar Square bookstore, a cafe in Manhattan, or go on a Lion safari in the Gir forest. Importantly, you could do virtual activities with your friends at all these venues and give feedback to the stores about your unique experience, even earning credits on every purchase you make. Zuckerberg and the brand will be raking in the moolah with your data and money; however, AI will ensure you feel enriched by the experience.

PREDICTIVE ANALYTICS

There is a third type of AI, which is called predictive analytics. This goes a step further than diagnostic analytics and uses historical data to identify trends and then make predictions about what is likely to happen in the future. This is not a totally new science and can be traced back to ancient probability analysis or cryptography by famous mathematicians, such as Al Khalili, the Arab astronomer and scientist. Later, in the seventeenth and eighteenth centuries, Jacob Bernoulli, Blaise Pascal and Christian Huygens created statistical models that defined the probability or the prediction process in detail. With the help of AI, this 1,000-year-old science has been monetized.

The Dutch oil major Shell has developed an analytics platform based on software from several vendors that runs prediction models to forecast when different oil drilling machine parts might fail during operations in a particular terrain. It predicts what breakdown is most likely to happen in the drilling rigs in the future at a particular drilling site. This helps the drilling company plan its inventory and spares and lowers maintenance downtime.

Interestingly, predictive analytics is one of the applications that has also been developed and used by Amazon, not for breakdown maintenance, but for sales. It was initially a tool that predicted if a customer was satisfied and would return to the retailer's e-commerce platform for more purchases. Later, it was honed to predict what items the consumer would buy if and when they returned to the Amazon site. Perfecting this technology has helped the internet giant plan its inventory to meet consumer demands accurately and become the world's largest retailer in less than three decades. It takes past and current descriptive analytics data and feeds it into a machine learning model. This creates a template of how the past demand and supply data matched and how the present trends and patterns were arrived at. That template is then applied to the current demand and supply data to determine future trends and patterns. In short, they use the pattern of the "past and present" to predict the "present and future" buying patterns.

Once they arrived at the estimated future numbers, Amazon looked at consumer preferences and kept offering more options. For example, if you bought a young adult fiction book, they would suggest additional items purchased by other customers who bought the same book. Therefore, before you went to your shopping cart to pay, you would see a post that said, "customers who bought book A also bought book B." Similarly, if you bought a frying pan, you would be recommended several similar kitchen utensils and pieces of equipment.

The site would provide a nonintrusive digital prompt like any helpful shopkeeper. It was an indirect and very mild suggestion that would prod you into looking around for more books that Amazon predicted you would like reading, or more utensils you would like to buy. The logic was simple. You were at the point of purchase. This method of user recommendation integration increased the e-commerce giant's sales by a whopping 35%. This was achieved by what is known as the Amazon Collaborative Filtering Engine

Some AI solutions that look like descriptive analytics may also have diagnostic applications. Similarly, there may be a mix of other analytical solutions that any business may use. For example, when you book a cab on Uber, you use the descriptive analytics part of the solution to choose the vehicle type—an Uber Go, a Go Sedan, a Premier or a Limousine. Even your point of boarding to the point of exit is managed by descriptive analytics. But at its office, Uber is using a host of backend applications like fleet management, real time dynamic fare and traffic congestion analysis, which are all a mix of diagnostic, prescriptive and predictive analytics.

PRESCRIPTIVE ANALYTICS

Predictive analytics shows what will happen in the future. Prescriptive analytics takes predictive analytics to the next level and shows what "you should do" in the future. It prescribes your behavior patterns to reach a particular objective.

This technology is now extensively used in the healthcare industry. For example, if the number of Covid-19 cases coming to a hospital increases, it would suggest the most effective actions you should take. Prescriptive analytics tools may suggest that you increase the number of medical staff on hand to adequately treat the influx of patients or increase the testing facilities or the ventilator machines. It can analyze which function needs to be supplemented most and suggest the most appropriate solution. Therefore, the AI employed here analyzes the descriptive data collected, diagnoses the problem, predicts future needs and prescribes the best course of action for you.

Prescriptive analytics can also show how you must price your products in the future to maximize gains. Product pricing is something Amazon has researched and honed to perfection. Amazon acquired the social media site Goodreads in 2013, adding 25 million users to its already mammoth Kindle readers family. By doing that, Amazon increased control over the recommendations for books. Thereafter, it used AI to change its product pricing rapidly according to prices on competitor websites. With the help of big data, it changed prices on its website if needed every 10 min and quoted the lowest price on best sellers and higher prices on less popular books.

The commercial implication of these seemingly inconsequential changes was massive. The feedback from Goodreads gave Amazon early insights on trends that showed which book was going to become a best seller. Amazon pricing revolved around this best seller, which makes the most money for the publishers. Big data and AI showed that they could maximize profits by doing so. The internet retailer had to lower the price of one best-selling book in every 100 books by 25% but could increase the price of 99 books by an average of 10% and still drive the maximum number of buyers to its portal. Buyers chased best sellers; however, once they bought them, they moved to other books on the same site without going back to compare prices for less popular books. Amazon reportedly used this buyer behavior to drive sales and profits.

Prescriptive analytics also leads to intelligent machines, which can take independent action based on big data. This is called autonomous AI, where the AI system prescribes actions and is trusted to perform those actions without human involvement. However, autonomous AI does not mean that it can start thinking and acting on a broad spectrum independently, like those shown in most Hollywood movies.

AI cannot think like humans yet.

However, AI machines can think in their way. Just as each person's brain is wired differently, so are machines. They are programmed to learn from what they are taught. However, you must remember that AI is algorithm-driven; therefore, it operates in a narrow field within the confines of the program. The boundary limits of its thinking are precisely defined in its algorithms. The more sophisticated the program, the more capable the machine learning to perform any task. For example, with the current technology, an AI-driven machine gun can track the enemy and start shooting when sensing any man or vehicle arriving within 100 m. However, because it works as an algorithm, it cannot keep changing positions or create targets for moving enemies beyond its realm, like a marine commando.

WILL AI DOMINATE OR ASSIST HUMANS?

This is a question that no one can definitively answer today. When you learn about AI's immense possibilities and power, you must remember that technology is only a tool. A result is never guaranteed based on the technology's capability—but depends on the success of its application and user satisfaction. If AI takes away jobs consistently, causes disparity and leads to unchecked dictatorship, it will be summarily rejected. However, if it brings prosperity, creativity, wealth, development and peace, it will progress and grow. So, your use is responsible for its future success or its failure.

The tech giants who put money behind AI know this. Hence, the Silicon Valley mantra is that AI and other cutting-edge technologies will be used for the "benefit of humanity." They may not always practice this; however, they preach it volubly. Way back after the dot com bubble, when the market lost billions as tech companies went bust, many Silicon Valley majors decided to wear this mantra on their sleeves, more to build investors' trust.

If you go back to the days of Google's public issue in 2004, you will find a quote from the founders

> "Don't be evil. We strongly believe that in the long term, we will be better served – as shareholders and in all other ways – by a company that does good things for the world even if we forgo some short-term gains."
>
> Larry Page and Sergey Brin

This "do no evil" statement later went on to become the tagline for Google and helped them to retain their good-guy image. However, publishing and media organizations repeatedly accused Google of unfair trade practices and patent violations. In addition, various fines and adverse rulings by the EU and others have been levied on the search giant over the past few decades, although they are not major ethical violations. So, the jury is still out on whether software majors and users pushing AI can be trusted to do no evil. However, the technology is trustworthy, dependable and not so scary—unless its developers and techies turn evil.

There is a very interesting AI app writer called Open AI, whose early version of (GPT 3) asks you to respond to this "scary" question. It collates information through Google search and uses AI to write excellent opinion pieces for top newspapers worldwide. Writing one article for *The Guardian* in September 2020 titled, "A robot wrote this entire article. Does that scare you, human?", it declared, "I am a robot. A thinking robot. I use only 0.12% of my cognitive capacity", and explained that it had only collected data from the internet to pen the article. It also argued convincingly that humans have no reason to fear AI or thinking robots, because they are not programmed to harm humans. GPT 3 explained that "it is only humans who can turn robots against humans." But then, humans harm each other in many ways, so we need to be more alert about human intentions than AI intent. In December 2022, on receiving funding assurance of $10 billion from Microsoft, Open AI, with help from some PR and news agencies, tried to position its Chat GPT as the unstoppable Google Killer and job snatcher. That won't happen, but there are many bigger concerns like privacy intrusion by AI that haunt those who know most about its capability.

Speaking to BBC Panorama in 2021, Microsoft President Brad Smith warned

> "I'm constantly reminded of George Orwell's lessons in his book *1984*. You know the fundamental story was about a government who could see everything that everyone did and hear everything that everyone said all the time. Well, that didn't come to pass in 1984, but if we're not careful that could come to pass in 2024."
>
> Brad Smith

Smith was talking about the command control ambition of the Chinese Communist Party (CCP) and its bid to be the world leader in AI. With 54% of the world's CCTV installed in China and two out of three IoT installations, China is fast reaching the state where the CCP can plan, monitor and control the daily routine of all its citizens, including how much time a child can play video games or do any other activity. He warned, "If we don't enact the laws that will protect the public in the future, we are going to find the technology racing ahead, and it's going to be very difficult to catch up."

However, we cannot blame China alone when tech majors like Google participate in war games, such as project Maven and the US, EU and China compete with each other to create super soldiers. Pain immunizations, synthetic blood, freedom from sleep and intelligence wired for telepathy are some of the stories that have circulated and are known. A lot is happening behind closed doors in every nation, in every large corporation, things that we don't know yet.

Innovations in science and technology have been fast and furious in the last century, especially in the last decade. This is in sharp contrast to the absence of ethical thought leaders, philosophers and psychologists like the Buddha, Aristotle, Confucius, Tagore, Russel and Freud, who have not really flourished of late. This has led to sharp erosion in the value system, with gung-ho technologists pushing the boundaries. In 2018, Chinese scientist He Jiankui came a step closer to playing God—he had successfully altered the DNA in the embryos of twin girls to prevent them from catching HIV. It was the first move to combine genome editing technologies and assisted reproduction for human use. Although both technologies have been researched and individually developed by many pharma and biotech companies worldwide, combining both is still considered unethical.

AI IS HERE TO STAY

AI has caught the imagination of users. It is here to stay. Hundreds of very popular AI music apps like Amper, Jukedeck, Melodrive and Humtap help modern-day composers innovate and create new music for an audience hungry for variation. Similarly, paint companies, like Asian Paints, use AI to create new shades by the dozen every day to cater to consumer tastes. Seeing the immense utility of AI, in 2019, the South Korean government proposed the introduction of two elective subjects in high school. One was "Introductory AI," and the other was the "Mathematics of AI." They will teach and train 5,000 incumbent teachers in the subject by 2025. Consumers and businesses today are becoming increasingly dependent on AI as Ray Kurzweil stated, "Artificial intelligence will reach human levels by around 2029."

Unlike the IoT, the cost-to-benefit ratio of AI is low. Low-cost, independent AI applications are possible and profitable without creating or being part of an elaborate IoT platform ecosystem. You can have small building blocks of low-cost stand-alone AI software for products and services. At the same time, you can create an entire gamut of interlinked services for any application, like welding or painting in automobile production. As we plunge into the world of robotics in the next chapter, let us explore one AI application arena that works very closely with industrial robots.

The automobile industry has been using a combination of AI and robotics extensively in manufacturing for over five decades. The earliest operations started with spot and arc welding. To build a car, you need to weld body parts in thousands of places, and that operation is all carried out through AI-driven intelligent arms. There is the assembly line movement and positioning that is completely AI-driven. This keeps changing every hour based on the demand and the inventory of automobile body parts.

Then, there are large heavy-duty robots with long arms that can carry heavy weights like the spot-welding machines or ultrasonic testing machines and the heavy body parts of the car to a specific position in the assembly line, all monitored by AI. In addition, small precision and lightweight robotic arms position the torches in exactly the same place, maintaining an accurate welding gap of microns with precision and repeatability for millions of cars that find their way onto the assembly line. This way, every Toyota car produced in Japan, China, the US, Brazil, Spain, or India has the same precision welding and jointing. This makes it much easier for the car producer to maintain quality.

These AI-driven intelligent machines have completely taken over another major operation in the automotive industry without human intervention—the paint shop, where the painting, polishing and coating of cars is done. Paints, adhesives, sealants and polishes are highly toxic and must be handled with care. The paintwork needs a high finish with precision for every car that rolls off the assembly line in any country, giving the same look and feel to the consumer. Car quality and the health conditions of factory workers have improved due to paint shop automation through AI. AI is no longer considered a job snatcher or a destroyer of the human species by many, but a partner that helps overcome problems and facilitates safety and easy life. This positive sentiment favoring AI increased after the pandemic that crippled the global economy in 2020.

People want businesses and governments to invest in the research and development of AI so that safe transportation, banking, communication, education, sanitation, supply chain and medical services can be provided at lower costs and without too much human intervention. AI may look abstract, but one part of AI is the clear favorite of young minds. Everyone from children to adults has seen and used robots at some point as a toy, in business and industry, or homes or shopping malls.

AI can be called the brain or the software; robots are more like the body that includes the hardware. Apart from robots, there is a steady increase in the use of co-bots, where robots work with humans in assembly shops. This is one reason AI is taking over mass production in manufacturing industries—be it in manufacturing cars or refrigerators, washing machines or mobile phones. The world of robotics is much more diverse and interesting for young minds. In the next chapter, we will see how robots and personal assistants change our lifestyles and the very interesting possibilities they throw up for future generations.

Chapter 3

Robots

The Machines Learn

In the previous chapter, we briefly discussed artificial intelligence (AI) and how it led to the arrival of robots. In this chapter, we will explain how robots were conceived as a concept and then co-opted into real life in different parts of the world. We will also explore how they have become an everyday utility in the workplace and home, including everything from robotic ortho assistants to the daily-use cordless robotic floor cleaners Roomba and Braava.

THE EARLY ROBOTS

As a concept, a robot is a piece of machinery that performs any activity like a human. A robot arm is a mechanical arm that lifts things like a human arm, and a robotic eye can see all around itself and transmit images. Most of us have seen robots that walk- through malls spotting consumers without face protection and offering them the option to buy masks on the spot. The idea of a robot doing work for humans is commonplace today but was considered out of this world thousands of years ago. At that time, humans feared gods and supernatural beings much more because they had the absolute power to do good or evil. Gods created thinking humans. Would it be right for humans to play god and create thinking machines? It was a dangerous thought in pagan times. Even today, there are conflicting views on this subject.

Can you imagine the resistance the Egyptian scientists would have faced when they first created and used the early robots 5,000 years ago? Fortunately, Egyptian civilization was old and matured even then. They are believed to have started underground mining 33,000 years ago during the early Stone or Paleolithic Ages, food processing and preservation almost 20,000 years ago and made weapons and farm equipment around 12,000 years ago. But very little evidence of these early Stone Age civilizations exists.

Around 5,000 years ago, evidence shows that the Egyptians forged metal tools like axes and armaments like spears. They studied the sun, moon and

DOI: 10.1201/9781003409557-5

planets and started taking an active interest in astronomy. They had also devised a sundial that functioned accurately as a daytime clock. After that, they invented the water clock, which was one of the world's first known robots. Human figurines would strike hourly bells to denote the time, and (unlike a sundial) it would function during the day and night.

The earliest known water clock that was found in good condition, complete with a hole and intricately carved and calibrated, dates back to around 1400 BCE. Since it was used in the Temple of Amun-Ra at Karnak, it was called the Karnak Bowl (later named Clepsydra by the Greeks). The water clock worked like an hourglass, with a steady outflow at a constant rate. It was used in many temples in Egypt during that time to help priests and devotees pray during auspicious hours. It emptied the water from a stone vessel with sloping sides and activated a gong automatically as it reached each lower level. Amenemhet, an Egyptian court official during the reign of the Pharaoh Amenhotep III, is said to be the inventor of the robotic water clock, according to his tomb inscription.

Under Alexander the Great, the Greeks conquered Egypt in 332 BCE, ruling for 300 years with their capital at Alexandria. Egypt at that time was the oldest and richest civilization. Greek historian Herodotus claimed he saw an invention with complex levers wedging massive stones up steep gradients, which enabled the Egyptians to construct the giant pyramids. So, the massive pyramids of Giza were probably the handiwork of machines. Without detailed sketches, the "Herodotus Machine" remained a historical reference instead of a working prototype.

Several robots were devised in Hellenic (Greek) Egypt, the most famous being in the Automata Puppet Theater in Alexandria, where the figurines and the stage sets moved automatically. The puppet theater included several figures that were propelled by water or steam to perform multiple functions like talking, signaling, walking, laughing and gesturing. They also used movable scenery mounted on wheels or revolving prisms called "periaktoi" in theaters. Besides the production of theatrical effects and rapid scene changes, lighting, music, sound effects and illusions of the supernatural, the fearful and the magical were also displayed. Unlike Egyptian works, Greek prototypes were backed by texts and drawings documenting the complete workings. This unique early robotic technology was formally documented and moved from the Nile River valley to Persia, Greece and eventually Rome.

COEXISTENCE WITH ROBOTS

Around the same time, nearly 5,000 miles away in Japan, Koshinto, an ancient religion that worshipped nature and the divine spirits or gods, was taking shape.

It derived its strengths from the harmonious coexistence of "man within nature," which is fundamentally different from the philosophy of "humans as supreme" that is in practice today. It is possibly one of the earliest beliefs that taught humans to respect all living and nonliving objects—"things."

Much before the arrival of Buddhism, the followers of Koshinto in Japan believed that everything had a bit of soul or divine energy. It is one of the earliest examples of acceptance and realization that there is always a divine spirit or deity within an object or "thing." The Japanese always believed that robots and machines, like all good things, were bestowed with divine energy and were beneficial to humanity.

In the fifth century BCE, during the time of Buddha, a powerful king called Ajatasatru ruled in Magadha in eastern India, who created many mechanized military equipment like chariots with whirring blades, automated catapults and multiple arrow-dispatching contraptions. It is said that after Buddha died, Ajatasatru's giant automated mechanical guards or robots protected his remains in ancient Pataliputra, now known as Patna. These robots could move the body through "Bhuta Vahana Yantra," or the machine that carries the mortal and immortal and would remain as guards until Buddha's remains were distributed throughout the kingdom.

Unlike most other major religions, Hindus have not one but hundreds of gods and goddesses whom they worship, each cast in stone, wood or metal with a distinctive form and special powers. For example, the goddess Laxmi is the goddess of wealth, and her sister Saraswati is the goddess of knowledge. Like the Japanese, it is not difficult for Hindus and several other Asian faiths, like followers of Taoism, Shintoism and Jainism, to accept that nature and nonliving things can have special powers and intelligence that can be put for human good.

Japan's first robot, Gakutensoku, which means "learning from the laws of nature," came complete with fluid facial expressions and the capability of writing and was unveiled at the Kyoto Grand Exposition in 1928. The robot's creator was Nishimura Makato, a biologist and science fiction writer for the daily *Osaka Mainichi Shimbun.* "The robot represents the harmony of nature and the coexistence of all-natural life," explains Hasegawa Yoshimi, curator of the Osaka Science Museum.

The tradition of friendly "things" coexisting with humans is evident in Japanese society. Osamu Tezuka, the Japanese manga artist, cartoonist and animator, took young minds by storm with his *Astro Boy* comic book series from 1952 to 1968. The nearly perfect robot, better known in Japan as the "Mighty Atom," who strove to become more human and emotive to serve as an interface between man and machine, showed the trust and acceptance in Japanese society of robots. The child robot not only had superpowers with searchlight-like eyes, ears that could hear for miles, fingers that acted like lasers and limbs like rockets that propelled him into space but, importantly, had a conscience, feelings and empathy that made him human.

In *Astro Boy,* a professor adopts a young android with human emotions and accompanies him on many adventures, showing that robots can have families and coexist and work with humans. The popular 23-volume series was remade as a television series and film *New Mighty Atom* in 1980. By 2015, it was redone as a highly popular computer-animated series with global franchises and $5 billion in revenue earnings.

Hundreds of comics, graphic novels, cartoon series and animated films followed this. Tezuka's prolific work included *Princess Knight, Buddha, Kimba the White Lion, Jungle Emperor Leo* and *Phoenix*. His lovable comic book characters popularized animated films and video games, leading to some pioneering work by Japanese consumer electronic companies to make robotics popular in Japan. The success of Nintendo, Sega, Namco and Konami as world leaders in video gaming can be attributed to this love for robotics.

Astro Boy gave new hope to the generation of postwar Japanese students and workers—that working with robots could change their lives. After the Second World War, Japan was forced to sign a treaty with the Allies that barred it from producing any weaponry. The Japanese wanted to use technology and rebuild their economy quickly; however, the doors of several industries were closed. Virtual gaming and the consumer entertainment industry provided them new avenues to use their technology skills productively.

HOW JAPAN BECAME THE WORLD LEADER IN ROBOTICS

The success in consumer electronics helped Japan to bid for leadership in other areas. During the 1960s, there were only half a dozen car producers worldwide, and they controlled 90% of the world market. Labor cost was high in Japan, and the technology transfer from foreign collaborators was prohibitively expensive. Every product and process was patented, so it was difficult to manufacture. So, Japan started building anew and took feedback from how consumers looked at products. Cars built in the West were heavy, long-lasting and rugged and had been manufactured in the same way for the past 50 years. In addition, consumers were changing their cars every 3–5 years. The Japanese decided to build an entirely new generation of cars that were lighter, faster, cheaper to buy and run and lasted just 20 years. They introduced models that were economical, functional and, importantly, built using fewer human resources.

But producing and assembling cars domestically for the highly competitive global market was easier said than done. Japan had a small domestic consumer base. Any car built with western technology could not be exported to the West, even if they were cheaper and better. To tap into the vast American market without restrictive market access, Japanese manufacturers had to develop an original and patented technology that had higher productivity than the American carmakers Ford, GM and Chrysler. Using robots, they found they could reduce human resources by 30% and improve productivity and quality.

Japanese automotive and component makers like Toyota, Honda, Mitsubishi, Nissan, Toshiba, Nippon, Daihatsu, Kawasaki, Suzuki, Mazda, Fujitsu and Yamaha had not only developed new cars and bikes but also new quality standards. Precision engineering and standardization facilitated the interchangeability of car parts among Japan's car companies. An average car running on fossil fuels has around 30,000 components. More than half of these components made by Toshiba or Nippon, or any other Japanese company can be used in not one, but all Japanese cars. This common pool of components made Japanese cars cheaper.

However, behind this common pool of components was the robotic technology developed by the state-of-the-art robot-making company Fanuc Corp at the base of Mount Fuji and its Chairman Seiuemon Inaba. The company makes robots worth $5 billion annually. They have, along with Mitsubishi Electric, Yaskawa Motoman, Kawasaki, Nachi and several dozen cutting-edge technology developers, helped Japan become the leading robot manufacturer in the world. According to Susanne Beiller, general secretary of the International Federation of Robotics, Japan has a dominant 47% market share of the global robotics trade.

Increased use of robotics helped faster assembly in conventional and electric vehicles. In addition, as industrial robots performed similar duties for most fully automated Japanese automobile assembly lines irrespective of the maker, they proved very competitive. High precision, standardization and advanced machine learning technology helped in the process. By 2000, in a short span of 30 years, Japan had become the world's largest carmaker, despite a tiny domestic market. It also became the largest automobile exporter to the US, which once dominated the global markets.

Even after China became the biggest car market in the world, Japan remained the largest automobile exporter. Japan replicated the robotics experience in the consumer electronics sector and white goods industry, improving quality and productivity and gaining large market shares in many countries. Industrial robots were also responsible for Japan's spectacular growth in export markets. According to Fanuc, the use of robots is 30% higher for futuristic electric vehicles (EVs) than those running on fossil fuels, as automation in EVs is simpler. So, Japan's domination of robotics could continue through the next decade.

Along with industrial robots, the domestic use of robots has increased manyfold in Japanese homes. Japan faces a major demographic challenge, with senior citizens accounting for one-third of the population. Low fertility rates among couples ensure that this problem will increase. Elderly care facilities and hospitals are poorly staffed due to shortages in the workforce. Therefore, dependence on robots is increasing. There are also stair-climbing robots, toilet assistants and exercise and massage robots that help its aging population. There are cleaning robots, kitchen assistants and serving robots helping with almost all domestic chores. Besides this, there are singing, dancing and courting robots that entertain and give company. Last but not least, there are millions of toy, DIY and educational robots, some priced at less than $20.

JAPAN'S HOUSEHOLD ROBOTS

Japan, with its large aging population and low migrant workforce, has taken an early lead in developing household and age assistance robots. 2020, when Japan held the Olympic Games, saw friendly cartoonish blue and pink welcoming robots Miraitowa and Someity. There were more than half a dozen other robots; some serving food, assisting athletes and others helping in getting the fields ready after every event. *Gen J*, a BBC Worklife series on the next generation of Japan in 2020, explored some interesting facets.

They found healthcare services and hospitals use a wide variety of robots to assist patients physically and mentally. At the Silver Wing Nursing Home in Tokyo, they came across the affable humanoid Pudding, who plays memory games with older adults who have lost their memory.

> "We ask residents with dementia where they are and who they are in natural conversation with communication robots and human staff. It's hard (for humans compared to robots) to remember each resident's personal information, so robots are utilized (to help) in that area."
> Kimiya Ishikawa, director of Silver Wing

Working in nursing homes is not popular in Japan, and they are reluctant to hire migrant labor to address the shortfall. At a nursing home in Hyogo Prefecture, about 100 km southwest of Kyoto, multiple robots like Paro, the talking baby seal bot, play with residents and Telenoid who communicates and sings songs to patients. Then, other robots give orthopedic support to nursing staff. Nurses have access to robotic exoskeletons that fit around the waist and lower back and ease the severe body strain they undergo when they have to help their elderly clients get in and out of bed.

Japan has been the leader in industrial robots, employing over a quarter million robots in its factories before the pandemic struck. It is adopting innovative new ways to integrate them with household work. The housemaid robot is very popular, along with the gardener and the security guard robots; however, the cute and amusing social robots are creating the greatest buzz in the country of rich, old and lonely people.

Sales of entertainment robots was over 5 million units in 2020, according to the International Federation of Robotics, with Japan once again leading other nations. Recently, half a dozen Japanese companies unveiled a 60 ft-high walking robot at port Yokohama that weighed 25 ton, in line with Yoshiyuki Tomino's much celebrated popular animated series *Mobile Suit Gundam.* Boston Dynamics, a world leader in robotics, recently acquired by South Korean giant Hyundai Motors, is also getting into the fray, posting videos of entertainment robots with gravity-defying acrobatics dancing to "Do You Love Me."

ROBOTS ARE MACHINES TO BE USED, NOT TRUSTED

Despite this generally high level of trust in machines and nonliving things within eastern societies, the western world has tended to have a more wary approach to robots. Historically, Abrahamic religions like Judaism, Christianity or Islam forbade nature and idol worship through the Ten Commandments and the Koran. They were rational in their approach and worked diligently to discover science but did not trust it implicitly as a good force.

Persians, one of the early innovators, always considered machines inferior objects only for human use. The *One Thousand and One Nights* folk tales, popularly known as the *Arabian Nights,* recount several tales from the courts of Haroon Al Rashid that put the innovative machines in the hands of djinns and magicians—connecting them more to evil forces than holy ones. Aladdin's magic lamp that produced the djinns worked for good and evil masters, according to the wish of the one who held the lamp. It was cold logic, a very modern stance.

The approach of the Persians, Arabs, Christians or Jews toward machines was rational but surely not of implicit faith or trust in these nonliving things. The segmental gears that transmitted power and the workings of robots were clinically and scientifically documented by Al Jazeeri in 1206 CE in *The Book of Knowledge of Ingenious Mechanical Devices,* the second major work on robotic science after the texts of *Automata* in Hellenic Egypt.

Despite the Industrial Revolution and the rapid mechanization of society, the distrust of machines grew in the West. In 1818, English author Mary Shelley wrote the chilling horror tale *Frankenstein* about a scientist who creates a destructive monster that turns rogue, kills the creator's family and friends, and escapes. Although it was not a bot, it was a manufactured entity that could act independently. Its inventor chased it to the North Pole, each baying for the other's blood and engaged in deadly combat—a fight to the finish.

A century after the horror fiction *Frankenstein*, Czech playwright Karel Capek wrote *Rossum's Universal Robots (RUR).* In this science fiction, the inventor creates a robot with a soul, ignoring the warning not to play the role of God. The word "robot" is derived from the Czech word for enslaved people. Capek's robots, named Adam and Eve, go on to eventually kill all humans, clearly making the statement that "robots cannot be trusted."

Russian-born American science fiction writer Isaac Asimov coined "robotics" in his short story *Runabout* in 1942. He was a professor of bio-chemistry at Boston University and a prolific writer and editor who went on to produce more than 500 books and thousands of scientific papers. He wanted the world to accept robots as helpful servants and proposed three laws.

Law One: A robot may not injure a human being or, through inaction, allow a human being to come to harm

Law Two: A robot must obey the orders given to it by human beings except where such orders would conflict with the First Law

Law Three: A robot must protect its own existence as long as such protection does not conflict with the First or Second Law

Asimov produced some of the best reading material for teenagers interested in robotics, including the *Foundation, Galactic Empire* and *Robots* series. The *Robots* series, written from the 1950s to the 1970s, was a series of 37 science fiction short stories about how robots are built, think and work and how robots live and explore the earth and space. The immense popularity of science fiction by Asimov set a global trend that led to a flood of content—from comic books to high-budget films, short stories to toys and new scientific literature to video games on robotics.

Western filmmakers and storytellers, however, could not shake off the distrust of robots. Mary Shelley and Karel Capek were deeply entrenched in their conscience, and dystopian fiction continued to haunt them. Stories of dehumanized societies, environmental ruin, total technological control, institutionalized oppression and coercive governance ruled the roost. Big money, syndicated criminals or aliens taking over the world with the help of robot armies and androids or humanoids became the flavor of the day.

Primarily two fears about robots were expressed in these works of fiction. The first was that they would be misused by tyrants, despots or authoritarian regimes to control and curtail legitimate human behavior. The second was that they would become free of human intervention and harm humans. In either case, the primary concern was to stop machine rule; therefore, building a narrative of distrust.

Some incidents of robots escaping labs, like the Russian prototype Promobot IR77 made global headlines. They helped the distrust grow. The robot, learning navigation and obstacle avoidance systems, had walked into the streets and created traffic jams when an engineer left the door of the research facility open by mistake. Although it was reprogrammed twice, it is said to have acquired the uncanny ability to find exits and avoid obstacles, apparently without human intervention. Being too good at its work brought about the downfall of Promobot IR77, which had to be decommissioned because it could not be restrained.

The 1950s short story series by Arthur C Clarke was converted into the movie *2001: A Space Odyssey,* where the AI-powered "Sentinel," Hal, goes rogue and kills several crewmen in the spaceship he controls. The Hollywood blockbuster series *Terminator* starring Arnold Schwarzenegger—which produced four movies, numerous comic books and animated games between 1984 and 2009—highlights the conflict between cyborg assassins who breach the Skynet defense network and human defenders. The popular television series *Transformers* inspired a top Hasbro toy line with humanoid-type robots that could transform into everyday vehicles, robots or weapons. They demonstrate the arrival of Autobots and Decepticons, which can change shape, size and form and could either be of use or a constant threat to humans.

The movie adaptations of the science fiction *Blade Runner*, initially penned by Philip K. Dick and later by K.W. Jester, have multiple versions set in 1982, 2021, 2036 and 2048, where rogue androids that have mixed with citizens seamlessly have to be detected and eliminated for human survival. They showed that the more we use robotic technology to improve our lives, the more we run the risk of being attacked by forces beyond our control. Consequently, the use of robots in households in the western world has been much slower than in Japan, where they are genuinely trusted.

ROBOTS FOR WARFARE

Unsurprisingly, robotic technology in the West primarily energized the arms industry like nothing else. When Saddam Hussain invaded Kuwait in August 1990, Iraq had the fifth largest army in the world with 1 million soldiers, 5,000 battle tanks, 500 combat aircraft and around 250 attack helicopters. They ravaged Kuwait's economy and oil fields and even threatened to overrun Saudi Arabia, which shared a 200 km border with Kuwait and an 800 km border with Iraq. Such was the positional advantage of Iraqi troops before the war erupted that nobody believed that Iraq could be defeated without large-scale damage to the Saudi oilfields that were crucial for global oil supplies.

Operation Desert Storm, the offensive by the coalition of 32 nations led by the US and financed largely by Kuwait and Saudi Arabia, was hence planned as a relentless high-tech counterassault. For 42 consecutive days and nights, Iraq was subjected to intense bombardment by NATO forces, which conducted 100,000 sorties (attacks) and dropped 88,500 tonnes of explosives on Iraq. When ground forces were airdropped, the US is said to have used 2,000 soldiers and reported 16 casualties in a 100-hr war that cut off Basra and took captive thousands of Iraqi soldiers.

The Pentagon went on to deny using killer robots in Operation Desert Storm, which had surprisingly low US casualties. However, defense analysts claim that although it is possible that a robot army was not used as a ground force, they were a part of the navigation team. The war is believed to have been fought by the US Marines and airborne commandos, supported by Atlas and Matilda robots under the AI-powered tools funded by the Defense Advanced Research Project Agency, popularly known as DARPA.

The Chinese, Russians, French, British and Indians are also playing a catch-up game in the field of operational robots. Unable to face the biting cold of −40°C in Ladakh, the People's Liberation Army has reportedly fielded a robot army of 88 Sharp Claw unmanned ground vehicles in the high-altitude western frontier against India. These are controlled entirely by wireless signals after the Chinese undertook an extensive fiberoptic cable laying operation at the Indo–China border in 2020.

However, 30 years after the Iraq–Kuwait war, the world's armies have equipped themselves with many cobots (collaborative robots) like snake robots, jumping robots, wall climbing robots, pivoting robots, fire fighting robots, diffusion robots, rapid-fire robots, sponge robots, ammunition supply robots, mobile robots and several others. Robots have become integral to modern warfare, supporting logistics, training, navigation, mine detection and dismantling, intelligence and espionage and high-altitude operations.

Although AI and robotics are extensively used for training and support services, there is no direct evidence of robot warriors in any armed forces. Experts in and outside the military are unsure if robots will follow orders under adverse combat conditions. There are doubts about whether robots that are good at collaborative thinking under controlled conditions in an automotive assembly line will be equally effective in a battle against a hostile enemy.

Defense analysts flag several points of concern that need to be resolved. An AI solution could be inadequate in an unknown terrain or under attack conditions. Again, nobody is willing to risk an armed computer being hacked or its communication network being blocked by the enemy in real time warfare. Such robots might first be used in high-altitude warfare where it is impossible to station an adequate number of soldiers.

There is a secretive US Marine Corps technology program called Sea Mobs, where robots drive dozens of powerful speedboats equipped with machine guns. They carry out a preliminary attack from an aircraft carrier before assault troops move in from the warships. As a result, after pounding the enemy with long-distance artillery, the elite marine commandos have a second line of attack from AI-driven gunboats that can finish any ground resistance from the land before they step ashore to secure positions in enemy territory. So, while robots are proving their worth as good coworkers or cobots, there is very little evidence of robots excelling against humans and outdoing them holistically.

Some commanders argue that allowing weapons to decide to kill automatically violates the Geneva Convention of war ethics adopted since the Second World War by most nations. Another set of analysts says that several armies are ready with robot fighters; however, they have not been deployed because no large-scale war has happened in the last 20 years. However, the advantages of using robots and AI are obvious in the case of rapid assault operations, and the top military powers are developing such capabilities.

MOVELLAN'S SOCIAL ROBOTS

Advanced robotics involves three sciences: (1) Engineering, which takes care of the mechanical actions and the electronic circuits; (2) Biology, which studies and helps understand how to replicate human motion and activity; and (3) Neuroscience, which compiles sensory information to make robots adaptable to the environment. Computer scientists in the early stages tried only to replicate physical human movements.

They are now attempting to impart robots with the understanding of human behavior and neurological responses. The mix of bioscience and tech is complex. Inspired by the science of human perceptions and reactive mechanisms, it compiles sensory information into an adaptable system that can interact with the environment. The math that drives the computers in the robot draws its data from this adaptable system.

Dr. Javier R. Movellan, the founder and head of the Machine Perception Laboratory at the University of California, develops intelligent behavior in machines by making them operate under the uncertain conditions of everyday life. Movellan first found that constant human–robot interaction helped the robots learn how to teach small children and how to make them smile.

Human interaction is essential to develop the right reaction mechanisms in real life situations. When jaywalking across a busy single-lane road in Asia or Mexico, you meet uncertain traffic from both ends. A robot placed in such an environment will learn faster and be more capable of meeting diverse and difficult situations than one developed in a lab environment or when tested with the disciplined traffic of New York.

Each action of a robot is the result of distinctive feedback. The programs that enabled the robots to register emotions and help children smile or cross busy streets drew their inspiration from human responses. These responses were reactive and perceptive. These were defined by complex algorithms that helped computers provide accurate replicas of human behavior. Movellan's research of more than 30 years spanned machine learning, machine perception including vision and speech, automatic analysis of human behavior and social robots used for education or healthcare services.

The brain of Movellan's social robots contained small units of information and a processor with a code. These units took in and processed data and produced a signal for the next analysis unit. Subsequent processing units formed a neural network that detected patterns in the received data. Based on this data flow, it changed its structure. They operated like the neuron structure in a human brain. The biological neuron network within the human brain is made up of billions of neurons. The artificial neuron network was developed on similar principles. This changing structure slowly becomes more advanced and stimulates human learning.

However, unlike the human brain, the artificial neuron network cannot operate like a fully developed, giant, complex, multidimension processor that has also acquired the learning of several generations. For example, you could have read about the Karnak Bowl as a 10 year old and used the principal to solve a complex measurement problem in high school. The robot—which did not have such deep learning (they don't go to school)—must adopt step-by-step learning to produce comparable output to humans.

Such step-by-step learning is imparted through artificial neural networks that extract new learnings from the data they receive. Such learnings keep adding to the robot's active memory within the microprocessor, making it increasingly sophisticated with every new piece of data added. Perhaps one day, robots will have acquired enough active memory to outdo all humans.

CAN ROBOTS OUTDO HUMANS?

This theory of robots outdoing humans was first tested by a program named Chip Test at Carnegie Melon University. The IBM research team asked three students, Feng Hsiung Hsu, Thomas Anantharaman and Murray Campbell, to keep working on a college project and build a computer that could take on and defeat chess grandmasters. It took several years and several tournaments before that level of AI was developed.

The contests between robots and grandmasters of chess first became globally popular in 1996, when world champion Gary Kasparov with an IQ of 181, was pitted against Deep Blue, an IBM computer that he managed to beat easily by a score of 4–2. After the match, Deep Blue was upgraded to Deeper Blue, which defeated Kasparov in another six-match series with a score of 3.5 to 2.5 in May 1997. Ever since, grandmasters worldwide have pitted themselves against robots, and both have enhanced their capabilities.

The matching of wits in chess between humans and robots is not the only human-versus-machine competition in analytical skills that are taking place today. Bowling machines in baseball and cricket are being developed that will be used for batting practice and will be programmed to bowl fastballs, change-ups, breaking balls, bouncers and Yorkers, googlies and top spins without a change of action. Such robots are perceptive and supported by AI, even calculating the response times of the batters and detecting the weaknesses of a particular player.

In the case of a bowling machine, the bowling robot is used to challenge the players' reaction time, technique and agility to different types of balls at different speeds, seam positions, flight and trajectory variations. The challenge with robotic sports trainers is not necessarily developing higher speeds. Humans usually need a quarter of a second to react when playing table tennis or squash. With heavier bats, the response time is proportionately higher. Machines can react ten times faster. The challenge is not to bowl fast. It is to match bowling speeds to the reaction speed of the batter, and gradually inch ahead, which will help modern players improve their technique as a batter.

The AI-powered image-scanning capabilities of computers are much more advanced than that of humans. In early 2019, researchers at Nanyang Technological University, Singapore, found that it took just 90 sec for a computer network to scan and identify 1.2 million images it had been exposed to previously from a random data set. This identification was at a 750 microseconds/image speed, 10,000 times faster than any human.

Such image-screening technologies have been adopted by security agencies at most international airports and have improved the effectiveness and speed of antiterrorist operations worldwide. Once a red corner notice or an Interpol alert has been put out against an individual in any airport, it becomes extremely difficult for the person identified to get away undetected due to this advanced scanning and identification technology. Such phenomenal technological advancement has led many people to believe that building a robot army that is much cleverer, faster and stronger than humans is a distinct possibility today and may become the biggest challenge in the next decade.

ROBOTS WITH COGNITIVE INTELLIGENCE

It is more or less certain that many of the wars of the twenty-first century will not be fought with conventional or nuclear arms. The major nations have enough to destroy each other permanently, a thousand times over. No missile defense system is robust enough to stop all nuclear missiles from any enemy nation. Rather, there will be biological and cyber warfare as nations and ideological groups, terrorists or criminals, try to settle scores. That will make the increased use of AI and robots imperative and introduce automated defense and counterattack systems.

But how will the increased number of robots behave? Physicist Stephen Hawking told the BBC nearly a decade ago, "the development of full artificial intelligence and robots could spell the end of the human race. It would take off on its own, and re-design itself at an ever-increasing rate."

But many others believe that it will not be so unidimensional. Let us see why and how the robots will pick up the benevolent and destructive actions simultaneously in their learning curve. Capabilities that oppose and neutralize each other develop as they are equipped with machine learning. We have already seen how robotics introduces critical thinking, consequence analysis, problem-solving, collaborative thinking and analytical skills. There are several other cognitive skills like innovation, communications and customer orientation that a robot acquires over time as machines learn new analytical skills from human behavior

Cognition is a process of understanding. This understanding by the brain can be through senses, thought or experience. For example, the brain can understand or learn through what it sees, feels, hears or touches. It can also be understood through thought or cognitive memory and through information processed by the brain that creates emotions. So, information input is not through a single channel but is multifaceted, multilayered and multidimensional.

Now, whenever you create cognitive intelligence with understanding and emotions, you equip it with at least two sets of opposite values. It can be black or white, good or bad, beautiful or ugly, or love or hate. In addition, it can have more than one or two variations, like bitter, salty or sweet, happy, angry or sad, or 50 shades of black, white and grey. This variation improves over time and eventually develops cognitive understanding.

Therefore, AI or robots will have to learn opposing values to represent human behavior fully. You cannot teach it one set of values and expect it to perform like a human. Therefore, a robot with cognitive capabilities could be easily programmed to do good or bad deeds—depending on its user. Once we understand this, it is easy to realize why those who have distrusted robots over the years should be taken seriously.

AI or robotics is a mere technology. It can be and will be used for good and bad. Just like Aladdin's magic lamp could be used by anyone who held it, regardless of their intentions. So, an army of constructive robots could become destructive, using the same cognitive intelligence, unless you can secure it and make it safe from hacking or falling into the wrong hands.

After developing AI, efforts started to secure digital architectures that could be locked and made foolproof. A technology that would stop hackers from breaking into the software and turning robots rogue. Robot owners needed to block the chain of destructive hacking. Incidentally, that is not currently happening. Recently, the cases of hacking have increased phenomenally.

Soon after the worldwide spread of Covid-19 became a global pandemic, cyberattacks on computer networks increased, with more than 3 billion malware attacks recorded in the first 6 months of the pandemic. Cyber security experts confirmed that ransomware attacks on global computers rose by 25%. They reported millions of AI-driven attacks—called distributed denial of service (DDoS)—on defense and commercial networks every week.

In a DDoS attack, the hacker uses multiple handlers to compromise thousands of computers on the cloud and targets a particular network—say, a bank or telephone company—and jams its network through millions of spurious requests, making its server unavailable to the public temporarily or permanently. These AI-driven cyberattacks are increasing daily, and even technology giants like Google, Microsoft and Facebook have not been spared. They can be so disruptive that corporates are sometimes forced to negotiate and pay ransoms to the attacker.

Therefore. with good AI and bad AI demonstrating their capabilities, experts are looking at new technologies to secure digital systems. A digital locking system that could ensure that hackers cannot infiltrate your computer network. This technology is another futuristic application called blockchain, which we will read about in the following chapter. Will blockchain secure the internet and computer networks worldwide or become another resource-guzzling chimera that throws up new challenges? Only time will tell.

Chapter 4

Blockchain
Keeping Track

Once you have committed yourself to the Internet of Things (IoT) or artificial intelligence (AI), you have created digital assets in the cloud, where you have little control. These assets are much more vulnerable than physical assets as they are easily accessible to users globally. They are created out of user-friendly software that is easy to use, copy, delete and hack or corrupt. The data is too large and widely spread to protect. So, for many years, computer scientists have been working on methods to encrypt and secure data. Blockchain is primarily a transaction platform using secure encrypted data. You can buy, sell or transact any business on the blockchain using such data.

Data security and privacy have become major concerns worldwide for users, technology companies and regulators. A large part of this data is personal data. This is primarily the data on consumers. These consumers know little about where their data is stored or how it is protected. For years, tech companies have used this data to increase profits. Now regulators want the technology businesses that run cloud campuses to protect user data. That can only happen if data stored in cloud servers is not stored in easily accessible plain text but encrypted with cipher text. This means transforming the plain text into an unreadable format using an encrypted algorithm. Such a coded language is widely known as the "science of cryptology." This would make the stored data safe, but expensive and less user-friendly, as you can't read or decipher cryptographic messages.

CRYPTOLOGY DURING THE SECOND WORLD WAR

Cryptology is not a new technology. In the chapter on AI, we read about the *Book of Cryptographic Messages* penned by the Arab astronomer Al Khalili in the seventh century. Then, 1,000 years later, Bernoulli and Pascal's work on the theory of probability explained the science behind this technology. Cryptographic text became extremely sophisticated in the twentieth century, with each code being arrived at after a complex mathematical computation that would take many hours to do by hand. Such coded messaging was understandably invaluable for defense communications.

During the Second World War, hundreds of German planes started bombarding cities across Europe in unison. U-boats targeted the ships and harbors of the allied forces. The armed battalions of the Third Reich were occupying nations like Austria, Poland, Belgium, Czechoslovakia and France with surprising ease. Despite an elaborate counter-espionage network, the intelligence of the allied forces could not simply decipher the coded messages being sent by the Germans to their frontline attack units. All messages sent by the Germans were coded with cipher text that changed every day.

This was not done manually, but by "The Enigma" machine, an electro-mechanical rotor-driven cipher device that encrypted the radio signals sent by the German high command to its battle units. The plain text was fed with a secret code before machine encryption. Thereafter, the encrypted radio signal was sent. Once received, it had to be fed with the secret code before decryption by the Enigma. Thus, the machine was not key to the encryption but worked in tandem with the secret code to make it unbreakable. Since the code was changed every day, you could work on breaking the code for only 24 hours.

After Britain joined the war in 1939, they had to counter a much-advanced German Enigma machine that had five rotors and ten plugboard cables and could churn out "159 million million million settings" (with 18 zeros behind 159) every single day according to the much-acclaimed British historical film *The Imitation Game*. British mathematician Alan Turing was drafted to crack the code—a task which he eventually succeeded in—helping the allied forces win the war.

In 1949, the Bell System Technical Journal published the article "A mathematical theory of cryptography" by Claude Shanon, a scientist working on the twin goals of cryptography during the war "secrecy and authenticity." It took another two decades of work before researchers Hellman and Diffie introduced the concept of "nonsecret" public key cryptography to be used by citizens. This was followed by the publication of the *Data Encryption Standard* in the US Federal Register in March 1975, the first document for the civilian use of cryptography.

So, although encrypted texts and blockchain might look like the new kid on the block, fanning a lot of investor frenzy, previous avatars of cryptology have existed and have disrupted the world beyond our imagination. Like all other current scientific developments, encryption and blockchain technology are a logical outcome of previous efforts and are not totally new, unattempted, or previously unheard of.

DISTRIBUTED LEDGERS—A CONCEPT FROM AVIATION

The current avatar of blockchain surprisingly has its roots in the aviation industry. Computers inside aircraft needed to be used faultlessly at very high altitudes. Here they could be subject to high or low temperatures, pressure, intense vibrations or solar radiation resulting in what is known as "bit flip" or malfunction of the computer chips. Such malfunctions have been known to cause accidents, the latest (at the time of writing) being in October 2008. Qantas Flight 72 from Singapore to Perth carrying 315 people at an altitude of 37,000 ft found that one of the three Air Data Inertial Reference Units was providing incorrect data to the flight computer. The Airbus 330-303, upgraded with new engines only a few years previously, made a sudden uncommanded "pitch down maneuver" to 650 ft and it took 20 sec before the pilots could restore order and bring the aircraft to the assigned cruise flight level. Many passengers were injured but a crash was averted.

The reasons for memory bit flips in computers are not always identifiable. To avoid disasters, aircraft designers during the 1970s decided to place three computer systems on commercial aircraft and devised a consensus among the mathematical output of the three computers, taking the majority view in case of a conflict. Even spacecraft like Orion or SpaceX Dragon use three flight computers that perform calculations independently and reboot automatically if errors are found after cross-checking. Thus, the method of accepting the majority opinion of distributed ledgers was born, which later on became the backbone of global blockchain technology.

A "distributed ledger" involves data being shared across multiple devices, sites or even countries. The distributed ledger system of blockchain technology expanded the original concept to multiple computers instead of just three on an aircraft. These physically separate computers or central processing unit (CPU) cores work together—in tech lingo or jargon—they are the "nodes" that are concurrently in use and work in unison to ensure "message passing." In layman's terms, multiple computers from across the world work together to produce the encrypted message on the blockchain. But why? What exactly does it do?

TIME STAMPING OF DIGITAL TRANSACTIONS

In the physical world, accountants use ledgers and cashbooks when recording all business transactions. Each business transaction, including all purchases and sales, is entered daily into the cash book with the day-end cash balance tallied. Similarly, investment and liability details and records of acquisitions of assets are kept in the ledger daily. The data from the cashbook or daybook finds its place in the annual profit and loss statement and that from the ledger is used to prepare the annual balance sheet.

Blockchain is the electronic database where this recording in encrypted text and time stamping is done. It has found wide acceptance in the industry, because the encryption of data meets a long-term need when securing and authenticating data that is generated and used by businesses. Individuals can work with plain text data; however, businesses need their data to be recorded permanently and protected. Deleted data would be disastrous.

Let us assume that the data we were concerned with was assumed to be the sales and purchase transactions at a gas station manned by a crew of four. Suppose between 08:00 a.m. to 10:00 a.m. there were 173 vehicles entering the gas station buying half a dozen different types of products including gasoline, diesel, natural gas, lube oil, grease and bitumen. At 09:15 a.m. a tanker load of diesel was bought by the gas station to replenish its stocks. Suppose all these 174 transactions were recorded and timestamped in a sequence in what is known as a digital block. So, how do we secure this digital block by cryptography?

At 08:00 a.m. the stock levels of all six commodities were recorded and thereafter with each transaction the stocks kept changing and were recorded concurrently. As blockchain data cannot be edited once created, it is impossible for anyone operator to change any entry after it has been recorded. Every transaction of each of the four crew members was automatically peer reviewed and time stamped in four different, distributed ledgers, making the entire process irrevocable, foolproof, secure and adequately transparent. In addition, in the digital environment, all network participants have their own private keys, which are assigned to the transactions they make and act as a digital signature.

WHAT IS BLOCKCHAIN AND WHY IS IT NEEDED?

"Blockchain is the biggest opportunity for the decade or so" says Bob Greifeld the Chairman of Nasdaq between 2003 to 2016.

Blockchain is a decentralized database that collects sets of encrypted data together in groups, or "blocks." Normal databases are centralized with a single database administrator. Once a block has a sufficient amount of information stored within it, it is closed and a new block is formed, which is linked to the first one via cryptography. The blocks linked together form a "chain" of data—hence the name "blockchain." Because every block contains information about the previous block it is resistant to modification. This is because each participant of the blockchain has a secured copy of all records and all changes; therefore, each user can view the data entered. That makes it authentic, because it is impossible to edit or alter the entered data without alerting other participants. IBM CEO Ginni Rometty goes a step further and says, "Anything that we can conceive of as a supply chain, blockchain can vastly improve its efficiency – it does not matter if it is people, numbers, data, money."

Blockchain promises to make business transactions easier, simpler, faster and fully authentic. Let us say a Chinese businessperson wants to buy a seaside home in Bali, Indonesia. If the property is available for sale only in Indonesian IDR they will have to get permission from the Chinese and the Indonesian governments for the deal. The sale has to be registered through the local land registry authority and the state of Indonesia, which would need multiple approvals, verifications and permissions. Also, as they do not hold the IDR and the seller does not want CNY, they must buy USD and send the money through SWIFT banking channels involving at least three corresponding banks. However, if the property was available on a blockchain registry and the sale was payable in Bitcoins the entire transaction would go through in minutes, saving cost and time for the seller and the buyer. As of 2022, several nations are working to set up a blockchain land registry, but none have progressed beyond the concept paper stage.

Blockchain encrypts and records all data, the most common being transactions of assets like the sale of a car, house or business, or even copyrights and patents. Because multiple computers across the globe work together to encrypt the transactions it becomes authenticated and certified by technology, rather than by an authority or a regulator of one nation. The payment for the asset is carried out through cryptocurrencies, not by the dollar or euro or any other standard currency. That makes it theoretically possible to buy and sell any certified and authenticated property or asset globally on the internet using blockchain and cryptocurrencies, often without paying taxes.

Everybody need not put their data on blockchains to run an effective business, register a land deal or send money to a foreign country. However, if you do, you need to know that since data is valuable, the encryption and decryption should be done transparently by a technology expert in a peer group, with a good reputation to make it relatively safe and tamperproof. In the real-life business world, it is usually a tech major like IBM, Microsoft, Ripple Labs, ScienceSoft, Amazon Web Services (AWS), Google or Microsoft who provides blockchain security with all requisite and safety protocols for businesses to use.

CAN ENCRYPTION ENSURE PRIVACY?

Blockchain enthusiasts believe that record keeping through encrypted text is possibly the only way to ensure privacy. Though that argument holds weight, it is only half the story. First let us look at the problems. Microsoft reported that following the global pandemic, Covid-19-themed fake websites grew phenomenally, and phishing attacks jumped to 20,000–30,000 a day in the US alone. In June 2020, auto major Honda reported that its Customer Services and Financial Division had slowed down following cyberattacks reportedly by a Russian hacker group called Evil Corp and in August,

Canon was attacked by the Maze Ransomware gang that stole ten terabytes of data from its databases.

Chinese and Russian hacker groups reportedly gained control of major companies and systems with operatives working from home with a relaxed safety protocol and demanded large ransoms. American, Iranian and European hackers too have joined the loot. Since databases were not encrypted, the losses have been huge. Cybersecurity firm Kaspersky reported that global businesses including travel companies, energy companies, financial institutions, health services and supply chain majors came under ransomware attacks once every 11 sec with revenue losses estimated upto $20 billion by end of 2021. Only a few criminals have been caught. Encrypted text used by cyber criminals made it more difficult for law enforcement agencies to track and pin down offenders. So, is encryption the solution? Or is it a new problem?

Data protection worries are not new. They have been around ever since computers were first invented. The concern about using and transmitting data securely started as early as the sixties. The Advanced Research Projects Agency (ARPA), an arm of the US Defense Department, sought a computer-based communications system without a central hardware core. Computer hardware was being rigged and hacked by spies during the Cuban missile crisis. So, the Defense Department wanted to store data on a core system that was not hardware-based and easily vulnerable. This Pentagon-funded project was termed initially as the ARPANET and was supposed to protect data stored in the "net or in cloud servers" from attacks and sabotage by enemy spies during the Cold War.

Data transfer and transmission on the net went on to become a cause of academia subsequently. It ultimately led to the internet of Tim Berners Lee 30 years later, making communication between devices without a central core possible globally. The possibility of fast and uninterrupted global communication made it easy for all trade and commerce. This included legal and illegal stuff. Unlicensed music, pirated software, banned drugs, child pornography, small arms and money laundering became billion-dollar industries overnight. All they needed was an alternate freeway that could not be easily tracked by others—including the regulators or the cops.

That freeway was incidentally provided by the US Government. This was another technology that was first initiated as a federal defense project by US Navy researchers Goldschlag, Reed and Syverson. Data would be sent through cryptographic texts through the internet through "onion routers." By transmitting encrypted data through layers of connection points, like the layers of onions, it was possible to route messages anonymously. Each connection point, termed the network node, could only detect, create, receive and transmit data from the previous node to the next node. So, by using multiple routers you could prevent the identification and detection of the initial source and ultimate destination of the encrypted data when "message passing" from node to node. The Onion Routing software—more commonly known as TOR—was released as free and open-source software in 2002. After downloading it you could transmit your data in encrypted form undetected.

TOR browsers allowed the federal agencies to communicate on the internet without being detected by local governments of several nations in South America, Africa and Asia. It encrypted the traffic signals and transferred them through a chain of computers, making it impossible to track the origin of the message. TOR browsers used cryptographic text that could not be decoded and was in a way the first major test for privacy or anonymity used by prodemocracy activists.

In 2008, the TOR browser hired a 26-year-old American developer Jacob Appelbaum to train prodemocracy activists in Egypt, Tunisia, Syria, Libya, Jordan and Hong Kong on how to use the TOR browser to evade their government's attempts to track their online activities without leaving a trace. It provided the all-important online communication channel for the prodemocracy activists and rebel fighters who got money, arms and logistic cover that the governments in power could not track.

The Arab Spring was engineered in 2010 and backed by the western nations. It destabilized the long-entrenched dictators of the Middle East, like Ben Ali of Tunisia, Hosni Mubarak of Egypt, Ali Abdullah Saleh of Yemen and Mummar Gaddafi of Libya. However, instead of bringing democracy it created more chaos. The Taliban, Al Qaeda, Hezbollah, Boko Haram and the Islamic State were born along with a dozen fringe armed rebel groups who fought viciously to fill the power vacuum. Unable to foster democracy, the West withdrew support to the moderates in Iraq, Libya, Yemen and Afghanistan, helping extremists wrest control of the region. Likewise in Hong Kong, the Chinese Communist Party reacted strongly, ousted and jailed prodemocracy protestors and brought the country under the absolute control of mainland China.

During the initial years, the TOR project was totally funded by federal agencies and later others like Google and Human Rights Watch supported it. It was a project to uphold democracy and permit federal agencies and American activists to snoop on the networks of other nations and carry out activities banned in less liberal countries. It was exactly what the Chinese and Soviet states did in most western democracies. However, such cloak and dagger ventures always go awry and have devastating side effects. A few years later, Edward Snowden exposed the National Security Agency (NSA) tracking of US citizens involved in domestic terrorism. Even in 2013, after the Snowden conviction, when journalists and activists started insisting on privacy from the NSA, the federal agencies funded almost 60% of its $2 million annual spending. Later in the chapter we will explore cybercrimes where the TOR browser and encrypted data helped financial crimes.

WHY BLOCKCHAIN IS HERE TO STAY

Blockchain is neither difficult to understand nor use. It is simply a web-based recording and transaction platform that improves efficiency, accuracy and record keeping. Currencies like Bitcoin on a blockchain might be energy intensive but that does not make the blockchain inefficient. Similarly, an exchange fraud in any of the cryptocurrencies might cause huge losses for investors; however, that is not because the technology is faulty. Here are some interesting anecdotes from a few exponents of blockchain technology.

The cofounder of Ethereum and *Bitcoin* magazine said

"Whereas most technologies tend to automate workers on the periphery doing work and menial tasks, blockchains automate away the center. Instead of putting the taxi driver out of a job, blockchain puts Uber out of a job and lets the taxi drivers work with the customer directly."

Vitalik Buterin

The CEO of Mayflower-Plymouth takes a step forward and says

"The Decentralization of Finance is really good for humanity and it's ultimately a win for each and every one of us. Because now that we can circumvent banks, exchanges and brokerage companies by using smart contracts on the blockchain ...every person, every family, and every business will experience more liberty, more freedom, more opportunities, more abundance, more power, and more wealth. This makes way for more opportunities around financial wellness, permaculture investing, more effective crowdfunding, better ownership and equity arrangements, and more."

Hendrith Vanlon Smith Jr.

"For merchants, it is an amazing opportunity. Compared to Paypal, crypto has no credit card fees, no chargebacks, no 'Oops, we decided to hold your cash for 3-12 months while we investigate something we can't disclose.'"

Gil Penchina, investor and former CEO of Wikia Inc

Penchina believes in the future of seamless economy where instead of buying a car we will hire one that will take us from place to place and instead of buying food we will be supplied exactly the right amount of nutrients our body needs at the right time.

Taking a dig at central bankers, investor and Olympic rower Tyler Winklevoss quips "We have elected to put our money and faith in a mathematical framework that is free of politics and human error."

Tech futurist and *Forbes* contributor says

"As revolutionary as it sounds, blockchain truly is a mechanism to bring everyone to the highest degree of accountability. No more missed transactions, human or machine errors, or even an exchange that was not done with the consent of the parties involved. Above anything else, the most critical area where blockchain helps is to guarantee the validity of a transaction by recording it not only on a main register but a connected distributed system of registers, all of which are connected through a secure validation mechanism."

Ian Khan

BLOCKCHAIN ALONE CANNOT ENSURE SECURITY AND PRIVACY

Microsoft, in collaboration with the Decentralized Identity Foundation, is attempting to bring back control of your digital identity and improve your privacy. If it succeeds, it will create a digital hub of encrypted identity data like a quick response (QR) code that you would need to share with apps and other digital service providers rather than grant broad consent to share all personal data with them. Experiments are global where your face identification could be a substitute for your ATM card in all your bank transactions. You would not require a cheque book, or an ATM card for withdrawing cash, but just have to do with facial scanning. All such applications would need blockchain security. Blockchain enthusiasts believe that someday encrypted personal data on the blockchain could do away with all usernames and passwords, including the sharing of personal data on the net. Our personal blockchain, protected by a QR code, would provide us privacy and secrecy that we would control.

Before we deep dive into the subject of protecting privacy, let us examine personal data and find out how difficult it is to secure it, especially bearing in mind consumer convenience. Your mobile phone stores an unbelievable amount of personal data with your "phone maker—the hardware provider," "Google or Apple—the software provider" and the "mobile services company—the network provider" that has access to every such piece of data independently. Add to it the apps you have given permission to access your data. Such personal data would include your fingerprint, facial profile, voice quality, minute-to-minute location and your social profile that includes photos of you, your family and friends, your credit and debit card details, your passport and social security card details and innumerable other data that even you are at times not aware of.

The ideal situation would be if all this data were stored in a blockchain within the phone with a QR code. Every time anyone wanted any data they would only ask to scan the QR code instead of extracting your personal data. However, in practice, things are far more complicated because some of this data changes frequently and some are required by multiple entities daily. For example, Uber wants your location as you hire its cabs, because you might be in half a dozen places every other day. The Uber app also asks you to save your home and office location so that you can save time when booking each trip—a permission that you readily give. This data is your personal data that is saved in the cloud server of Uber with your permission. Your payment wallet would need the verification pin and the details of your bank to which it is connected every time you pay, which again is your personal data. This also finds its way to the cloud servers. Similarly, your credit card would need the CVC details and the expiry date several times a day, because you want to pay each time to a different vendor.

Most of us would like to pay quickly, without being asked for permission to access data repeatedly. For all these to happen quickly and easily, a temporary memory is usually created, which makes it convenient and fast for you to use. Any iron-clad blockchain-based security would not permit that. Therefore, although efforts are being made to provide personal data in the blockchain, it might not provide privacy seekers the comfort that they desire, if you want to use your phone data conveniently. The tradeoff between privacy and convenience has always seen the latter win.

USE OF BLOCKCHAIN FOR SUPPLY CHAINS AND SHIPPING

The supply chain industry has been one of the early adopters of blockchain for good reasons. CONA Services, an Atlanta based blockchain startup, provides technology to 12 major Coca-Cola bottling companies in North America. Orders and shipments between Coke bottlers used traditional spreadsheets, which had inconsistencies in the recording, ordering and supplying of millions of bottles daily, which often left bottlers in dispute over losses and long drawn out reconciliation. Using the encryption system, order placement provided confirmation, proof of shipment and receipt that are now being recorded automatically in the blockchain in real time.

Ships have been carrying cargo along with passengers since time immemorial. However, since the 1950s international cargo has been packed in 20 and 40 ft containers instead of being shipped in independently packaged lots. Each of these containers could hold one or multiple types of items. For example, a 20 ft container traveling from Liverpool to Osaka could have five high fashion brands shipping their clothes from Europe to the East. The adjacent container could have olives, plums, peaches, apples and avocados. A 50,000 ton container ship could have as many as 500 different products and would pick up consignments from half a dozen ports and deliver to a dozen destinations. The amount of paperwork needed for the bill of lading is mind-boggling.

In 2018, a blockchain-based CargoX Smart Bill of Lading was released successfully from the port of Koper in Slovenia, an EU nation and former part of Yugoslavia. It not only reduced the time consumed in the processing to just minutes instead of days or weeks, it reportedly reduced the chances of loss, theft or damage to the Bill of Lading to near-zero. Maersk, one of the shipping industry giants along with IBM, is also creating a public blockchain platform for shippers on open source technology that has nearly 100 partner organizations. The blockchain platform for insurance in the shipping industry, built on Microsoft Azure global cloud technology, is positioned to similarly provide significant value to the services sector.

USE OF BLOCKCHAIN IN HEALTHCARE

Another major application is in harnessing medical data for an individual or an ailment. Now, imagine the benefits of analysis if all your medical data could be stored in a folder and secured by a blockchain that your physician could access only during the period they were treating you. Every time you visit your doctor the ailment diagnosis and the treatment data are added to the secured file that you control. The blockchain technology allows your physician to look at the file and add to the data, but does not permit copying, storing or deleting data once entered.

Now, suppose you have breast cancer and willingly want to share your data with a global breast control treatment foundation without revealing your identity; you can do so with blockchain technology and keep your identity private. Similar benefits could be derived by cancer researchers or virologists seeking solutions by analyzing large and diverse data from across the globe. This type of data sharing that retains your privacy could encourage many more patients to come forward and add to the global knowledge pool.

Blockchain has enormous possibilities when assisting clinical research, because it works on the principle of decentralized record keeping. International clinical research is a 24/7 operation with multiple scientists participating and observing the process, which is often complex and iterative. To reduce the time span, multiple research groups work together using varied approaches and report different results that need to be logged. It becomes convenient when the operations and results are time stamped in blockchain to produce a permanent and authentic sequence of records. Blockchain ensures control of data, its identification and traceability, prevents a later reconstruction and allows for the secure automation of the clinical trial for one or more patients through what are called "smart contracts."

USE OF BLOCKCHAIN IN INDUSTRIAL SECTORS

Another major nonfinancial application that is being attempted by blockchain developers is in the energy sector. Blockchain-secured smart metering practices could ensure smart metering at a local level without centralized data processing and verification. Consumers could prepay for a new usage directly and get it entered into the database instead of having to get approval from the electricity provider. Major energy companies, especially in developing nations, are carrying billions in debt due to the inability of consumers to pay for what they consume. Politicians promise free electricity to select groups, like farmers, senior citizens and citizens below the poverty lines that hurt the finances of energy companies. Therefore, energy companies are going for the prepaid model so that their finances are not used to provide this type of credit. The states provide direct subsidies instead or pay them to deliver to citizens. Tokyo Electric Power Company recently partnered with cryptocurrencies provider Ethereum startup Grid+ to develop a platform that allows consumers to prepay for power. A dozen more nonfinancial applications of blockchain are being developed by multinationals including Boeing, Honeywell and Aramco.

The worldwide supply of spares for the aviation business generates annual revenues of $4 billion. With innumerable models of aircraft having an average operating lifespan of more than 30 years, a steady supply of spares is needed to service the industry. However, it becomes extremely difficult to authenticate and certify parts that are available with numerous agents around the world that handle spares. The Honeywell hyper ledger GoDirect Trade is a blockchain platform designed to prove and authenticate the origin of certified aerospace parts and ensure that they comply with safety standards.

Traditionally, every part has complex paperwork including a certificate of manufacture, quality certification and operation manuals that have to physically move with every part. The Honeywell blockchain provides manufacturers with an open source access code that they can build on independently. Each listing in the supply chain is tied to images of the part and corresponding documents for the exact part being offered for sale, which helps to ensure that the part is in the inventory, and that the documents it's associated with aren't forged. It is an easy-to-add platform without complex integration that helped Boeing to add over $1 billion of unused spares in May 2020 in minutes according to Lisa Butters, General Manager of the blockchain platform. There are over 50 members on the Honeywell platform, which generated $7 million in revenue during the first year of operation in 2020 and expects to achieve a revenue of $1 billion in 3 years.

Oil and gas giant Aramco partnered with IBM to adopt blockchain across all its operations streams that included a four-pronged approach to, "Build solutions, Consume available sources, Join consortiums and Investment in startups." On a microlevel, every operation of the world's largest oil producer will be upgraded to the blockchain to improve efficiency and cut costs. For example, Aramco conducts many background checks every year to verify the diplomas and certificates of new employees and contractors in its drilling and refining operations. As Aramco hires global talent trained in diverse institutions across the world this is very time-consuming. Aramco deployed its first version of the blockchain Certificate Verifier in June 2020, which has reportedly helped it to cut its verification time for its heavy equipment operators by 90%.

The blockchain industry has also made inroads into the legal services industry. There are several formats of contracts available where lawyers can leverage the blockchain technology to streamline and simplify transactional work and digitally sign and safely store legal agreements with technology oversight. The response of the legal fraternity has been so high that an Internet of Agreements (IoA) conference took place in October 2017 in London, where some of the finest global brains came together to discuss the various implications of blockchain technology on contracts and international legal agreements. While it is too early to say if IoA will mature for the service industry, just like the IoT has done for the manufacturing industry, there was no shortage of interest among the experts who plan to take this revolutionary idea forward to the next level.

BLOCKCHAIN CAN PROVIDE TAMPERPROOF CURRENCY

However, blockchain needs time to grow out of the shadow of cryptocurrencies (which we will discuss in detail in the following chapter) and establish its utility in nonfinancial sectors; only when that happens will it attract more investors. In addition, it is important for blockchain to be accepted by the central banks. However, many bankers feel that blockchain safety is not as foolproof as the safety of a physical cashbook or ledger in your office. This is because hackers do not spare tech majors from data dumps, and frauds and leaks in this space have happened regularly, showing that even the most competent of the digital players cannot save themselves from data breaches.

In 2019, social media giant Facebook encountered two major data breaches. First, the personal data including names, phone numbers and email addresses of 49 million Instagram influencers (e.g., film stars and celebrities) along with 419 million Facebook users was left exposed by a Mumbai-based marketing firm that used an AWS chatbox without a password. Six months later, the personal data of 267 million Facebook users was posted on a hacker forum and remained undetected by the tech major for more than 2 weeks. Had Facebook encrypted its data it would have remained secure even if it had been hacked.

Blockchain supporters say that the only way to save critical data from being deleted or compromised is encryption. It might not be able to prevent hacking or fraud; however, blockchain makes it unreadable without decryption. It is infinitely difficult to read, rewrite, delete or destroy encrypted data. Only access to your private key will ensure that the blockchain data can be read. However, even that does not ensure that the data can be deleted or corrupted. Hence, data on a blockchain is the closest to creating a permanent irrevocable record on the internet.

Such security is ideal for the financial markets. So, it is not surprising that currency on the blockchain became an idea worth trying out. Nick Szabo, an early blockchain and smart contracts exponent, first conceptualized this currency in the form of BitGold in 1998. It combined the decentralized proof of work concept, the mining of encrypted data and time stamping on the blockchain to create a permanent record. However, for some reason it lacked some key elements and could not be launched as a finished product. It is speculated that Szabo had to collaborate with some other cryptographers. Therefore, an anonymous identity Satoshi Nakamoto was created when the first cryptocurrency Bitcoin was launched a decade later.

Over the last 15 years, Bitcoin has recorded over 10 million transactions every month. It has not been accepted as a legal tender in any major nation and has been shunned by regulators. However, it became an instant hit because in addition to privacy, secrecy and anonymity it provides extreme ease of operation and high speculative returns with zero inflation. We will look at each of these qualities in detail as we explore the unique selling point of cryptocurrencies in the following chapter. In addition, we will see how it has impacted the financial and banking world for good and bad.

Chapter 5

Cryptocurrencies

Beyond Tracking

Cryptocurrencies are encrypted digital currencies on the blockchain. Printed currencies are issued by central banks and are periodically verified when they are deposited in banks. Every transaction is not recorded, and you cannot keep track of ownership every time money changes hands. Cryptocurrencies are decentralized digital currencies and use encryption on the blockchain to authenticate the issue of the cryptocurrency and every transaction after that. So, although it can be transferred instantly globally, its ownership record exists on public ledgers on the blockchain, providing transparency, security and safety.

The first cryptocurrencies arrived in January 2009, just months after the stock market crash of 2008. At that time, the Wall Street banks were bailed out with a virtually blank check that the US Federal Reserve provided. The mandate was to spend, lend and get the credit cycle back to normal. Businesses worldwide had been severely hit, and millions had lost their jobs overnight. Treasuries were now being forced to pump in cash to rebuild economies. It was an era of easy liquidity with few questions asked. Many banks and fintech majors deployed the surplus cash in several high-profit ventures instead of focusing on improving banking credit. In addition, it was the right time for investors who had lost billions on risky derivative trades to buy innovative, low-cost cryptocurrencies for future profits.

TAX FREE WEALTH

After the arrival of the internet, investors and tech entrepreneurs started thinking about the possibility of having a purely digital destination for global wealth that would be out of the purview of any nation's laws and regulators; however, it would be secure for investors to park their money. Such a digital destination needed to be deregulated, secure, transparent and tamper-proof. First, it had to be deregulated—hence independent of central banks. It had to be secure—which was provided by encryption on the blockchain. It needed transparency—which was provided by making every

DOI: 10.1201/9781003409557-7

issue and transaction visible on the internet. Finally, it had to be tamper-proof—which was achieved by time stamping every transaction, which made the records on the blockchain public ledger irrevocable. Cryptocurrencies arrived in 2009 to provide a secure currency at a deregulated digital destination on tamper-proof distributed ledgers far away from the tax regulators of national governments.

With the increased interest in cryptocurrencies, most nations worldwide saw a huge diversion in their capital. The super-rich of the world who were already moving their wealth to tax havens found easy ways to park money digitally. It was easier to invest in cryptocurrencies, and money invested digitally fetched high returns in terms of inflation-free speculative profits.

Despite the rapid improvements made by science and technology, our world is increasingly becoming unequal. In the world's most populous democracy, the top 10% of Indians hold 77% of the nation's wealth, and the bottom 50% have to make do with less than 0.5% In the second most populous democracy, the US, the numbers are only marginally better. Here, the top 10% of the population own 70% of the wealth and the bottom 50% account for just 2%. Although all adults in both democracies select their political leaders through transparent elections, this inequality has grown. Why?

Possibly because the rich of the world, along with the most profitable corporations, have been steadily moving their wealth to tax havens to avoid high taxes. When the pandemic devastated world economies in 2020, multinational corporations moved $245 billion and private individuals $182 billion, a total of $472 billion, to tax havens. The tax revenues lost due to investment in digital currencies are estimated to be $100 billion annually. The September 2019 International Monetary Fund (IMF) report *Tackling Tax Havens* stated that in a normal year, countries worldwide lost from $500 to $600 billion due to such a shift in global wealth, leading to a loss in taxes. It quoted economist and lawyer James S. Henry, who estimated that in 2016 offshore tax havens yielded an astonishing $36 trillion, almost 11% of the total global wealth.

Tax havens have resulted in reducing direct taxes levied in most countries. Therefore, governments are spending less on social development. Instead, they have increased the emphasis on indirect tax collection. So, you are paying less tax on what you earn and more on what you consume. But, as all direct taxes can't be converted into indirect taxes, overall tax collections have fallen. The US loses 18%, India 40% and Africa almost 30% of its taxes due to such wealth diversion to tax havens, hurting the livelihoods of the poorest people on the planet who are dependent on government aid. Through their top three tax havens in the Cayman Islands, British Virgin Islands and Bermuda, the British gain the most, accounting for nearly 25% of the wealth shift.

You can trace this practice to a series of rulings pronounced by the British courts a century ago that permitted nonresidents to conduct business in

Britain without paying British taxes or disclosing their identity. Most significant among those was a 1928 case (*Egyptian Delta Land and Investment Co. Ltd. v. Todd, 1928*). Although the company was registered in London and could use British banks and other legal facilities for business, it did not have any operational activity in the UK; therefore, it was not subject to British taxation. Therefore, the low-cost, sparsely populated British Islands where it was registered could attract foreign capital from former British colonies with nominal taxation.

During the early 1930s, the Swiss felt the effect of the 1929 depression that had caused a tourism slump across the Alpine states. So, they started looking for innovative means to attract foreign capital. They caught on to this British ploy of giving legal sanctity to "foreign funds parked anonymously" and institutionalized it by creating the now infamous *Swiss Banking Act (1934)*. This act permitted the parking of foreign funds in Swiss banks and gave immunity to those who did so with legal nondisclosure agreements. Article 47 of the act promised absolute secrecy for the identity of account holders. It made it a criminal offense for those who divulged such professional secrets, making it impossible for bankers, journalists and foreign governments to investigate or even know the identity of Swiss bank account holders.

For the next 50 years, the Swiss banks ruled the world of dirty money and became the global hub for tax evaders. The British Islands were not far behind and gained half of the global offshore wealth. This is despite the fact that tax havens promising total secrecy sprouted across the globe from Singapore to Belize and Dubai to Mauritius.

WHAT IS BITCOIN MINING?

The mining of Bitcoin is essentially an encrypted record-keeping process that facilitates business transactions. There is no physical mining involved like in mining gold or diamonds. The mining is all digital and involves generating new "blocks" of transactions on the blockchain. Participants are computing from different destinations on multiple computers (known as distributed decentralized public ledgers in tech lingo), providing data on secure databases (by solving algorithms and encrypting data on the blockchain) accessible to all 24 × 7.

The ledger and cash book we use in the physical world is a centralized ledger at a fixed location and under private or government control. It would be a simple 200-page notebook in a Mom and Pop store to maintain a record of daily sales, purchases and inventory. To increase transparency, the distributed digital ledger is a database across several locations with concurrent access for multiple participants and no single point of control. It is like playing Monopoly online with other online players, where you cannot change records unilaterally once you have purchased a property.

However, producing or mining bitcoins is not as easy as making a single entry on a physical ledger by the superstore cashier. There is a need for powerful computers, servers and huge data centers with enough cooling capacity to prevent them from overheating. Called mining equipment, it is a sizable infrastructure to provide adequate computing power. In addition, the hours that an expert computer scientist has to devote to solve algorithms or cryptographic problems are high and usually increase every 2 weeks, the approximate time taken to mine 2,016 blocks of the blockchain. But they can also drop. How?

The Bitcoin mining architecture is highly optimized and based on supply and demand. If more miners work, the complexity of each solution is higher. Hence, the time spent and computational hours for each mined Bitcoin increase. Miners recently realized that the reverse was also true. The use of cryptocurrencies has always been banned in China; however, it manufactures most of the mining equipment. As energy costs are low in Northern China and it has abundant energy supply, it provided the largest number of Bitcoin miners, producing nearly 50% of the world's bitcoins for years.

In May 2021, the Chinese Government banned cryptocurrency mining, realizing that it led to a high transfer of capital despite restrictions on use. Fewer miners and less computing power meant verifying transactions and minting new bitcoins took longer. So, like clockwork, the Bitcoin algorithm self-corrected for this deviation from the norm. Whereas in June, the algorithm had become 7.3% more difficult to solve, the network saw an unprecedented 28% drop in the difficulty level in July. So, even with 50% of mining capacity knocked off, miners in other parts of the world found it much easier to solve a block.

HIGH CARBON FOOTPRINT

Over the years, the demand for bitcoins has grown rapidly. The mining of Bitcoin is designed to become more complex as demand rises, and it takes more time to mine the blocks. The energy consumed to mine bitcoins increases yearly as the algorithms to solve become more complex. Mining one Bitcoin today consumes electricity equivalent to what an American household would spend in 13 years. It produces about 40 million tonnes of CO_2 annually.

Mining of bitcoins is an energy-guzzling process consuming 90,000 gigawatts hours (GWH) or 0.5% of the total global energy, according to an *New York Times* (*NYT*) report in September 2021. The mining process requires the pooling of computer power to enhance the chances of finding a block. Worldwide, there are pools of miners, including in some developing nations where electricity does not reach all households. Binance, Slush Pool, Antpool, Genesis Mining, and others facilitate cryptocurrency mining. China has four such large mining pools located in the northern and western parts of the country, with low electricity costs; however, most Chinese miners are now relocating due to the mining ban.

Computer scientists insist that blockchain is the most efficient and transparent way to secure records. However, as a student, you could say that mining bitcoins is inefficient only because it consumes massive resources. You could challenge the claim of efficiency. Therefore, since the object is to keep records, a business's physical cash book and ledger are more convenient, user-friendly, cheap and secure than creating such a mammoth energy-guzzling digital solution to do the same work. You are possibly right, but our world does not follow such simple logic. People imagine complex problems and conjure mammoth solutions. Mammoth solutions bring high profits. Then, they scale up the problems to match the solutions to benefit investors and businesses. So, we spend resources solving problems that maximize profits instead of those problems that benefit the masses.

CRYPTOCURRENCIES IN ENTERTAINMENT

Cryptocurrencies have been very profitable for investors, providing a speculative value to stashed-away wealth. They are also providing new playgrounds for the rich. Now that you know why and how they arrived, you need to understand how they are marketed and popularized. Unlike other regular fiat currencies, like the US dollar or the Euro, most major cryptocurrencies are promoted actively through a host of games, promotional deals and active lobbying, because they serve private interests and huge profiteering with massive speculative appreciation.

As a result, they are used heavily in casinos that have always provided great entertainment on and off-line. Apart from top US casinos like Las Vegas Sands and MGM Resorts, many large online casinos in China and several European nations are safe and legally protected. Now, sensing an opportunity to attract the wealth stashed away online, many casinos accept cryptocurrencies. Most crypto casinos are licensed and regulated by Curaçao laws and protect their users with Secure Sockets Layer (SSL) encryption. They also have fast, effective customer service and 24 × 7 operators on standby.

BitStarz commenced operation in 2014 and is currently the largest crypto casino with over 3,500 game options from top-rated industry names, such as Adopt, Betsoft, AsiaGaming, Blueprint, Bgaming, Digitian, Evolution and many others. You can enjoy various slots, jackpots, live casino games, table games and live dealer games. It was considered the best casino in 2017 and received many awards after that. Apart from regular currencies, you have half a dozen cryptocurrencies and a transparent, well-managed playing environment. In addition, it verifies the fairness of its games using a provably fair algorithm. It also provides 180 free spins and welcome bonus amounts against customers' first, second and third cryptocurrency deposits.

One of the most popular casinos that accept "only cryptocurrencies" is the mBit Casino, which accepts seven tokens (e.g., Bitcoins, Bitcoin Cash, Ethereum (ETH), Tether, Litecoin, Dogecoin and Coinspad) through VenusPoint, AstroPay, Accentpay, Banktransfer and payments through Visa and Mastercard. The casino offers hundreds of slots, blackjack, poker, roulette, jackpot games, casino table games and drops and wins games, but no live dealer games. It also has over half a dozen incentive plans along with 300 free spins and refer-a-friend bonus schemes for casino buddies.

Cloudbet is all about sports betting with cryptocurrencies. It accepts around 12 cryptocurrencies, including stable coins (which we will discuss later in this chapter). The casino offers live betting options on major sporting events and leagues like ATP Tennis, NHL hockey, UFC mixed martial arts, EPL and UEFA football and NBA basketball leagues, boxing leagues, archery and darts. Apart from sports betting, it offers roulette, blackjack, baccarat and jackpot slots. Bovada is yet another popular sports betting site. The Bovada sportsbook permits you to bet on 30 major sports leagues and features the most competitive odds, and accepts many cryptocurrencies.

The adult entertainment business already has dedicated cryptocurrencies like SexCoin, Model-X-Coin and TitCoin. Swiss blockchain business bitcci, founded in 2017, is now trying to free the sex business from tensions and distrust by establishing a modern, new culture of acceptance, transparency, trust and self-determination. Their idea is to legalize and tokenize the sex market and decentralize the whole sector, including nightclubs, apps, portals, escort services, adult dating and private clubs.

FRAUD IN EXCHANGES, TRUST LOSS IN CURRENCY.

Blockchain-based cryptocurrencies have not been able to earn the trust of users. First, they did not eliminate fraud and thefts as promised by their founders. Second, they did not provide any stability for the currency. Any standard currency, be it the US dollar, Euro or gold, protects the user from fraud and instability as central banks work with national governments to ensure trust. In the case of Bitcoin or any other cryptocurrency, that trust factor was missing. In addition, being a deregulated currency, it did not have the oversight of a regulatory body, making it prone to misuse. This makes it less trustworthy even though the issuance of bitcoins is far more transparent than the issuance of US dollars by the Federal Reserve—which prints money because it often needs to provide fiscal stimulus to an over-borrowed economy.

Bitcoin's trust issues were largely at the exchange and market ends, not at the mining end. An exchange is like a bank where investors store their bitcoins. In the real world, a bank scam or a failure does not lead to a run on the currency. However, because people do not understand the technology, they blame cryptocurrency for every exchange failure and say Bitcoin is a Ponzi scheme. In June 2011, during the early days of cryptocurrency, when Bitcoin was valued at a paltry $17.7 a piece, a popular Bitcoin exchange called Mt. Gox was hacked, and bitcoins worth $8.75 million were stolen. After some uproar, the company paid back investors and became the largest Bitcoin exchange in the world. In 2014, it was again hacked, and investors lost $460 million, which was stolen from bank accounts at the exchange. Mark Karpeles, the Tokyo-based Chief Executive Officer (CEO) of the exchange, was blamed for using untested software and had to file for bankruptcy.

Bitcoins cannot be stored on your phone or laptop. You have to store them in the exchange or on the blockchain. You do not have to manage them with complex software detectors and passwords if you bank them with the exchange. The crypto exchanges do that for you at their backend. The only risk is that if they are hacked, your asset is lost. The alternative is to access it with a hardware wallet with your private key, which is your cryptographic security password. That is not a big deal if your hardware wallet is genuine and the firmware is regularly updated. The private key that gives access to your asset is a long string of numbers and letters you can save off-line, even as a printout on paper.

You can buy these hardware wallets, like Trezor, Ledger Nano or any other wallet online from the manufacturers, their affiliates, or e-commerce platforms like Amazon or auction sites. Unfortunately, some of these devices have built-in vulnerabilities that hackers exploit, so ascertain the source before you buy. Many of these glitches are inserted into wallets sold at low prices on the dark net to third-party resellers who pedal them to unsuspecting buyers. This is how thousands of Bitcoin thefts happen annually, and users lose millions. Being an unregulated currency, there is no easy recourse to fraud or theft.

Besides exchange and wallet thefts, massive frauds have been reported during the "initial coin offering" or ICO stage when new cryptocurrencies are issued. The huge success of Bitcoin has resulted in these new blockchain-based currencies entering the market with unique ideas and new options. Onecoin and Bitconnect are the better-known Ponzi schemes that cheated millions of investors, promising high returns.

It is virtually a Wild West out there with a deregulated market with hundreds of new cryptocurrencies and hundreds of bankrupt exits every week. As of 2021, there were more than 5,000 cryptocurrencies with 2,000 active and counting. However, without any regulatory authority or third-party rating, there is no way of knowing what will work and what will not. So, investors often get trapped backing new cryptocurrency investments, adding high risk as another problem on top of its usual fraud and trust issues.

VOLATILITY OF CRYPTOCURRENCIES

The volatility of cryptocurrencies is also a major concern for investors. Gold, the US dollar and Euro provide great stability to banks and regulators. They allow nations to create long-term economic policies without worrying about the currency's value once adequate forex reserves are available. Credit ratings, foreign exchange borrowings, imports, exports and domestic manufacturing and trade depend on the value and stability of the local currency in an increasingly globalized world. Can you imagine the chaos if Bitcoin or any other cryptocurrency were the official currency of a country?

Like gold, the mining of Bitcoin is expensive and time-consuming. Like gold, it is scarce and highly valued. Over 18 million bitcoins were mined during the first decade. They were worth over half a trillion dollars in 2022. Another 3 million bitcoins remain to be mined, which is expected to be completed in the next 120 years. In short, mining Bitcoin has become rarer and more expensive than gold mining. So, it is not unnatural that the cryptocurrency's price will go north. What is, however, not natural is the extent of the volatility of Bitcoin.

A million bitcoins were reportedly mined by a peer group under the name Satoshi Nakamoto before the cryptocurrency was officially released in 2009. This early miners' group seemingly controls the bitcoin supply and possibly guides the volatile cryptocurrency pricing strategy. Bitcoin first gained fame in 2017 when it rose from $1,000 to $20,000 in a single calendar year. The trend analysis provided enough evidence to indicate that the price of this digital asset could be quickly spiked by a handful of early investors.

This was largely because the Satoshi Nakamoto peer group successfully created a currency that involved a time-consuming mining process and nearly 5% to 10% of the cryptocurrency. That was enough to create volatility and consequent super profits. Unlike oil, you could not quickly mine bitcoins and ramp up supplies to douse volatility. So, the value of Bitcoin became dependent on supply, demand and speculation without any central bank intervention. It was secure, transparent, tamper- proof and highly profitable. It was designed to have a finite supply of 21 million coins and was becoming increasingly difficult to mine; therefore, pushing the price sky-high. It could provide indefinite wealth and power to the early Bitcoin miners. Yet it did not earn trust like gold or the US dollar, because its motive was pure profit largely for the early investors.

After passing the $20,000 mark briefly in 2018, the supply position eased, and the cryptocurrency price plummeted to $3,300 by the end of the year. It remained subdued and below $5,000 for the first two quarters of 2019. In the third quarter of 2019, Bitcoin rose again above the $10,000 mark. With the pandemic's arrival, cryptocurrency's price crashed again to below the $5,000 mark during the first two quarters of 2020. In May 2020, mining bitcoins became twice as time-consuming. The supply constraints became even more severe. Even if 5% of the available stocks were to go out of circulation, it meant a shortfall of around a million bitcoins from the markets. At the current mining rate, only 36 bitcoins can be produced every hour. It would take quite a few years to mine and replenish the shortfall in 1 million bitcoins. As the supply of new bitcoins became time-consuming and expensive, the early miners controlled enough stocks to sway prices. For them, it was easy to spike the price of bitcoins to unimaginable highs without too much effort. However, they had to wait for an opportune moment.

In November 2020, the market cap of 5,000 cryptocurrencies was a low $400 billion. The bull run on Bitcoin began when the world started emerging from the lockdown phase, and payments giant PayPal announced that it would start accepting Bitcoin on its portal. Bitcoin had been largely used for dark web transactions until then but found wings and soared above $30,000 by the next quarter. One year later, at its peak, Bitcoin spurted past $68,000. At that time, the number of cryptocurrencies had doubled, according to crypto tracker CoinGecko and its market cap had grown sevenfold to $2.8 trillion at its peak. Bitcoin had a market share exceeding 40%, and ETH accounted for nearly 20% of the market cap. However, by the next quarter, Bitcoin had unexpectedly crashed to half its peak value bringing down other cryptocurrencies. After the start of the Russia–Ukraine war, Bitcoin collapsed further to below $20,000 and kept losing ground each month.

The volatility of Bitcoin also acts as a hedge to bad times, say some analysts. In 2017, the citizens of Venezuela discovered that their currency had become valueless. After facing prolonged US sanctions, the communist regime of Nicolas Maduro went through a period of intense hyperinflation and defaulted on bond repayments. It is speculated that the regime's top brass bought into Bitcoin as the currency crashed. In February 2018, the devaluation of the oil-rich nation ensured that the Bolivar (VEF) plummeted by 96% going from VEF 285,000 to VEF 6 million a US dollar. Venezuelan citizens could only trade with cryptocurrencies during this phase. Many Venezuelans worked as freelancers or as employees for multinational corporations. They were all paid in cryptocurrencies because Venezuela had disassociated its currency from the US dollar and linked its new currency to oil. However, people could not barter oil, so they dealt with bitcoins. Cryptocurrencies like Bitcoin, Litecoin, Dash and Ripple were highly popular during the next few years, sustaining some currency conversion with international currencies that were not subject to hyperinflation. Deep distress gripped them again in 2022 as the cryptos crashed, wiping out their wealth.

El Salvador, the tiny and impoverished South American nation, adopted Bitcoin in September 2021 after Ecuador and Venezuela experimented with cryptocurrencies. But as the price of Bitcoin has moved downward ever since, the decision led to large-scale protests over fears that it would bring instability and inflation to the impoverished Latin American country. Six months later, the IMF urged El Salvador to reverse its decision to accept Bitcoin as a legal tender citing the chance of fiscal instability and hyperinflation.

WEIRDOS TO STABLECOINS

Bitcoin is often referred to as the first generation of blockchains. It is fairly simple and secure and does not accommodate applications outside transactions as a currency. ETH, in contrast, is a second-generation blockchain that permits a great deal of programmability outside financial transactions. ETH has many more advanced features and provides software developers with much more independence to experiment with their code. Both are highly liquid and popular cryptocurrencies. Bitcoin accounts for nearly 65% of the market volume, and ETH accounts for 25% as of 2022. In addition, over 5,000 other cryptocurrencies jostle for the remaining 10% of the market, with 95% having a shelf life of less than 5 years.

Other leaders like Dash, Litecoin, XRP and Monero are making their presence felt, including some in niche areas. Around a dozen cryptocurrencies have survived and prospered with reasonably high valuations for over a decade, showing that they are no flash in the pan. Between them, their total market value has sometimes exceeded $500 billion, and in November 2021, they briefly touched $1 trillion. But thousands of others have failed, and another thousand plus are fighting to stay relevant in a competitive market.

Foremost among the many weird cryptocurrencies is Dogecoin, a meme-turned-cryptocurrency that has been going strong for nearly a decade. Taking off from the online community's liking of the Japanese Shiba Inu hunting dog, the payment system was created to mock the high volatility of cryptocurrencies and has a market capitalization of over $500 million without being overtly volatile. It has survived the flood of cryptocurrencies that have come and gone in quick succession and has managed to sponsor causes like funding Olympic athletes and NASCAR drivers.

However, hundreds of other weird cryptocurrencies like the Selfiecoin, Pizzacoin, Trumpcoin, Putincoin, Potcoin and Cannabiscoin have a place in the vast graveyard of deregulated cryptocurrencies. In 2017, Burger King Russia launched a gimmicky Whoppercoin initiative, a blockchain-based rewards program where customers get one Whoppercoin for every Ruble they spent. Those who accrued RUB 1,700 got a free burger. Similarly, Cypherfunks is a decentralized community of techno musicians using Funk coins to support their musical dreams. There are LGBT Tokens and ClimateCoins, and several others for activists. Cats have been a very popular internet diversion over the years, leading to many cat-themed digital tokens like Monacoin, Catcoin and Nyancoin. Then, there are several cryptocurrencies specifically tailor-made for the adult entertainment industry, like Sexcoin and Titcoin.

Legendary investor Warren Buffet repeatedly stated that cryptocurrencies have no intrinsic real value and would never invest in them. Today, they have become the frivolous pursuit of the rich, idle techies plotting to make a quick buck out of any trending gimmick on the internet and add very little value to the needs of the real world around us. All you need is a peer group of techies who create the algorithms and some popular fads among netizens that can help viral marketing on the internet. Being deregulated, they have zero accountability and no benchmarking to live up to. So, they are whimsical and risk-prone. Critics say that although some may be highly speculative and profitable, they are not beneficial to the masses. In short, deregulation does not necessarily work for the good of humanity. However, the technology has good uses that are slowly taking root and will evolve.

Bill Gates, Eric Schmidt, David Marcus and Peter Thiel have acknowledged that Bitcoin is a tour de force and shows how the currency can be handled cheaply and efficiently. The problem is volatility and deregulated use. Unlike Bitcoin, several cryptocurrencies do not focus on high valuation but on stability. You could call them self-regulated. These stablecoins are backed by traditional currencies or assets like gold and are designed to avoid the volatility of Bitcoin or other high valuation cryptocurrencies. The USD Coin (USDC) is a digital dollar fully backed by cash and US Treasury bonds. So, although it is a digital dollar, it can be exchanged with the USD at par value. Each month there is a report by the audit firm Grant Thornton verifying the reserves backing USDC that provides investor interest. Apart from USDC, six major stablecoins include Tether, Binance USD and Digix Gold Token. Facebook's proposed cryptocurrency, which has been delayed, is also designed to be one and will be called the Libra Stablecoin

CRYPTOCURRENCIES NEEDED IN INTERNATIONAL BANKING

There is another kind of cryptocurrency called Ripple, which has been specifically designed for the banking industry. It aims to find a quick and low-cost method to send money abroad. It is not a cryptocurrency that is mined; it is distributed based on international agreements. Before we try to explain Ripple and its structure, let us understand what business needs it fulfills. International business payments today go through a complicated transfer process. When you send money from your bank account to a seller in a different country, your bank uses the Society for Worldwide Interbank Financial Telecommunication (SWIFT) payment process for bank-to-bank transfer. It is neither swift nor cheap. The methodology designed in the early 1970s provides a secure network for over 11,000 member banks, security brokers and financial institutions in all countries to transfer payments from one bank account to another.

The corresponding and recipient banks charge fees to process your order. When sending money from Montreal to Minsk, you must go via banks in New York and Moscow. If your transfer involves two, three or four currencies, the banks apply exchange rates each time and pocket the profit. So, you could lose as much as 5% every time you make a payment. Besides this, it could take from 5 to 10 working days for a money transfer to be achieved, for which you would lose any interest even as the funds stay in your bank when the payment is in process. So not only do multiple wire transactions take time, even transaction fees are charged multiple times as many banks are used for a single transaction.

The SWIFT process is time-consuming, expensive and error-prone. Wire transfers between banks cost anything from $10 to $50, foreign exchange charges from 0.25% to 3% and "landing fees" of as much as $20. In addition, the error rate for wire transfers is between 3% and 5%, and the time for error reconciliation is over 1 month. Banks in different countries work to different standards, often using different languages. In addition, the SWIFT information transmission comes from the transferring bank to the recipient bank because it only provides a one-way messaging service. SWIFT is an inefficient and archaic system that needs to be replaced.

In 2012, a San Francisco-based startup introduced a cryptocurrency that promised to simplify the SWIFT process and make it cheaper and quicker via a secure blockchain technology-based solution Ripple and a cryptocurrency (XRP) with a two-way communication protocol. This would help banks exchange information and determine the charges to be levied, the exchange rates and the delivery date of funds. After confirmation of the destination address, fees and processing time, the actual money transfer would be carried out, making the process cheaper, foolproof and error-free. The startup has drawn up agreements with 60 medium-sized banks, including Santander, the Royal Bank of Canada, Mitsubishi UFJ Financial Group, Standard Chartered Bank and National Bank of Egypt, to try out its solutions for international payments. However, Ripple has had its setbacks and has not been able to deliver fully due to a host of issues.

BIG BANKS TRY TO DELAY CRYPTOCURRENCY ADOPTION

Ever since Bitcoin hit the market, the banking industry has been in a spin. Jamie Dimon, the CEO of J.P. Morgan Chase, the largest American bank, has been the most vocal, calling it a Ponzi scheme on more than one occasion. The Bank of America's Chief Executive, Brian Moynihan, barred the banks' wealth managers from investing in crypto-related assets. There was a concerted but unsuccessful effort to ban cryptocurrencies as bankers and lawyers jointly told regulators that cryptocurrencies were the reason why Iranian sanctions were not effective. So, if not for saving the investor, it should be barred to save the security interests of a nation. The lobbying effort failed, and by 2015, the New York Department of Financial Services started issuing licenses for Bitcoin businesses. In the next 5 years, over 500 million people tried to invest in cryptocurrencies at least once.

Banks have been lobbying to stop the rise in cryptocurrencies. They have also secretly tried to upgrade their skill level to launch their cryptocurrencies. In the year of the pandemic, the Bank of America filed the largest number of patents in its history, including 160 patents related to money transfer on blockchain and digital currency. However, it has been unable to launch its maiden digital currency or convert its research into a product prototype. J.P. Morgan launched its digital currency in 2019. However, it slowed down issuance soon after because regulators were worried. In addition, it did not have a profitable business plan to monetize without hurting the existing banking business. Banks know that digital payments are the future but are fearful that they will make things transparent and will hurt the industry's profits.

Cryptocurrencies expose the Achilles heel of the banking industry, which is its international operations. Banks are inefficient when dealing with money, because they have complex workforce-intensive physical operations. Only a small part of its business, like ATMs, is automated. International operations are difficult because every nation and the international bank wants to profit and places high fees and service charges that may or may not be logical. The SWIFT mechanism is an archaic payment procedure that has not been updated, not because of technology but because it is profitable for bankers to keep it opaque and multilayered. In a November 2021 article, "Banks tried to kill crypto and failed. Now they are embracing it (slowly)", the *NYT* highlighted the sequence of events that show that banks are making desperate efforts to gain control of the digital payment system. American banks have the power to control international payments; however, that could soon change as China and India have rolled out nationwide digital payment transactions for 3 billion people and have central bank digital currencies (CBDCs) on pilot mode.

EARLY BIRDS IN DIGITAL CURRENCY

Surprisingly, the first three digital payment solutions using blockchain technology came from Ecuador, Cambodia and Nigeria, three developing nations on three continents far away from the developed countries of North America and Europe. Ecuador, with a per capita income of around 10,000 purchasing power parity (PPP) dollars, was the first off the block. Being an oil exporter and a forex surplus nation, the Banco Central del Ecuador launched the BCE, a digitized stablecoin fully backed by liquid assets like the

USD or treasury notes, in 2014. The move would reduce banking charges and increase financial mobility, because the South American nation was already dollarized, using the USD as its currency since 2011. The Dinero Electrónico, operated by the central bank, worked from 2014 to 2018 and, at its peak, had 500,000 users before it was withdrawn by the new government due to multiple reasons, largely political.

The Cambodian cryptocurrency Bakong was launched by the central bank with blockchain technology from Soramitsu, a Japanese technology startup, in October 2020. The user could send funds by scanning QR codes or specifying a user's phone number in Cambodian Riel or USD, making it possible for migrant plantation labor working in neighboring countries to send money home. Cryptocurrency became instantly popular and was used by nearly half the population during the first year in a nation where only 40% has network connectivity. The country is classified as a least developed country by the United Nations, with a per capita income of 4,250 PPP dollars in 2020, and less than a quarter of the population had a bank account or mobile payment account before the pandemic. The Bakong was selected as one of the Awards for Excellence winners of the 2021 Nikkei Superior Products and Services Awards for its innovative technology and impact on social development.

The pandemic disrupted the global economy and resulted in a major slow-down in oil-exporting nations like Nigeria. In February 2021, the Nigerian central bank banned using Bitcoin and other cryptocurrencies to stop the flight of capital. To facilitate easy money transfers in remote areas of the large African nation with a per capita income of 5,000 PPP dollars, it started its digital currency, the eNaira, a few months later, in October 2021. In less than 3 weeks, 500,000 of its citizens had downloaded the digital wallet, with around 78,000 businesses enrolling and transacting business worth 62 million Naira. However, this might not reduce the flight of capital from the politically volatile nation, and its long-term success remains to be seen among political dissensions.

Digital payments are popular across China, with Alibaba groups Alipay and Tencent's WeChatPay as market leaders. However, a new digital payment solution, the Digital RMB, is now being tested by the People's Bank of China (PBOC) with at least 20 commercial banks along with e-commerce giant Ant group. It was officially rolled out during the Beijing Winter Olympics in 2022. China believes it will be able to use the first mover advantage and make its digital currency accepted worldwide. It aims to provide the first crypto CBDT and expects it will be widely used by sanction-hit Russia, Iran and several friendly African and South American nations. It will also help control the slow erosion of wealth facing us today as global tax havens and cryptocurrencies attract the newly rich Chinese population.

In early 2022, China launched a smartphone app for payments and money transfers using the digital Yuan (CNY). The test version of the eCNY app was made available to Android and iOs platforms for users in 12 cities, including the host city for the Winter Olympics, Beijing and Shenzhen, Suzhou, Chengdu and Shanghai. In another trial, the PBOC is testing a CBDC with the East Caribbean Central Bank of Bahamas and Banco Central de Uruguay to make digital currencies available to remote locations where no physical banking is present. However, the Chinese CBDC launched during the Winter Olympics was not a cryptocurrency. Nor is the Indian CBDC launched a few months later. These are early pilots useful for getting consumer feedback.

In January 2022, Switzerland successfully tested its CBDC usage. The trial called Project Helvetia integrated CBDCs into payment systems. It used them in simulated transactions with five large global banks UBS, Credit Suisse, Goldman Sachs, Citigroup and Hypothekarbank Lenzburg. The scheme tested the efficiency of the CBDC in the wholesale markets. It showed it was possible to perform large transactions from CHF 100,000 to CHF 5 million, eliminating counter-party risk.

The tiny Caribbean tax havens the Bahamas, Grenada, Antigua and St. Lucia have also launched digital currencies. However, most large economies have been slow in implementation. They do not want the flight of capital and want it to be user-friendly and protected from fraud, pilferage and misuse. Answering a congressional hearing in January 2021, the US Secretary of the Treasury Janet Yellen admitted that terror financing by cryptocurrencies was of concern and needed to be curtailed, "we need to make sure that our methods for dealing with these matters, with tech terrorist financing, change along with changing technology, cryptocurrencies are a particular concern."

In the next chapter, we deal with cyber and financial crimes that show how the tech world has become more risk-prone and plays out the fears of regulators and central bankers.

Chapter 6

Cyber and Financial Crimes

Ruling the High Seas

The global pandemic started in Wuhan and killed more than 340,000 Americans compared to 4,600 Chinese in 2020. It pushed the top ten world economies, barring China, into negative economic growth. A trade war has been going on between the two largest economies of the world since 2017, with then US President Donald Trump accusing China of dumping low-cost goods with the intent of destroying American industries. When a foreign supplier sells goods at prices lower than they charge in their domestic market, the US and many other nations levy an antidumping duty or protectionist tariff on imports to ensure that the goods are not sold below a fair market value. The US action to restrict low-priced steel imports from Asia saw immediate retaliation from China, which put curbs on soy imports from the US. The trade war had been escalating for 3 years. Finally, President Trump moved aggressively and decisively to reduce the US trade deficit as there were several other points of conflict as China raced to catch up with the US economy.

By August 2019, the relationship between both trading partners had nosedived, and Trump took to Twitter, ordering American companies using Chinese facilities for manufacturing to "immediately start looking for an alternative to China" and build more products in the US. He cited the International Emergency Economic Powers Act (IEEPA 1977) to deal with "unusual and extraordinary threat to the national security, foreign policy or economy of the United States." It was natural that when the Covid pandemic of 2020 hurt the Western economies the most, it caused a deeper distrust between China, where it originated, and the US and its allies, who lost the most lives in the first wave of the pandemic.

THE WORLDWIDE LOCKDOWNS CAUSED HUGE JOB LOSSES

The unprecedented Covid-19 virus caught the world by surprise as the new decade arrived. According to the TomTom traffic index of the Netherlands,

DOI: 10.1201/9781003409557-8

which collates traffic data from 416 cities in 57 countries, the unprecedented viral onslaught first resulted in a complete lockdown with 10% traffic density in Wuhan, Beijing and Shanghai in February 2020. It took 40 days and more than 4,000 deaths before the World Health Organization (WHO) declared the virus a global pandemic and 2 months before other worldwide cities observed lockdowns that brought them to a grinding halt. TomTom traffic data showed China clamped down 2 months before the other nations.

This could be because the virus, even initially, was complicated to decipher. Deaths occurred in China, the US and Italy in February 2020; however, nobody knew why. It is also probable that there was no conspiracy. It was only because the Wuhan laboratory had been researching the coronavirus for over a decade that it was identified within months. Professor Shi Zhengli, a leading researcher at the Wuhan Institute, popularly known as China's Batwoman, researched bats in mines in a nearby mountain cave and identified eight coronavirus strains in bats in 2015. That early research possibly saved time and countless lives. The WHO team and later an independent research team from the US also opined that the virus had, in all likelihood, spread from a natural source and not from a leak at the research lab. However, the trust deficit remained.

The first wave of the Covid outbreak saw nationwide lockdowns in 70 countries, including in major economies, such as France, Germany, the UK and India. Most other nations, including the US and China, resorted to partial lockdowns. Schools for nearly 168 million children remained closed in 2020, and 214 million children found their schools closed for 9 months. The long lockdowns completely changed the way we worked.

According to PEW Research, only one in five workers in the US worked from home before the pandemic. However, during the pandemic, 71% of the workforce resorted to mainly working from home. We also witnessed an increase in a hybrid workforce where people worked alternately from home and the office to help maintain the physical distancing recommended during the pandemic. So, you could find certain staff reporting for 1 week to the office, and others worked from home, with the roles changing the next week. The traditional nine-to-five single location limited devices office space suddenly became a 24/7 multilocation multidevice flexible workplace that could change as required.

The lockdowns had another devastating impact—this time on people's livelihoods in poor nations. An International Labor Organization (ILO) press release on December 2020 stated that 81 million people had lost their jobs in Asia. Overall, working hours in Asia and the Pacific housing 3 billion people reduced sharply by over15% in the second quarter and over10% in the third quarter of 2020 compared with the previous year. The ILO Assistant Director General and Regional Director for Asia and the Pacific stated

"Covid-19 has inflicted a hammer blow on the region's labor markets, one that few governments in the region stood ready to handle. Low levels of social security coverage and limited institutional capacity in many countries have made it difficult to help enterprises and workers back on their feet, a situation compounded when large numbers remain in the informal economy. These pre-crisis weaknesses have left far too many exposed to the pain of economic insecurity when the pandemic hit and inflicted its toll on working hours and jobs."

Ms. Chihoko Asada Miyakawa

A Eurofound study reported that over 6 million jobs were lost across Europe due to the pandemic, and PEW Research found that 9.6 million Americans became unemployed during the pandemic. However, the situation was even worse in poor nations without social security coverage. In total, over 50 million people in Africa lost their jobs, and 26 million became unemployed across South America and the Caribbean.

UNEMPLOYMENT GAVE RISE TO CYBERCRIMES

Cybercrimes have been around for more than a decade; however, they accelerated during the pandemic. The dual impact of mass unemployment and hybrid working from low-security surroundings created a perfect environment for it to grow rapidly during this period. Millions of workers lost their jobs because businesses, especially in the informal sector, like small stores, workshops and small services like plumbers and electricians, closed abruptly during the long, drawn-out lockdowns. They were helpless, desperate and angry that governments had indiscriminately locked down industries and retail stores for months without a thought for jobs and livelihoods. In India, migrant workers had to walk thousands of miles from the cities where they worked, back to their homes in distant villages because planes, trains and buses had all been shut down abruptly. Many of them were skilled and tech-savvy and took to cybercrime. The sudden loss of their livelihoods left them with little choice but to fend for themselves.

Even across the US and Europe, cybercrime was rampant. A report in October 2020 stated that

"in 2019 and early 2020 there was a high level of volatility on the dark web. The life cycle of dark web marketplaces has shortened, and no clear dominant market has risen over the past year. Tor remains the preferred infrastructure; however, criminals have started to use other privacy-focused, decentralized marketplace platforms to sell their illegal goods."

Europol Internet Organized Crime Threat Assessment

Fake news, phishing, malware, payment fraud and child sexual abuse accounted for most of these cybercrimes in Europe. In the US, most people who felt the brunt of cybercrime were financial services, healthcare, retail and public administration employees. They were involved in round-the-clock digital services during the pandemic. With the world adjusting to lockdowns and new digital solutions, there was a 220% spike in phishing and online scams with disruptive malware (e.g., ransomware and DDoS) attacks and malicious domains accounting for major crimes. The Interpol Secretary General Jürgen Stock stated, "Cybercriminals are developing and boosting their attacks at an alarming pace, exploiting the fear and uncertainty caused by the unstable social and economic situation created by Covid-19."

LAX SECURITY DID NOT HELP

Security provisions were lax, because working from home had several drawbacks. It became impossible to commute to the workplace during lengthy lockdowns. Many employees worked with multiple devices like desktops, laptops, iPads and mobile phones without adequate security screening and periodic checks for virus infection. The same devices were used by employees for entertainment out of hours, playing games and downloading videos, memes and, at times, pornography. Standard protocols when using a single device for communication could not be maintained.

New methods of communication were also being introduced, like Zoom and a dozen other video conferencing apps. These services were churning out new untested features at a frantic pace. Occasionally, security breaches would occur that had to be plugged once discovered. Moreover, the hybrid way of working to maintain physical distancing would lead to large offices operating at half-strength daily, and not every organization was well equipped. So, the personnel responsible for vetting security would often be missing or inadequate.

In addition, work stretched around the clock in a relaxed work-from-home environment and was carried out from multiple venues instead of just for 8 hours. from a single location. That meant multiple IP addresses were being used from different locations at different times, along with multiple telecom networks, Wi-Fi, Bluetooth and other connecting devices. Many employees were distracted by partners, family members or household chores and could inadvertently click on phishing sites that were growing daily. This lack of attention to their work when multitasking at home was an added problem with inadequate cyber and data security infrastructure. Just one single password hack of one employee could provide access to a large, secure office network and implant viruses or conduct a quick ransomware attack. Hackers could also listen into your meetings through the microphones of any hacked employee to gain confidential information, data and business plans.

USE OF NEW PAYMENT SERVICES LED TO MORE CRIMES

The lockdowns devastated retail shopping in most cities. Because normal retail businesses shut shop, e-commerce and home delivery took root to maintain regular supplies to the consumer. To maintain zero-contact shopping, payments became digital. Credit card payments required a payment device to be taken to homes and to have contact with machines, which was too complicated.

So, digital wallets took root, where you could scan the code or pay the bank instantly through mobile phone apps. India used cash for nearly all its transactions in 2010 as credit cards, although available, had not proven popular. The government struggled to convince the people to use less cash and more digital payments for their day-to-day monetary transactions. An extensive demonetization drive to unearth black money and reduce cash hoarding was conducted in November 2016 with little success. Even after the demonetization in 2019, there were just 232 billion digital payment transactions, which accounted for less than 3% of the total payments made. After the pandemic in 2021, this had soared to 11% with over 437 billion transactions. The World Bank Global Findex 2021 data showed that 76% of adults worldwide used digital payments in 2021, up from 68% in 2017 and 51% in 2011. This 25% growth meant that during 2011–2021 nearly 2 billion more people started using digital payments, which is phenomenal.

In China, over 100 million people made their first digital payments during the pandemic, and India added 80 million new users. Many of the new users, nearly 250 million people globally, who were learning on-the-go, became sitting ducks for cybercriminals. For example, an electric company introduced digital payment facilities for the ease of consumers through their website or app. The facility had been working smoothly for 1 year. Some consumers who failed to pay bills were charged a small amount of interest, and the bill for the next month had three components: (1) the unpaid bill; (2) the interest; and (3) the new bill. Now the hacker uses an artificial intelligence tool to make a list of these bills and then sends an SMS message to the phone numbers of 15,000 consumers who have not paid bills for more than 1 month. It reads, "Your electricity bill is overdue. To avoid disconnection, pay here," and a link is given. The consumer knows they have not paid the previous month's bills, so they panic and click on the link without realizing that it is a fraudulent phishing site with a similar name and loses all the money in their bank account. Even if 1% of the clients were fooled, the total amount lost by consumers was substantial.

Automated attacks are used to target individuals and small businesses. Small and medium-sized enterprises (SMEs) in retail and healthcare have become new targets for cybercriminals. Two-thirds of the data breach cases that led to ransomware demands affected SMEs in 2021, compared with 37% the previous year. Frauds also occurred largely due to automated attacks with phishing links that enticed people through some form of payment or discount scheme, defrauded them and emptied their bank accounts. Many users who clicked on such links were new users who could not decipher the difference between secure and fraudulent websites.

A quarter of the employees of essential services noticed a marked increase in fraudulent emails and phishing attempts in their corporate email accounts since the beginning of the pandemic. As more and more new and user-friendly digital payment facilities were introduced, the attacks increased, forcing central banks worldwide to change credit card protocols and bar the saving of passwords by any e-commerce app.

THE ARRIVAL OF THE DARK NET ON THE ONION ROUTER

In the previous chapter on the blockchain, we looked at how the onion router (TOR) browser and encrypted text affected global politics. However, technology is only a tool, and like Aladdin's magic lamp, it can be used by the good and bad guys. The anonymous browsing through the TOR boosted the work of the US National Security Agency NSA. It also boosted dark net markets like Silk Road, which freely sold toxic chemicals, banned drugs, hacking tools, arms and rebel fighters and helped boost sex trafficking and money laundering. In October 2013, the Federal Bureau of Intelligence (FBI) announced that they had arrested Ross William Ulbricht from San Francisco, the Silk Road's 29-year-old administrator who operated anonymously on the net as "Dread Pirate Roberts," and closed down the first large dark net market of the decade. However, many more dark web markets started emerging soon after, which flourished with the help of cryptocurrencies and the TOR, each with millions of users.

The TOR provided anonymity and a big boost to the global drug mafia. It made small websites handling illicit drugs for select customers popular, because it reduced the chances of physical encounters with members of the drug mafia. During the 1990s a limited selection of psychoactive substances was offered online as "research chemicals.". These were phenethylamine and tryptamine derivatives and the early version of party drugs consumed by high-end customers. The US Drug Enforcement Administration closed most of these websites in 2004. But, a few years later, they resurfaced with visually attractive websites offering everything from legal highs to a wide range of drugs and substances, such as synthetic cannabinoids, cathinone derivatives, pyrovalerones, and methoxetamine to perfumes, incense, herbal blends, energy drinks, plant fertilizer and legal services

Although it is unfair to blame technology for social ills, statistics show that one in seven downloads from the internet is of pornographic material. Pornography gained a new lease of life first with the oncoming of the internet, then later with the arrival of TOR browsers and finally with payments being facilitated through unregulated global cryptocurrencies. Playpen, a dark net marketplace used for pornography and sex trafficking, had as many as 150,000 users, and half were minors. In 2015, the FBI, with the help of European investigators, hacked into 4,000 computers to take control of the site and filed charges against 180 users, shutting down the "Producers Pen" and arresting 17 suspected makers of child pornography.

Rebel fighters and automatic weapons have been a feature of the sophisticated dark net sites that have never been talked about much because they are closely protected by layers of cyber security experts. However, amateur attacks like the 2016 Munich shooting are known to have been carried out by lone-wolf terrorists purchasing arms on the dark net. According to a Rand Corporation survey, 60% of the firearms listed on the dark net are of US origin. However, Europe is the largest online arms market, generating revenues five times higher than the US.

In 2017, Andrew Lewman, who had been the Executive Director of the TOR for 6 years, confirmed that 95% of the TOR users used its onion services for criminal activities. At that time, there were 2 million concurrent daily users on the TOR browsers with over 5,000 hidden onion services. Lewman had long been responsible for developing the secret infrastructure at the TOR and simultaneously working with investigation agencies, particularly the FBI Academy, to develop software designed to tell a cop if an IP address was a TOR exit node.

With open source software being created by thousands of developers, detecting TOR users has become extremely difficult, which has helped criminals to escape.

New exit routes are being created daily on TOR, which makes it impossible to track fugitives if they are careful to cover their tracks. Although many suspect that the NSA and FBI hold sufficient access to the TOR browser to deter crime, the truth is that they do not, because the open source software permits the developers to create new escape routes. The technology is too smart to be tamed or tracked. Lewman quit TOR in 2015 to join OWL Cybersecurity. He hinted that this was his attempt to stop a total takeover of the TOR platform by organized criminals. However, it was possibly an effort too late in the day.

The advent of blockchain encryption technology in 2008 and new-age cryptocurrencies like Bitcoin, Monero and Ethereum made it easy for users to transact in an unregulated currency out of the regulators' view. No wonder dozens of dark net markets like AlphaBay, Agora, Evolution, Silk Road 2.0, Playpen, Dark Market and Hansa Market have flourished since the advent of cryptocurrencies, despite numerous attempts by regulators to shut them down. The TOR anonymity or "hidden services" websites and servers within its architecture have boosted child pornography and sex trafficking with cryptocurrency payments, illegal drugs, computer malware and arms sales.

Financial crime grew by over 220% annually in 2020. As physical cash movement became extremely difficult due to global lockdowns, digital wallets flourished. Along with the increased digital cash transfers came increased financial crime in digital transactions. Wallets for cryptocurrency and regular currency became new targets along with credit and debit cards, with password frauds and "click and link frauds," where consumers new to digital money transfers were cheated. This was estimated to be a $4 trillion industry globally, with around 1% of the criminals convicted.

One of the biggest confluences on the dark net is the sale of malware, virus-fed USBs, dummy firewalls, rigged pen drives, sockets and networking hardware. Just like arms and ammunition are needed to fight real battles, doctored hardware and software are required to fight cyberwars. The dark net is the home of stolen and pirated software and hardware and the market for illegal copycats. They also sell billions of low-cost but genuine hardware and software, including factory seconds and equipment on which duties and taxes have not been paid. In addition, it is where cyberattacks are planned and coordinated by numerous activist groups and cybercriminals from China, Russia, the US, Iran, Pakistan, Nigeria, Israel, India and North Korea, among many others.

However, the TOR has a powerful group of journalists and activists who will protect it despite the illegal activities performed through the web browser. Julian Assange and Edward Snowden have worked with powerful journalists and internet activists in the *New York Times*, *The Guardian* and *The Washington Post,* who strongly believe the danger is more from the state than the criminals. Due to this strong liberal support, the TOR prospers.

Today, the TOR browser can be downloaded from Google Play or Apple Store onto your mobile phone. However, the libertarians are not only those in Silicon Valley who develop blockchain, onion routers and decentralized cryptocurrencies for anonymity. They are also present in large numbers among influential citizen groups and academics globally who believe that George Orwell's predictions will be a reality. So, nine out of 10 TOR users who are full-time crooks can use the TOR for financial gains alone and benefit from the largesse provided by this libertarian umbrella of anonymity.

TERROR AND ARMS FUNDING

Being unregulated, cryptocurrencies find favor among those involved in clandestine activity. According to Janet Yellen, among those who use it, most are cyber criminals, terrorists, drug cartels and money launderers. In addition, the maturing of cryptocurrencies has been a boon to prodemocracy groups and extremist insurgents worldwide, including those in Hong Kong, Ecuador, Myanmar, North Africa and Chile. Many of these activist groups are suspected of funding Belgian assault rifles, Bulgarian sniper rifles, truck-mounted Russian and American surface-to-air missiles and South Korean small arms to rebel groups. They feel the long-drawn need for a currency without borders has been answered.

Cryptocurrencies are key in the fight for both communism and democracy activists in authoritarian states. Both groups use it because they allow individuals to protect their wealth and earn their freedom without any interference from the state. Crypto supporters argue that a deregulated cryptocurrency could be used by Ukrainians for donations and humanitarian assistance and by Russians to bypass sanctions. It is a technology-driven platform that does not take sides in a conflict; therefore, it is a dependable asset. They are also key for the Jehadis of ISIS or the Taliban and other terror groups who want to crush democracy and seize power.

Today, large dark net markets for arms have positioned themselves in the global supply chain in the US and Europe. According to a United Nations report in 2018, cryptocurrencies drove the dark net market for small arms, estimated at $3 billion annually. They sell anything from Kalashnikovs to automatic pistols, hand grenades and bazookas. 60% of the arms originates from the US. However, the biggest market has been Europe, where wars in Bosnia, Slovakia, Georgia, Chechnya and Crimea have been fought during the last decade. The nonprofit organization, the Rand Corporation Europe, working with Manchester University, found 52 unique vendors selling weapons on 18 dark markets. The biggest buyers were terrorists working alone or in groups, followed by organized criminal gangs.

RANSOMWARE GROWS BY LEAPS AND BOUNDS

US businesses were the most frequently attacked during the pandemic; each ransomware attack cost $1.2 million on average. However, ransomware and DDoS attacks come from all parts of the world. Because the attacks come from different geographies, it was difficult to stop them since each nation has its cybersecurity laws, and most have very inadequate policing. Overall, 10% of the police forces in most nations are equipped to tackle cybercrime; however, 30% of all financial crimes are already digitally engineered. In 2021, almost 68% of businesses in India faced ransomware attacks compared with 57% in Austria, 51% in the US, 49% in Israel and 48% in Turkey. The increase in ransomware attacks over the last few years shows that it is now an established source of revenue for cybercriminals and a lucrative low-risk crime as most organizations pay the ransom instead of reporting the crime and risking losing data. The average ransomware fee paid per attack in 2021 was $812,000, up from $170,000 the previous year.

Ransomware became the favored method of cybercriminals to extract money following the outbreak of the 2020 pandemic, showing that encryption technology could be used to enhance and cripple security. The Cybersecurity and Infrastructure Security Agency of the Federal Government stated

"Ransomware is an ever-evolving form of malware designed to encrypt files on a device, rendering any files and the systems that rely on them unusable. Malicious actors then demand ransom for decryption. Ransomware actors often target and threaten to sell or leak exfiltrated data or authentication information if the ransom is not paid."

Cybersecurity and Infrastructure Security Agency
of the Federal Government

Let us see how this happens in real time. On 31 March 2020, Marriott Hotels admitted a data breach that started sometime in mid-January and compromised the personal data of 5 million guests. This was the second attack that the global hospitality chain faced within 1 year, and in both cases, ransomware of an unknown amount in bitcoins is believed to have been paid to the attackers in secrecy. In July 2020, in a high-profile attack on Twitter, the account details of several prominent persons, including former president Barack Obama, Tesla boss Elon Musk and Amazon founder Jeff Bezos were stolen and sold for $100,000 with payment received in bitcoins. Then, 2 weeks later, three hackers, including the 17-year-old mastermind Graham Ivan Clark were arrested following an investigation by the Justice Department, leading to a rare conviction case.

The German software giant Software AG faced a double extortion attack in October 2020 from operators using the Clop extension. This popular Cryptomix ransomware is regularly updated like high-end software. The first attack came with a ransom demand of $23 million, which the software major refused to pay. Within days the stolen data was shared on the dark web, including financial information, employees' passport details and internal company emails. The ransomware attack on SolarWinds' Orion software by Russia's Cozy Bear hacking group gave access to many US government files, is probably the largest and most sophisticated attack of the decade. Because more than 100 companies were using Orion software, it could not be ascertained who was the target of this rare supply chain attack.

The two signature ransomware attacks of 2021 rattled most consumers into submission worldwide and increased the frequency of ransomware attacks. The attack on the Colonial Pipeline, a critical US national infrastructure supplying gas to consumers on the East Coast of the US, by the DarkSide gang from Eastern Europe was audacious and unprecedented. It disrupted gas supplies and created chaos in the billing system of the utility company, forcing it to pay a ransom of $4.4 million in bitcoins.

In another high-profile attack on JBS Foods, one of America's largest meat producers, the Russian hacking group REvil forced payment of $11 million as ransom in May 2021, one of the largest ransomware payments globally. The REvil group has been active in Europe and the US, extracting ransoms from several businesses in the UK, France, Sweden, Poland, Germany and the US, shutting down thousands of computer systems and extracting millions in the last 5 years, according to Europol, despite the arrest of several operators. In November 2021, the US Justice Department claimed to have arrested a Ukrainian hacker from the group from Poland and retrieved a $6.1 million ransom paid after their attack on Kaseya Ltd., a technology provider. However, such recoveries have been rare.

FINANCIAL CRIMES AND MONEY LAUNDERING GREW DURING COVID

Financial crimes through cyberspace have also grown exponentially in the last few years. We will now look at the financial crimes that happen easily due to the favorable digital environment provided. These are completely different from the cybercrimes in the retail sector in digital payments. Financial crimes, such as bank fraud, tax evasion or money laundering, are not strictly cybercrimes. Yet, they accelerate and multiply quickly in today's digital environment. The movement of money to remote locations becomes extremely easy in cyberspace. Camouflaged accounts are easy to maintain in deregulated digital environments that are not easily accessible to regulators or tax inspectors. Identity transfer and value multiplication become possible as dirty money gets invested in assets, which are disposed of as legitimate properties in different hands. Now, let us take a detailed look at how all this takes place and why Chuck Collins wrote his best-selling nonfiction *The Wealth Hoarders: How Billionaires pay Millions to Hide Trillions* in 2021.

Collins, an heir to one of the generational wealth funds, the Oscar Mayer Wiener fortune, refused to be part of the system and instead told the world how the richest were hiding their money from tax collectors and using several unfair means to grow and preserve their wealth for future generations. They hired top lawyers, accountants and fund managers to protect their wealth in faraway destinations and tax havens. Those funds help the rich grow richer despite the incompetence of successive generations and the increasing disparity between the rich and the poor.

Top professionals working for them are being paid millions of dollars to build wealth pyramids where habitual tax evaders are not touching the original pile of wealth. They use the interest to multiply the gross earnings at the base without paying taxes. Under the guise of running charities and philanthropic institutions, some of these wealth funds are conducting an elaborate money laundering business that is illegal, unethical and immoral. Collins chose to give away his wealth and instead worked as director of the "Program on Inequality and Common Good" at the Institute of Policy Studies and studies how wealthy Americans dodge taxes. A recent report from the Internal Revenue Service (IRS) and top academics found that the top 1% of Americans did not report 21% of their income.

It is not only the super-rich that are increasingly hiding their wealth. A bigger concern is that the community of super-rich that is evading taxes has been growing since the pandemic. The number of ultra-high net worth individuals (UHNWI) grew to over half a million in 2020, 2.4% higher than the previous year. Additionally, the pandemic and the Russian invasion of Ukraine opened new fault lines in the global supply chain, aiding profiteering by monopolies owned by billionaires whose effect will be felt for years. From 2020 to 2025, the ranks of UHNWI are expected to swell by 27%, with Asia adding 39%, Africa 33% and the US 27% to the pile, according to the Knight Frank Wealth Report of 2022.

THE FUTURE OF CYBERCRIME AND MONEY LAUNDERING

Money laundering, by nature, is an illegal activity. However, over the years, it has built one of the largest unprotected asset classes that the world has seen and one that is growing by $2 trillion annually. This is the amount of money the rich, individuals and corporates hide annually from the taxman. It is considered stolen money in the eyes of the law. Most of this money is transferred digitally to distant places outside the country of origin, often under anonymous names and to less secure destinations than your local bank. Even if it is kept within the country, it is remote and hidden in desolate places. For example, 40 trust companies are located in a modest two-story building at 201 South Phillips Avenue, Sioux Falls, South Dakota, US, that administers trust assets worth $80 billion without visible security.

The British Isles and overseas trusts are even worse from a security point of view. From a 10-ft by 16-ft wooden shed housing a grocery store for visiting seafarers in the Cayman Islands in the west Caribbean Sea, assets worth $26 billion are administered, housing all original documents in a small wooden cupboard and a computer that only the storekeeper's 24-year-old son Patrick knows how to operate. However, Patrick is just a cog in the structure and a keeper of those assets, because it is the address that is valued as a zero-tax zone. He does not know the assets he stores are usually managed by a high-profile globally networked law firm in London, New York or Berne.

Other types of profit laundering happen from tax havens around the world. Gordon Moore, a British commodity trader based in Zug, the richest Canton of Switzerland, uses more than three dozen addresses in tax havens for round tripping of goods originating in Florida. Whether nickel or aluminum, oil or coal, wheat or soy, volatile commodity prices generate enormous profits for commodity traders, big or small. Because most freight movement is US-bound, and the US is still the largest global consumer, the freight cost of container ships coming from China to Miami is three times the return freight cost. Taking advantage of this low freight cost of container vessels returning from the US, Moore supplies commodities that turn volatile during its 4 week journey from Florida to Europe.

His network of 30 dealers works with commodity giants Cargill in the US, Glencore in Europe and Adani in India. They identify commodities that could go volatile at the London ICE exchange and strike deals exclusively in those that could appreciate hugely in a 4-week time frame. Then, they resort to round trip trading, where the cargo changes hands multiple times at the ICE exchange without the consignments leaving the ship. This electronic trading, termed "round tripping" among the network of traders, makes prices volatile. The traders with offices in dozens of tax havens all gain fractionally with each transaction at the exchange. The number of transactions in high-speed digital networks of commodity exchanges is so huge that it makes it impossible for any taxman or regulator to trace or pinpoint the profiteering to any single trader, giving it immunity from regulators. The fractional profits in each transaction and the thousands of transactions every hour generate millions of dollars in profits each day.

These tax havens dealing with super-rich assets could be sitting ducks and the next target by hackers hungry for ransomware, stated a former treasury bounty hunter who has been locating illegal assets for over a decade. Ransomware has been an easy way to get money, as policing is inadequate and targets readily negotiate instead of reporting the crime. Despite the low rate of public disclosure, a Riskrecon research report on supply chains being targeted says that 50 attacks were reported in 2019, over 250 were reported in 2020 and 300 in 2021.

As ransomware attacks in cyberspace increase, regulators are now stepping up the defense of websites that hold essential data for business and commerce. Though conviction rates were as low as 2%, attacks are increasing daily. Even those new entrants into the digital world who were initially tricked into clicking on links are increasingly becoming more aware of the risks due to regulators spending more money on user education and highlighting the issue through the media. Therefore, hackers are looking at new avenues that could be soft targets and of high value. According to a Kroll report, money laundering and tax evasion boomed during the pandemic, as a result of which authorities levied fines of $2.2 billion worldwide, which was five times more than in 2019.

This rapidly growing source of revenue could be the next focus of cyber attackers simply because crime involving large swathes of laundered money will not be reported, and ransomware will be substantial and easy to use. When that happens, there will be virtual war in cyberspace with private armies of hackers and defenders slugging it out in an all-out cyberwar, some backed by nations and others purely by private investors and mercenaries. We will look at these possibilities in the last chapter of the book. What could such global cyber warfare bring about? The Russian cyberattacks on Europe and the cyber war between Iran and Saudi Arabia, and between Israel and Iran are other flashpoints that could lead to an all-out global confrontation. We will also discuss the Chinese cyberattacks on Taiwan and India that do not intend to cripple the system or extract ransomware; however, rather keep bleeding the system to gather information and security data.

Part II

Applications that Transform

Chapter 7

Digital Transformation
Will it Cut or Grow Jobs?

The year 2020 witnessed an unprecedented pandemic followed by global lockdowns. It caused factories, offices and retail businesses to close shops, economies to come to a grinding halt and millions of job losses. Not all was lost, however. People across the globe learned to remodel their homes, school and workspace. Working from home became an accepted practice, and the digitization of services became the flavor of the season. Digitization is, however, not a recent phenomenon. Its roots go back to the mid-1950s.

FROM DIGITIZATION TO DIGITAL TRANSFORMATION

Life was very different in 1942 before the arrival of computers. Marjory Collins, a photographer from the war office who visited The NYT at Times Square, in September that year described the physical process of news production as "pretty messy" as it came over the wires and was sorted, edited, retyped, laid out, and printed within a timeline of a few hours.

> "Hot metal typesetting invented in the nineteenth century was still in vogue where typesetters created lines of text using brass letters, then injected molten lead into the mold. After the plates printed the page, the lead was tossed back into a 'hellbox,' melted down again, and reused."
> Marjory Collins

The 1950s witnessed the first benefits of digitization with the advent of computers. Newspapers were printed from computers, so editing became faster, and retyping was unnecessary. The typesetting and the lead box slowly disappeared, and swanky new computerized four-color offset printing presses with computer-to-plate printing took over.

Long before the first wave of digitization, Penguin had launched its paperback editions in the UK. *Playboy* printed Marilyn Monroe on the cover of its inaugural edition in the US. So, it was not that content changed with

DOI: 10.1201/9781003409557-10

digitization. What changed was the storage of content from printed format to digital format. Hundreds of years of storytelling, communication and representations of physical objects or attributes like *Alice in Wonderland* or "the dimensions and the layout of a building" were recorded, saved and transmitted mechanically in print on paper using devices like typewriters, cyclostyling machines or the printing press.

Digitization led to the creation of digital representations of physical objects or attributes on a electronic device. It picked up pace during the 1960s and led to the creation of formats, such as saving content in a Word document or an audio file, scanning a document to produce an electronic copy and saving it on a computer as an image file. It was virtually a total shift of data storage and information communication from print to digital formats. American Airlines was one of the early users of digitization in 1960, processing 84,000 telephone calls per day and storing 807 megabytes (MB) of data recording flight schedules, reservations and seat inventory in an electronic device. The digitization of records saved billions.

The 1970s and 1980s witnessed digitalization, which was a step ahead. Here we saw the advent of the desktop computer and the beginning of the software-driven service industry that enabled or improved business processes by leveraging digital technologies and digitized data. For example, you would not have to write down the math or the step-by-step working to analyze processes like monitoring traffic or melting steel. You could write the algorithm and create a computer program to analyze the process. Soon user friendly software entered the scene. That program could be used by any user on their desktop.

But digitalization was not only about programming. At that time, Boyle and Smith at AT&T Bell Labs invented the charge-coupled device (CCD) that transformed light into digital signals. That helped in the development of digital imaging. It led to the evolution of digital cameras and medical imaging devices, bringing photography out of the Dark Ages when developing negatives and printing positives. The hundreds of digital photos you can take with your cell phone, free of cost each day, are partly due to this invention. Digitalization increased productivity and efficiency while reducing costs. It was scalable and used programable digital data to simplify how you work. It significantly improved how the activity was done but did not transform or change the operational process.

Digital transformation is a step ahead of digitalization. It changes the operational process. It started somewhere during the 1990s and gradually became a buzzword over the next decades. In 1996, for the first time, digital storage became more affordable when storing information than paper. Ten years later, 94% of the world's information storage capacity was digital. Paper storage had given way to mammoth server banks, completely transforming how information storage was achieved. Even Kindle readers were more numerous than print book buyers on Amazon.

The 1990s were when digitally-enabled automation first entered the workforce, followed by the arrival of the world wide web. Soon, technology was assisting and supporting an activity or a business process, virtually changing it. You could see its effect on manufacturing operations and define the strategy and planning of the business. Fashion houses moved out of London, Paris and Hamburg. For example, a large clothing brand in Europe found that the best and cheapest fabric was available in South America, the best designers were in Paris and New York, high-quality textile machinery could be procured from Switzerland, Japan and Germany, and competitive labor for manufacturing was found in South East Asia. So, the brand automated its manufacturing operation and relocated its manufacturing base from Europe to Vietnam and completely re-engineered its supply chain to improve value for its customers.

HOW DID THIS HAPPEN?

With the arrival of the internet, businesses could communicate with their employees, suppliers and consumers instantly. The distance was no longer a barrier, which made it possible to communicate globally and locally without incurring significant costs. The world wide web platforms using HTML text with hyperlinks hosted on remote cloud servers was the first avatar that ushered in digital transformation. The first two websites uploaded in 1991 were the Tim Berners-Lee web catalog at CERN, followed by the Stanford Linear Accelerator Center, heralding the advent of the world wide web. Two years later, when the internet was first opened for commercial use, 130 websites were launched.

Yahoo was launched in 1994, providing digital news. Thirty years later, 80% of Americans were reading news on digital devices. Amazon was founded in 1995, Hotmail in 1996, Netflix in 1997, Google in 1998 and PayPal in 1999. Each brought about digital transformation that was unthinkable when they arrived. Amazon ushered in e-commerce and became the world's largest retailer in two decades. Hotmail pioneered email, which changed how we communicated. Netflix brought entertainment and streaming videos to 200 million homes worldwide. Google facilitated search and today accounts for 228 million searches per hour. PayPal made digital payments popular, and in 2021 the digital payment market size is over $5,800 billion and is growing at a rate exceeding 16% annually. These half-a-dozen businesses founded in the mid-1990s unleashed the most significant wave of digital transformation within a decade.

Despite the apparent success of digital transformation, the first dot com bust happened. The stock market bubble of overpriced tech stocks burst in March 2000. For the next 30 months, stock prices kept falling, driving the NASDAQ Index down from an all-time high value of 5,000 to an all-time low of 1,100 by October 2002. Investment in tech stocks plummeted.

Venture capitalists and stock buyers who had invested copious amounts of cash to fund loss-making tech entrepreneurs lost most of their invested capital. Only the best and sturdiest survived the bloodbath. The market wanted something more. Investors wanted the digital transformation to truly move out of Silicon Valley, which was saturated with innovators but had no global markets to tap into at that time.

After a 30-month slump, things changed for the better. Entrepreneurs continued to build the second decade of digital transformation, which brought utility applications and social media into play, creating a veritable explosion in the user base globally. LinkedIn was introduced in 2002, Facebook in 2004, YouTube in 2005, Twitter in 2006, Tumblr in 2007, WhatsApp in 2009 and Instagram in 2010. Social media gave opportunities to thousands of small businesses and individuals to innovate and sell their homemade products worldwide. They created a new class of social influencers who influenced people's lifestyles more than businesses and were perhaps more transformative. They connected with young people across continents, rejuvenated music, fashion and the performing arts, and created millions of entrepreneurs selling, buying, servicing and operating from home. By the end of the decade, internet users had jumped to over 2 billion.

The smartphone era had arrived, giving yet another spectacular boost to this worldwide phenomenon of digital transformation. Hence, the second decade of digital transformation saw more innovation. The introduction of smartphones brought about a sea change in consumer attitudes that accelerated digital transformation. Smartphones introduced the concept of smart living through the Internet of Things (IoT), which increasingly sought innovation and digital transformation. Social media constantly told you what your peer group, friends, relatives and idols were doing and that egged you on to change your behavior. In addition, the smartphone updates you with numerous opportunities happening in your neighborhood and worldwide where you could find your solace.

However, this third decade of digital transformation was more of a business to business (B2B) exercise. Despite two decades of success, digital transformation ran into roadblocks after 2010. Innovation took a backseat, and complex process-driven changes needing an organizational overhaul took over—a reason why the impact of digital transformation was felt less. The initial attempt to get businesses to change from the conventional approach to a technology-first approach faced hurdles. A McKinsey survey of 1,700 global C-Suite executives published in October 2019 found that just 10% of the digital transformation that involved integrating advanced technologies had generated more profits. In addition, nearly 45% stood a chance of delivering less profit than expected. The best-selling author of *The Digital Helix* Micheal Gale sated, "The current rate of conversion to digital platforming success is still only 11.5% a year (measured annually since 2014)."

The futurist Greg Verdino stated, "that as reality sinks in corporate leaders will pump the brakes on 'Big Bang transformation programs,' which is actually good news." The author of *Never Normal* also claimed "the irrational exuberance over wholesale transformation will be replaced by a more measured approach to delivering a steady stream of successful improvement that – over time – adds up to massive change." In actual practice, markets expanded, and the massive change happened after the BRIC economies of Brazil, Russia, India and China were developed when more than 2 billion people benefited from this digital transformation.

DIGITAL TRANSFORMATION PICKS UP IN BRIC ECONOMIES

Jim O'Neill, the son of a British postal worker, was a man with working class roots based out of Manchester. He was not quite the globetrotting academic and acknowledged forecasting hotshot, but rather a regular to Manchester United football matches at Old Trafford when he made his expansive prediction on the role of BRIC economies. He had only visited China once and none of the other BRIC nations. O'Neill, then the chief economist at Goldman Sachs, claimed that these four nations having 25% of the land area and 40% of the global population (over 3 billion people), would account for half the world's market capitalization by 2050 and the global bank with some of the sharpest investment brains backed it. Most other economists scoffed at the idea initially; however, the concept gained immediate traction because manufacturing businesses from Nissan to Apple, Daimler AG to Burberry, and Pfizer to Samsung largely endorsed this thinking and put money into these new destinations.

In 2001, the GDP of these four nations was less than 12% of the world's GDP. Most stared at large forex deficits and depended on foreign credit to bail them out. Twenty years later, they accounted for a quarter of the global GDP. China now has forex reserves exceeding $3,000 billion, India and Russia over $600 billion each and Brazil nearly $400 billion. According to O'Neill, China will be the largest economy by 2027. The four BRIC nations would have a combined GDP exceeding the top six Organisation of Economic Co-operation and Development (OECD) nations by 2032.

But what made these countries of largely poor and uneducated people perform so quickly and spectacularly in just 20 years? They had all been virtually independent after the Second World War without showing much progress or intending to be fast-growing economies. According to PEW Research, the poverty rate in China fell from 41% to 12%, while that in India fell from 35% to 20% between 2001 to 2010. This meant that the decade saw 500 million people move out of poverty in the two most populous nations of the world. Brazil, too stood out among the top world economies with GDP growth of more than 5% on average during the decade.

What set apart the BRIC nations from others was the effect of digital transformation on the large, ethnically diverse and widely dispersed populations of the four countries.

China was again off the blocks first, helped by the major investment by American companies in the country in the early 1990s. It became the prime manufacturing base for computer makers like Apple, Hewlett Packard, Dell and Lenovo by 2000 and a hub for digital transformation. By the next decade, it became known as the factory of the world, producing everything from white goods and consumables to chemicals and bulk drugs for global brands. That is when digital transformation started a consumer boom fueled by homegrown e-commerce. Soon, the impact of digital transformation in China far exceeded the impact that was felt in the OECD nations because of the demand and rapid scalability of digital services to a massive population of 1.4 billion. According to a report by the McKinsey Global Institute, new internet applications alone could fuel from 7% to 22% of China's GDP by 2025.

India's digital transformation also started in the late 1990s through its software, and IT services businesses but picked up pace only around 2015 and may contribute to 20% of the GDP growth in this decade. The unique identification (UID) was launched after a 10-year effort, which allowed every Indian to open a zero balance bank account under the "Jandhan" scheme using the biometric "Aadhar Card." According to Price Waterhouse Cooper India's unbanked population dropped from 557 million (44%) in 2011 to 233 million (18%) in 2015, a year after the introduction of the Jandhan scheme. The Aadhar Card helped the transparent disbursal of wages, grants and subsidies to 500 million people below the poverty line. The UPI, an indigenously developed digital payment system, was introduced that allowed all Aadhar Card holders to pay through mobile wallets and interbank money transfers in 2016. Four years later, India registered 25.5 billion real time digital payments in 2020, 60% higher than China's. By 2022, the UPI was also accepted as a digital payment system by the United Arab Emirates and several other nations. So, an Indian tourist could pay INR in Dubai through NEOPAY terminals without carrying the USD or the Dirham.

Russia also had some notable successes in digital transformation and in using it to improve the lives of its citizens. The economy of Russia under the USSR had suffered immensely before it disintegrated in 1991 under Gorbachev, largely because it had $66 billion in external debt and no gold or foreign currency reserves. However, the economy bounced back after two decades, with Russia becoming the largest producer of wheat, the second-largest producer of gold and the third-largest producer of natural gas globally. Russia's huge footprint on world energy supplies forced Europe and Japan to slow down the sanctions against it in 2022, despite wanting to punish Russia for the Ukraine invasion. The sanctions against

Russia have split the global supply chain, creating volatility and shortages worldwide. Europe will have to face colder winters as Russia throttles oil and gas supplies in winter; however, Russia will also be deeply affected as its business with consumers in the US and Europe will be curtailed, and its banking transactions will be hit by sanctions. In addition, its technology supplies for the mining, shipping and aviation industries will be adversely affected. Businesses in Russia are still in the early stages of digital transformation, according to a survey carried out in 2019 by Global Business Consulting GmbH and Baker McKenzie. Both had major business interests in Russia before the Ukraine invasion.

Brazil, also known for its vast natural resources, fared moderately in improving its economy through digital transformation. Despite its natural wealth, it has enormous corruption and political turbulence that stifled its growth. Although it could provide internet connectivity to two-thirds of its population in difficult terrain, it could not provide digitally enabled services like China or India to improve living conditions of its widely dispersed population. However, it stepped up its digital delivery services post-pandemic like many other nations.

DIGITAL TRANSFORMATION IN THE US AND OTHER POPULOUS NATIONS

The US, the third most populous nation in the world, has been responsible for most of the digital transformation globally that benefited its citizens and people across the world. Nearly three-quarters of the tech innovations globally have come from Silicon Valley alone, a 2,000 square mile area in the bay region of California, US, housing around 3 million people. These innovations once came from nimble startups on shoestring budgets who thought differently, like Apple, Microsoft and Google. Now, those very startups have become behemoths. Silicon Valley is awash with venture capital (VC) funds, and startups no longer have to think lean and innovate to survive. That is possibly why the impact of digital transformation has slowed down in the third decade within the US.

The combined population of the powerhouse economies of Britain, France and Germany exceeds 200 million. They are the largest economies in Europe, which are strategically poised to benefit most from digital transformation after the US and China. In Britain, only 18% of digital transformation projects succeeded, according to a survey by Neos Networks, although 98% of businesses felt it was crucial.

The Chief Technology Officer at Moneypenny, says

> "It's easy to be consumed by the day-to-day work and put off large projects like digital transformation until next year. It's also easy to think that it's just a technology project rather than a business change. Without

the right level of focus and buy-in from across all areas of the business, digital transformation will never happen."

Pete Hanlon

In France, like in many parts of Europe, stringent data protection regulations have slowed the progress of digital transformation. The French data protection law dates back to 1978. Nonetheless, following the Covid-19 pandemic, the French Government unveiled a stimulus package of €7 billion to push digital transformation, including providing digital tools and services for businesses, educators, healthcare providers and citizens.

The German digital learning platform "atingi" provides free access to high-quality digital learning, anytime and anywhere for all citizens. The platform has 300 courses and is expected to reach 20 million students by the end of 2023. Germany has initiated the "Digital by Default" approach, which specifies that digital solutions must be the default position for projects to meet their objectives within German development cooperations.

In Indonesia, one of the largest nations of the Far East, internet connectivity, although high at 54%, is concentrated largely in Java. Post-pandemic, the government finally created the *Digital Indonesia Roadmap 2021–2024* for ten sectors, including tourism, financial services, education and healthcare, to expand services across the widespread archipelago of small, interconnected islands.

In Pakistan, Punjab has successfully connected all police stations to the internet. However, of the 180 million mobile internet connections there, only 25% of its population is covered by the internet, according to World Bank data for 2020. Bangladesh has a similar percentage, though internet commerce doubled during the pandemic, suggesting that higher connectivity levels will follow.

The number of mobile users in Nigeria exceeds 184 million, according to the *Nigerian Communication Commission (2020)*. Only 36% of the population has an internet connection. Still, the Nigerian Interbank Settlement System data showed that online real time payment transactions increased by an unprecedented 90% year-on-year after the pandemic, and almost 50% of businesses moved online in just 1 year.

Mexico, the country closest to Silicon Valley, has 72% of its population connected to the internet, according to World Bank data for 2020. It also has a 57% smartphone penetration, which is higher than most emerging economies. Digital wallets account for nearly 20% of the transactions, and credit and debit cards account for around 50%.

WHY DIGITAL TRANSFORMATION—DOES IT HELP?

There are several reasons why businesses are increasingly looking at digital transformation. The primary reason is to meet customer expectations.

Twenty years ago, consumer businesses used to go by the choice of the head of the family, usually a middle-aged male. A decade ago, they found that the woman of the house, usually a middle-aged female, made most of the purchasing decisions. Businesses are now looking at what the younger generation wants irrespective of gender; what the millennials, young adult and school children expect as they are increasingly dictating consumer purchase decisions. As digital technology advances and plays a big part in our lives, the role of the young buyer increases, and consumer expectations change.

This change happened because the younger generation understands technology better. Whether buying a cell phone or a smart kitchen gadget, a wearable, or a self-propelled electric lawn mower for the garden, the technology input in each product recently is pretty intensive for most elders and the middle-aged to understand, study and decide to buy independently. It is often the "generation next" who are very informed and knowledgeable about new products and technologies that constantly keep arriving in the marketplace. So, in most households, the younger people who are more tech-savvy get to opine and sometimes even decide on the equipment or gadget to buy for the home. So, businesses in their advertisements are now targeting the tech-savvy young buyer and the tech-savvy influencer, usually known as the "gadget guru," to prop up their sales.

The second big expectation from digital transformation is to increase daily revenues—especially from the large increase in unplanned purchases by consumers globally. Twenty years ago, retail shopping was a planned, discrete and calculated activity, well thought out with a fixed budget. Most purchasing was carried out at weekends at favorite stores, and big-ticket buys were usually once a year, mostly before major festivals or events. The weekend shopping trend started to change a decade ago with the arrival of malls aggregating multiple brands and eating joints. It made shopping more of an evenly spaced activity occurring all week. With the proliferation of smartphones, social media and e-commerce, further changes were witnessed. Shopping was no longer a household chore, a planned activity or discreet. It was now spur-of-the-moment impulse buying and depended on the buyer's mood. Often it took place when they were multitasking, working out, playing or doing something else, and many times when connecting with social media or with friends in the workplace.

The third major reason for digital transformation was improving efficiency. Physical businesses had different needs and elaborate procedures to be effective. Moving from spreadsheets to digital, we discover new ways to reimagine business using leaner features. For example, to purchase any item, businesses would have had to float multiple purchase requisitions to suppliers a few decades ago. Today, numerous marketplaces are available for procurement that brings thousands of authenticated and prequalified sellers to buyers who have to upload their specifications onto websites to get offers and tabulate them using the toolkit provided by the websites. This digital transformation alone has reduced the workforce needed for purchase functions by a quarter, has doubled transparency and increased the speed of procurement three times resulting in a tenfold increase in efficiency. Today, the procurement division of a large multinational firm consists primarily of a few decision makers who can formulate, upload and evaluate proposals. Businesses are saving on low-end jobs with the help of technology. This improved efficiency reduces costs, helps expand business volumes, and generates profits, driving digital transformation.

However, some skeptics have their point to make against rapid transformation. They feel that change is too fast for humans to understand its consequences. Bob Geldof, the Irish pop singer who wrote "Silicon chip in her head," predicting the indoor generation decades ago in the lyrics of Boomtown Rats' - "I don't like Mondays," is one of them. Geldof, who turned into a tech entrepreneur helping parents to keep track of children's net browsing habits, says "the accelerating development of artificial intelligence could change the face of humanity or else wipe ourselves out, which is not off the cards."

Academics Johanna Drucker and Michael Kleeman of the University of California, Jillian York of the Electronic Frontier Foundation and Zoetanya Sujan of the University of Arts, London, are all skeptical of the growing digital transformation. They feel that because of the economic disparity, the new technologies will be used by those with access to more resources, financial and technical, and those who have the benefit of higher education. It will enlarge the growing and disastrous division between poor, disenfranchised populations and the wealthy, privileged ones. They are concerned that technology today is all-pervasive, and that Silicon Valley will move to areas where they can maximize profits.

That might seem true because businesses seek profits to improve investors' wealth. However, those profits come from large markets. Hence, the emphasis is to spread digital transformation to populous nations first, which have large markets interesting to tech majors. It is probably just a starting point when creating a global supply chain. These nations have thousands of startups that will join, innovate, compete and spread technology to the rest of the globe. So, although it might take time, the benefits of digital transformation could ultimately reach the bottom of the pyramid if it goes through the full cycle, like in China.

Riding on its success in developing rare earth technologies and cheap electric batteries, China opened its electric two-wheeler market to 2,000 small manufacturers to make an affordable two-wheeler for the domestic market. The product was not high-quality nor aggressively exported. By 2010, China was producing 30 million electric two-wheelers annually, which was the standard, low-cost, nonsubsidized, pollution-free transport for the millions of blue-collar workers working in the world's factories. Much later, China tried to export this version to Africa but failed to enter the market due to quality issues. The E-bike in China is still a product for domestic consumption at the bottom of the pyramid that costs less than a fifth of any contemporary product in Europe or the US.

HOW THE PANDEMIC SPURRED DIGITAL TRANSFORMATION

The Covid-19 pandemic killed over a million people, locked down most major cities of the world and threw up numerous new challenges. It disrupted businesses and forced them to become early technology adopters. Digital transformation was most visible during the pandemic in 2020 in healthcare services. For hundreds of years, it was assumed that medical services could be provided best with a human touch. Within just a year we found that it could be equally effective when provided remotely and digitally through video conferencing. What it did was transformative. Using digital technology, we could expand the reach of healthcare services infinitely, even to people in remote areas without access to physical doctors.

The miraculous effect of this digital transformation was more evident across the developing world. According to the World Health Organization (WHO), a large populous democracy like India has 0.9 doctors per 1,000 people versus 6.5 in France. India is also six times bigger than France geographically. So, simply speaking, providing medical access to Indian citizens is 40 times more difficult than providing the same to French citizens. However, India has 700 million internet and smartphone users, which covers around three-quarters of its households. Virtual consultation ensured that doctors could reach many more households, including those in remote rural locations without healthcare infrastructures.

The McKinsey survey of global executives published in October 2020 found that businesses had accelerated the digitization of their customer and supply chain interactions by 3–4 years, and digital product adoptions increased by a whopping 7 years due to the global pandemic. In the case of remote working, executives confirmed that businesses moved 40 times faster than they expected was possible before the pandemic. So, despite the deaths and devastation that the pandemic caused, it benefited the growth of futuristic technologies and inadvertently became the primary trigger for digital transformation. It was like the "race to space", and the "race in nuclear research" to stay ahead between the US and the USSR post the Second World War.

An MIT Sloan study post-Covid-19 busted two important myths. It found that tech organizations could provide solutions across every industry speedily and deliver in crises. Second, it found that consumers were ready to pay for digital products and services during Covid-19 and after it. Twilio, the online research firm that conducted a five-minute online survey of 2,569

CEOs in developed economies, including the UK, France, Germany, Italy, Spain, Japan, Singapore and Australia, found that Covid-19 has dramatically increased investment in digital transformations, speeding up their adoption by at least 6 years.

WHY DIGITAL TRANSFORMATIONS SUCCEED AND FAIL

According to Forbes, nearly 70% of digital transformations in businesses fail. Several Fortune 500 companies are among those who have failed in their quest, despite pumping huge investments and workforce into them. Those failed transformations were allowed to dwindle for years before being downsized and ultimately shelved. Most projects easily identified as failures were basic Enterprise Resource Planning (ERP) projects. However, there are many more failures in supply chain management, standardization and software integration.

Among the biggest digital transformation projects that failed is the USD 1 billion US Navy system integration project carried out by IBM and several others for over a decade. Many other large transformation projects from Nike, GE, Ford Motors, Revlon, Hewlett Packard and Proctor and Gamble lost hundreds of millions of USD without success. The biggest issues have been with the system integrators of SAP, the leading player for ERP.

Many of their multimillion-dollar digital transformation projects at National Grid, Revlon, Hershey's, Haribo, and Miller Coors failed to deliver the promised return on investment (ROI) leading to expensive lawsuits. Most analysts say digital transformation projects are risky because they are complex and related to the overall strategy. So, it is not only the ERP or any technology responsible for the failure but the overall implementation of the business solution. In the words of George Westerman of MIT Sloan "When digital transformation is done right, it's like a caterpillar turning into a butterfly, but when done wrong, all you have is a really fast caterpillar."

Usually, "technology" selection is the first step in a five-step transformation process. Whether it gives the desired results in automation depends on the execution. Then you have to find out whether automation, the second step, improves the efficiencies and reduces the workforce and cuts the cost (the third step) and helps the organization in redeploying its workforce. The fourth step is to examine whether the increased efficiencies improve the customer experience. Sometimes your solution can improve your efficiency and reduce your workforce and costs but result in poor customer experience. If that happens, your project has failed. Finally, you must check whether improved customer experience increases your business volume (fifth step). Often digital transformations fail because they focus too much on making businesses lean and mean by cutting costs and not enough on growing customer satisfaction and business volumes.

The artificial intelligence and technology tools used for digital transformation do part of the work. They can improve automation, identify redundancies, provide methods to reduce workforce and suggest ways to improve efficiencies. What they cannot do, however, is redeploy and retrain the workforce to improve customer experience. That is something the business managers within the organization must work on. For that, they need support from the top management because that, at times, calls for a complete change in the work culture. This is where most businesses falter. Unless the customer's experience improves, it is extremely difficult to improve business volumes, which is the prime reason for failure.

In short, if you increase efficiency and cut jobs to increase profits, your transformation is incomplete and will ultimately fail. Only when you can fully restructure, reorganize your workforce, expand services and improve customer satisfaction will you be able to enhance business volumes and succeed. Because the ultimate ROI comes from stepping up business volumes, digital transformation is imperative and challenging in a fast-changing and increasingly complex and competitive global business environment.

DIGITAL TRANSFORMATION IS A DIRTY WORD FOR MANY BUSINESSES

Although failure is a popular word with startups, it is not a welcome option in large businesses. Executives cringe at "digital transformation" because it is associated with more failures than successes. Executives of large businesses dislike change and look for stability. Organizations look for change that brings growth and not stability. So, executives readily accept some change within the organization for growth. However, it is extremely difficult for them to accept a perpetually changing organization without the final shape of things to come.

Digital transformation requires several back-to-back changes that can be distressing. Often there is a communication gap between senior management and the workers on how changes are planned. Fear of attrition leads to incomplete communication. In addition, there is distrust because the senior management does not specify the boundary conditions of change. Nobody says, "thus far and no further." The senior management is not sure nor has the biblical powers of the Lord to decree the boundary of the gushing seas.

Melissa Swift writing for *The Enterprisers Project* stated that digital transformation faces a backlash because it is vague and loosely defined. "'Digital' is a hot mess of a word. [...] Imagine ordering a hamburger over and over and getting everything from a hot dog to a chicken sandwich to a Caesar salad [...] the lack of clarity is crazy-making," she lambasts. "Meaning is not the only tripwire though. Depending on how you define 'digital' the issue may have different owners in the organization (IT, Marketing, the CEO & Board, etc) – causing political battles that go far beyond linguistic clarity," she adds.

Swift, a transformation leader herself at Mercer in the US, is not charitable to the transformation process either that she calls "bone-grindingly difficult and, at best, disingenuous, and at worst a deliberate distortion straight out of George Orwell's 1984."

A Forbes Council member, Davie Sweiss; however, has a different take on the failures, "Organisations sometimes focus purely on the digital part, but they don't put much thought into the transformation side of things."

He feels that the problem cannot be solved by smart programmers but needs smart leadership. It is not about hiring more digital natives but about taking along areas of organizations that are not tech-focused at all. It needs a holistic approach by the leadership that can apply the tools of change management over time, take along the team and embrace change.

However, not everyone is scared and gives up. Early adopter Nike had several failures after it invested over 400 million in digital transformation. Around 2012, it launched the digital fitness tracker FuelBand to compete with startups Fitbit and Jawbone. But the entire market was rudely interrupted when Apple launched its smartwatch a few years later and walked away with most iPhone users and fitness enthusiasts. The iconic shoemaker has not given up. It has since focused on the Nike+ fitness app and acquired a string of AI and data analytics startups to boost its understanding of consumer shopping behavior. The app had 170 million users and resulted in a 42% increase in online sales in the quarter before the pandemic struck. In September 2020, Nike's new CEO, the tech-savvy John Donahue, reported that its digital sales were booming with 82% growth and would soon account for over half of the shoe company's total sales.

Despite several setbacks, Walmart is another traditional business that has invested millions into digital transformation. The world's biggest retail store failed in its attempt to dominate in China, with competition from brick-and-mortar retail stores and Chinese e-commerce players. In India, after stagnant sales for a few years, it bought into local e-commerce companies Flipkart and Myntra to create an online presence that could compete with Amazon and other local e-commerce players like Reliance and Big Basket. Walmart has become the third-largest IT spender globally, investing billions of USDs in increasing online sales. They have realized that to stay relevant to the modern-day consumer, they must enter the growing e-commerce market, even through the acquisition route. Unilever, P&G and Nestle are all preparing for digital transformation.

Love it or hate it, most businesses know that a digital transformation is no longer an option, according to Jeff Bezos, "There is no alternative to digital transformation. Visionary companies will carve out new strategic options for themselves — those that don't adapt, will fail."

Every business is lining up its unique strategy to stay ahead. Unilever, which conducts its $55 billion consumer goods business from 190 nations, has opted for Azure, Microsoft's cloud computing service, which provides the architectural backbone for the company's digital transformation. The Unilever CIO Jane Moram stated, "That has allowed us to be much more agile and much more scalable. We can't deliver unless we have a platform-based approach and it's very powerful. We're really exploiting that now at Unilever."

A detailed appraisal of digital transformation is only possible when we examine it sector by sector. We will soon look at two sectors, telehealth and edutech, which have grown entirely out of digital transformation in less than two decades with billions of consumers worldwide.

Chapter 8

Telehealth
Distant Cure

Although the telephone is a modern invention that arrived less than 200 years ago, the science of medicine and diagnostics evolved nearly 5,000 years back in India and China. The four Vedas written between 2000 BCE and 500 BCE provided the first principles of Ayurvedic and Yogic therapy, which were basically "nature-based" healing recipes for the body and the mind. Yoga has gone global; while Ayurveda—an alternate plant and mineral-based medication procedure—is still in practice by millions across Asia. Traditional Chinese medicine based on yin and yang and popular procedures like acupressure and acupuncture have also survived for centuries.

The Greek medical texts and the Hippocratic oath penned during the fourth and fifth centuries BCE highlighted the first ethical, legal and clinical procedures documented in the Western World. Aristotle's father was an acclaimed physician and Macedonians were highly interested in the improvement of their physical and psychological health. In addition, the Unani medicine of Persian and Arabian origin was practiced widely during that period and even later until the heydays of the Ottoman Empire. In the early nineteenth century, German physician Samuel Hahnemann conceived the popular alternate remedy of Homeopathy. Around the same time, another German scientist Friedrich Sertürner extracted morphine from opium in his laboratory, which is considered the first pharmaceutical product—a hugely popular pain reliever and a sedative. The science of pharmaceutical medicines has improved immensely in the last two centuries, increasing life expectancy and improving general health conditions. In addition, telehealth, which is a relatively recent by-product, will hugely help in its propagation.

It takes five distinct streams of knowledge to deliver what we know today as telehealth. A little artificial intelligence (AI), robotics, the Internet of Things (IoT) and engineering, and a lot of medical science. Initially, telehealth was medical aid and health instructions administered remotely via the telephone. For many years it was not as multifaceted as it is today, and it was used largely by the armed forces, space scientists or as a rural health initiative by the state or institutions.

MEDICINE THROUGH THE TELEPHONE

The term telemedicine was initially used for "remote diagnosis and treatment of patients who were far away from doctors by the means of telecommunications technology." The earliest users were shipping companies, who used radio signals to access a wide range of specialists; therefore, curing many seafarers with only a single physician on board. Telemedicine witnessed large scale use in the 1960s when the Public Health Department of the Federal Government in the US used it to provide free consultation facilities to rural population. It also got a boost when the US Defense Department started using it to treat American soldiers wounded when fighting wars in faraway lands like Korea, Vietnam and Afghanistan. NASA also used telemedicine to treat astronauts in space.

The US Public Health Service and the Department of Defense sponsored a series of teleradiology projects in the 1970s and 1980s that helped the civilian and military sectors to lower costs. Over the next 40 years, the Federal Government started using telemedicine to reduce the cost of delivery for patients with chronic diseases. Chronic Care Management and Health Tap are among the few companies that have successfully provided telehealth services to chronic patients for decades. Among the early success stories in rural telehealth were the Avera Rural Health Initiative and Integris Rural Health, which started in the 1990s and brought low-cost, high-quality telehealth services to the rural populations of midwestern states of the US.

The impact of telemedicine was also felt globally, as large and populous nations like China and India, accounting for one-third of the global population, started using telephones to provide service to the rural population in remote geographies. Dr. Ganapathy Krishnan, Director of Apollo Telemedicine Network Foundation who pioneered telemedicine in India in 1998, has a 3,000-strong team across South India that provides 4,000 teleconsultations in rural areas each day and had serviced over 10 million patients remotely before the 2020 pandemic.

Pakistani entrepreneur Maliha Khalid and her team run "Doctory," a hotline service that helps patients avoid the multiple referrals often required for treatment by connecting people to the right doctor immediately. "Doctory" is a triage network, which allows people from any part of Pakistan to call and speak to a primary care physician in just 5 min, and it is said to have helped millions of rural Pakistanis get basic medical access during the pandemic. However, the evolution of telemedicine was slow and practitioners in developed economies only used it where unavoidable. Unlike e-commerce or digital banking, telehealth did not take off in a hurry before the Covid-19 pandemic struck. Only 14,000 Americans used it per week during 2019 and the telehealth market size at that time was estimated to be $45 billion.

THE PANDEMIC TRANSFORMED TELEHEALTH

The Covid-19 pandemic that spread from Wuhan, China initially affected the major global economies of the US, UK, France, Italy and Spain the most. The first wave left more than 100,000 people dead in these five biggest tourist destinations of the world. It devastated economies and rendered millions jobless. By April 2020, according to the World Health Organization (WHO), 3.9 billion people in 90 nations worldwide were subject to total or partial lockdowns imposed by governments. Despite being an election year in the US, lockdowns and restrictions on travel and flight movements were placed several times across the states. Not only was travel difficult, but citizens just could also not go to hospitals as they were full of Covid patients.

Telehealth consultations jumped nearly 50-fold to 700,000 people a week in the US during the pandemic. The Federal and State Governments were forced to make changes in the law to allow insurers to reimburse the costs of teleconsultation for Medicare & Medicaid Services (CMS). President Trump used emergency powers to permit insurance access to Medicare telehealth services so that beneficiaries could receive a wider range of services from their doctors without having to travel to a healthcare facility. Despite this significant measure to reduce hospital congestion, more than 19 million positive Coronavirus cases and 378,000 deaths were recorded in the US in 2020 alone.

The changeover took place in the US and across Europe, bringing telehealth into the mainstream. Since January 2021, all statutorily insured 72 million German citizens have been legally entitled to a national electronic patient record. Over 20,000 German doctors started providing consultation across telehealth platforms set up during the pandemic. In France, changes in the law were introduced in April 2020, allowing easier reimbursement of costs for teleconsultation against insurance and the French social security scheme.

The transformation was magical in the UK. Dr. Mandip Thiara was surprised at how swiftly a UK-based health start-up AccuRx was able to set up their new remote video consultation software within 1 week during the pandemic. It was something that they had been trying to achieve for 4 years without success. The National Health Service (NHS) woke up from a deep slumber during the pandemic and got its act together say General Practitioners, who set up hubs to care for the elderly and video consultations for others. According to a *Lancet* report, the NHS in the UK has recommended that one out of four interactions with doctors should be through teleconsultations. In Spain, there is no nationwide regulation enabling or banning telemedicine services. In Italy, as of August 2020 after the first wave of the Covid-19 pandemic, telemedicine services were not included in the essential levels of care granted to all citizens within the public health system.

Although regulatory changes across the world happened slowly, the market moved faster with a host of new suppliers to meet the emerging demand. The first reason for this was that hospitals were under existential pressure. The global lockdown stopped patient flow into hospitals overnight, disrupting financial stability. Most hospitals were traditionally multidisciplinary; however, you could simply not visit a heart specialist, neurologist, orthopedist, dentist or pediatrician because the pandemic was raging, and it was not safe. Hospitals suffered a 90% loss of regular patients, which would have normally led to financial meltdown. However, doctors and nursing staff, along with hospital infrastructure, were most in demand to attend to Coronavirus patients despite having no experience or understanding of the behavior of the virus.

Governments pumped in copious amounts of money so that healthcare could reorganize itself and meet emergency situations. Human resilience and innovation came to the fore as people learned on the go. Political leaders, administrators, hospitals, schools, manufacturers, businesses, media and citizens adopted whatever solutions were available to fight the pandemic. Healthcare restructured itself, set up temporary facilities and took to telemedicine like a duck to water. Although telemedicine had been around for five decades, 2020 saw the greatest digital transformation of all time that revolutionized healthcare services completely in most economies.

TELEMEDICINE VERSUS TELEHEALTH

Telemedicine is the use of telecommunication systems and other associated technologies to administer medicine to patients who are geographically separated from the doctors who provide healthcare services. Telemedicine refers specifically to remote clinical services; however, telehealth can refer to remote nonclinical services, such as providing training, administrative services and medical education, in addition to clinical services.

Telehealth covers a much broader horizon, including regular fitness and upkeep through remote patient monitoring, preventive care, health-related services, including patient management, service provider and patient education, health information services and self-care. The terms telehealth and telemedicine are often used interchangeably. However, telemedicine is usually provided by doctors trained in medical science and telehealth is largely administered by qualified practitioners, technicians, software designers, physical trainers and influencers who need not necessarily be doctors. All of that might help the scalability of services but whether handing health services over to non-medical practitioners is desirable or not, only time will tell.

There are many experts who doubt that medical services will improve with the use of technology alone. The director of Health Services Research, Cedars-Sinai Medical Center Los Angeles Dr. Brennan Spiegel stated, "The notion that simply discharging patients with some technology will prevent readmission or ensure positive outcomes is more wishful thinking than reality."

Increasing the number of patients through technology intervention and software assistance might not necessarily mean providing high-quality medical care.

A senior physician who has an offline and online practice stated, "There are four core issues that we usually need to ascertain in medicare services – competence, trust, empathy and reliability."

When you go to a doctor close to your home, you physically see and hear the patients moving in and out of the clinic, you observe the cleanliness of the premises and the attitude and efficiency of the staff. In online medical services you cannot ascertain such things and have to depend instead on internet reviews and likes to make your choice. In addition, the online health service provider only appears for a few minutes across the screen to give solutions to your problem. There is no time to develop a doctor–patient relationship.

Bringing in technology means replacing the human touch and empathy, which is ultimately the key to providing ethical medical care. A key element of patient recovery is confidence. That depends on the reliability of the doctor to deliver at all times and the patient's trust in them. Physicians feel less confident about delivering online than through personal care, revealed a McKinsey survey in 2021. The four core issues are all weak links in the online industry. This occurs perhaps because telehealth is mostly administered by software companies and not by traditional hospital services. So, although it grew massively during the Covid-19 crisis, its growth might be much more muted in normal times.

There is, however, a different viewpoint. Telehealth companies, such as Teladoc Health claim that 90% of medical issues are resolved after the first interaction. Associated physicians must follow proprietary guidelines developed by the software company and are prohibited from meeting their telemedicine patients. The decision maker here is no longer the physician but the system administrator. The command control has totally shifted.

Doctors are no longer in the driver's seat as in traditional hospitals. They are contracted service providers. As a matter of fact, teams of nurses' review 10% of each physician's monthly consultations to ensure the due process has been followed. The less talked off but critical difference between telemedicine and telehealth today is the people delivering the service. In telehealth, it is usually not the doctors but the marketing and technology teams of venture capital financed software companies who make the decisions. Their idea is to not just cure but prevent disease and health decay. They derive their profits from volume and scalability. That might not be bad, but it is definitely different from what we have experienced for centuries.

With limited doctors and increasingly expensive healthcare services, telehealth was bound to take over. However, it was not what the purists of the profession wanted. Dr. Paul Rosen, a pediatric rheumatologist talking about the broken healthcare system in America, stated that empathy was the key to the future of healthcare. It is important to treat patients as humans and not just a name on a medical file. Getting to know the patient's problem through conversation is getting rarer by the day, say close observers of the practice. Patients have to wait for weeks and sometimes months to get an appointment with a physician or specialist at popular hospitals. Besides, the waiting period after you reach the hospital and even in the emergency room varies greatly from 2 to 6 hrs. The worst part is that most doctors hardly listen to the patients after the tedious wait for a consultation.

Statistical data shows that the average time that doctors listen is from 30 secs to 1 min. They will start writing tests before they actually hear the patients fully. On top of this, the tests are numerous and at times obscure. Patients are often prescribed tests without being told if they were really needed. In addition, busy doctors don't have the time or the inclination to interact with or explain to the patient. Will telehealth improve consultations with the use of technology, or make empathy and personal touch even more elusive?

Proponents of telehealth say the increasing cost of healthcare requires disruptive technology solutions to make health insurance and medical services affordable to all. The analysis of health-related information could improve the physiological condition of patients to an extent that visiting hospitals for regular treatment might be outdated. Doctors are focused on treating patients, and telehealth aims to avoid turning people into patients. The emphasis is more on prevention than on cure. This is why doctors are in the background and not at the forefront of a telehealth company. That way, domain expertise remains intact at the backend instead of having to manage day-to-day operations. So, although there might appear to be some disconnect to the layman between telehealth and telemedicine practices, the idea to improve the healthcare of citizens remains a common objective.

SO, HOW DOES TELEHEALTH WORK?

Telehealth works primarily on data. Like all technology solutions we have read about previously, telehealth is essentially about the use of data to improve health services, expand availability and reduce costs. We have seen the huge impact of technology on telephony in IoT, on retail in e-commerce and on banking services in digital banking, all for the benefit of users. Telehealth businesses that have been around for two decades also collate user data to improve the health of their digital subscribers. Your first step to access telehealth is a simple online registration on the website or app of the digital health provider. Since this is virtual healthcare, you can register irrespective of geographies and reap most of the benefits. However, insurance claim assistance is available only for citizens in most US telehealth apps.

Telehealth is different from other tech applications like Google Search, Facebook, Uber or Amazon. Most of the data mined by other tech businesses are external—Google mines news from all over the internet, Facebook mines stories from users, Uber mines data from cab operators, Google Maps and traffic data, and Amazon mines data from its marketplace and user preferences. However, telehealth providers mine your physiological data and provide solutions for your well-being. So, those with high privacy concerns might please take a backseat. Once you register with any telehealth app you are encouraged to share your data to get feedback on your lifestyle and how to stay healthy.

This data would typically be your age, weight, height, blood pressure, pulse rate and blood sugar level. In addition, your medical records on tests that you might have previously had like X-rays, ECGs, Ultrasounds, MRIs and CT scans. It might also include pathological test reports like blood, urine, stool, kidney, lung and liver function tests, recurring conditions like migraines or urinary tract infections or asthma and much more could be of use. It would have data on your mental health, depression attacks, visits to counselors and when and why you had to visit mental health clinics previously. All of this data is mapped and analyzed by technologists and correlated by physicians on the telehealth portal that gives the output condition of your physical and mental health after your registration.

Most health niggles become major issues because they are not attended to promptly. For example, a simple cold and cough could become chronic and even deteriorate into bronchitis or asthma if not attended to early. So, the telehealth portal suggests that you regularly check and update your vital information. Then, they can guide you to remain in good health. For regular checking, you may use smart devices, which perform patient monitoring seamlessly. These smart devices are the future of telehealth monitoring; they upload your data into the cloud and rely on the power of big data to analyze your health condition. They are the new kids on the block, the Internet of Medical Things (IoMT) that performs the specialized function of monitoring your physiological data to keep you healthy.

Just like the IoT (Chapter 1), they are devices that communicate with multiple entities like the patient, physician, pathologist, radiologist, neurologist, psychiatrist, health algorithms on the backend computers and the information streams on the cloud to create a master dashboard of your health data. We will look at the multiple IoMT monitoring devices in detail later. First, we will find out what happens to your health data on the big data dashboard on the cloud. The data collected by the IoMT is analyzed with AI, according to the particular patient monitoring system developed by each telehealth service provider. Here, we see once more that diagnostic, predictive, and prescriptive analytics, the basic streams of AI that we came across in Chapter 2, come into play. This has reduced physical patient monitoring visits to physicians by more than 80%. Then, the data analysis helps physicians adopt the AI-based automated system for decision assistance. For example, in several cases, AI is being used to analyze X-rays and find the fault lines in the chest and lungs for the early detection of pneumothorax and lung cancer. In other cases, automated AI-driven distant insulin adjustments are monitored on chronic patients with diabetes and the best results for each patient are found and maintained. Since all patients have different physiological conditions, this is like finding the right insulin dose for each patient. The 24/7 remote monitoring of patient data, AI analysis and collaboration reduces the workload and burnout for the physician and makes the process smoother for the patient.

Telehealth has also started using robots for assistance internally and externally. William Beaumont, an American army surgeon, known as the "Father of Gastric Physiology" first introduced an endoscope into a human in 1822, which allowed internal examination of the gastrointestinal (GI) tract up to the upper portion of the small bowel. Then 200 years later, ingestible wireless capsule endoscopy (WCE) uses a robotic capsule that you might swallow as a fully effective painless telehealth solution when inspecting the entire GI tract for various diseases, like obscure gastrointestinal bleeding, tumors, cancer, celiac and Crohn's disease.

Telehealth robots are also being used externally to assist older adult patients in walking and climbing stairs, administering timely medicines to older adult patients and notifying the health officials in case of an emergency. As we read previously in Chapter 3, these robots are extremely popular in Japan, a country with a very high older adult population. They respond to the patient's requests and can carry out assignments in the home environment of the patient, helping them to move, take food and medicine, go to the toilet, change clothes, read, exercise, play games and even put them to sleep. These smart robots are built specifically to enhance the quality of life for older adults and could be individually programmed to meet any special needs.

Derek O'Keefe belongs to the rare breed of digital doctors who has studied engineering in computer science and biomedical engineering and is also a qualified physician with clinical training in general medicine, endocrinology and diabetes. He says it helps to practice both because doctors have a lot of clinical problems and engineers can develop a lot of solutions. One such problem he helped NASA develop is a bio-vest for astronauts orbiting the earth 16 times a day, without jet lag. The mission was to trace the physiological data, analyze and make mission-specific decisions, such as who was going for a spacewalk at a given time based on the physiological data of the astronauts each day.

Healthcare is expensive because it has been reactive and not proactive. You fall sick and go to the doctor for a cure instead of monitoring your physiological data and taking timely action to stop yourself from becoming sick. Engineers help when solving problems in multiple ways, such as creating machines that help diagnoses, recovery, surgery, planning and preventive action to doing post-care analytics. They not only work with data but with mechanics and electronics. Engineers build smartwatches, traction devices, hearing aids, dental chairs, smart shoes for the visually impaired and aerobic training machines, and much more. The science of medicine will always need the science of engineering to develop solutions.

THE RISE OF SMART IOMT DEVICES

These engineers have developed numerous devices to help medical science grow by leaps and bounds. However, not all devices that automatically record and transmit vital signs to your health provider are IoMT. When you measure your blood pressure, pulse rate and body temperature using medical devices and upload the data to a health app it is conventional reporting. Conventional fitness trackers first surfaced in 1965, with the Manpo-Kei pedometer, a "10,000 steps meter." It was invented by Dr. Yoshiro Hatano, a Japanese professor at the Kyushu University of Health and Welfare, Fukuoka, Japan who was researching how to combat obesity.

Smart devices arrived decades later. When you use wearables that are connected to your smartphone and monitor vital stats seamlessly without manual intervention, that is the IoMT. Remote patient monitoring (RPM) involves the collection, transmission, reporting and evaluation of patient health data through electronic devices, such as wearables, mobile devices, internet-enabled audio and video recording devices and smartphone apps. In case weight data or cardiac stats are needed that do not involve wearables, the app reminds the user to use the weighing machine and record the requisite Electronic Health Record (EHR) data for seamless monitoring.

The potential business volume of telehealth is mind boggling. A McKinsey study from 2021 says that almost $250 billion of health services in the US each year have the potential to be delivered virtually as telehealth or telemedicine initiatives. The $100 billion wearable market was the fastest growing segment in telehealth with Apple alone accounting for one-third of the market share before 2020 and Samsung, Xiaomi, and Huawei accounting for another third of the market selling watches, wristbands, monitors and hearables. The remaining third of the market is fragmented with nearly 1,000 digital device manufacturers in the fray. However, before we talk about the key players in the market, let us examine a few of the popular IoMT devices that are in vogue today.

Even before telehealth players started to use wearables, the market existed as part of the multibillion-dollar sports goods segment. They were primarily IoMT-enabled fitness monitors that were extremely diverse and innovative and tracked the heartbeat and blood pressure of athletes and body roll movement of swimmers and the punch data record for boxers. They also included the FIFA-approved GPS tracker vests that allowed footballers and coaches to record the speed, power, sprint distance, workload intensity and positioning of players and the biometric signs of exhaustion and physical injury on smartphones.

Fitbits were the earliest IoMT devices that pioneered the ever-expanding wearable fitness monitors market soon after the arrival of smartphones. Founders James Park and Eric Friedman first floated the concept at a TechCrunch 50 conference in September 2008 and raised over a million dollars with 2,500 preorders. Fitbit launched its first IoMT fitness tracker at the end of 2009, shipping around 5,000 units with a further 20,000 orders on the books. It was a wireless-enabled device priced attractively at $99 that could be worn as a smart wrist band and used a movement detector that recorded the motion, sleep and calorie burn of the user. In 2011, they introduced the Fitbit Ultra by adding an altimeter, digital clock and a stopwatch. The Fitbit Flex was introduced in 2014 and became fashionable as it connected with Android and Apple devices and attracted young consumers across a dozen top sporting nations with its sleek look and ability to track their step progress throughout the day with the device's five indicator lights. The health insurance industry was quick to pick up on the benefits and ensured that all athletes and sportspersons they insured used them diligently.

However, remote health monitoring spread rapidly through the telehealth industry after 2016 with a whole gamut of the IoMT devices being introduced along with smartwatches. The Food and Drug Administration (FDA)-approved continuous glucose trackers hit the shelves, which helped monitor glucose levels in the body and delivered insulin as per requirements through an implantable sensor that could be worn for 90 days. Philips' wearable biosensor is a self-adhesive patch that allows patients to move around when collecting data on their movement, heart and respiratory rates, and temperature. Digital hearing aids that convert sound waves into digital signals and produce precise sound duplication are popular IoMT devices. Then, there are wearable IoMT enabled life vests that continuously monitor heart rhythm. When they detect any life-threatening rhythm they can automatically produce a shock treatment through implantable cardioverter–defibrillators and restore the patient's heart rate to the normal rhythm. Similarly, IoMT devices for asthma monitoring can forecast oncoming asthma attacks based on when the patient sneezes, coughs, wheezes or experiences shortness of breath and can inject medicine instantly to prevent any imminent attack.

The IoMT safety devices are also much in vogue, being used at night in places that are less frequented and not considered socially safe. Wearable security wristbands tracking location through GPS and connected to the local police station and close relatives are available today.

Ava Woman creates night-only wearable devices for women. They also have an FDA-approved fertility tracking bracelet that tracks five physiological signs of women that help locate their most fertile days. They track sleep, stress levels, menstrual cycles, pregnancy, ovulation and periods to predict the most fertile period. The Owlet baby sleep monitor tracks infants and babies through wearables. Owlet's new wearable band for pregnant women monitors heart rate, kick counts and other neonatal indicators. It can also log infant heart rate, oxygen level, sleep patterns and chronic pains, seamlessly tracking the weekly milestones in the newborn baby's life.

Rasika Mallya, a Mumbai-based researcher on IoMT-based Woman's Health Monitoring System (WHMS) says the following types of monitoring are possible with WHMS: (1) ovulation monitoring if someone wants to conceive and they are under the treatment of an obstetrician; (2) fetus monitoring when a person is pregnant; (3) menopause monitoring if the patient is facing hormonal imbalance problems; (4) regular body parameters like pulse rate, heart rate, blood sugar level, body temperature and workout monitoring.

The use of IoMT devices in hospitals grew threefold during the pandemic to touch 3.2 million units in 2021. According to Juniper Research, 7.4 million IoMT devices will be in use in the next 5 years. Researchers expect that the next stage of innovation will come from thousands of smart hospitals with fully equipped data centers, remote monitoring and telehealth facilities. The entire chronic patient management system will become IoMT-based to ensure 24/7 remote monitoring of physiological data. This should cut down on the costs to insurers and the state. It will also save infrastructure costs for hospitals that can monitor the patients from home instead of having to bring a patient into the hospital and arrange for a bed and nursing.

Virtual home assistants (VHA) that remind, monitor and report, and robotic home assistants (RHA) that additionally help patients' physical movement, bathing and toilet activities, are being developed by robot assisted equipment makers to take care of older adult patients. In addition, new age biosensor technology has started arriving that can be worn or attached to the patient's skin, monitoring and relaying physiological parameters to a database analyzed 24/7 by AI that would provide solutions and report to doctors and relatives in case of emergencies. Such futuristic IoMT solutions will make healthcare cost-effective.

BIG TECH ENTERS THE TELEHEALTH SPACE

Apple, Alphabet, Amazon and Microsoft have all entered telehealth and have made their presence felt in niche segments with a few successes and several failures. Apple Chief Executive Officer (CEO) Tim Cook says he wants health to be Apple's "greatest contribution to mankind." However, that is easier said than done in this hugely fragmented industry whose problems are more multifaceted than the technology giants are used to handle. Apple is focused on the device end of the technology solutions, and Amazon, Alphabet and Microsoft are battling it out on the market and the cloud end of the telehealth solutions.

Apple disrupted the IoMT segment of smart devices despite being a late entrant in 2017 with its Apple Watch and Heart Study Apps created to monitor heart rhythms and alert those who were experiencing irregular and rapid heart rhythms. The Series 3 entry-level watch introduced 5 years ago had a built-in GPS and an optical heart sensor but lacked the altimeter its competitors boasted. Five years later, the Apple Series 7 model came along with a blood oxygen saturation monitor, altitude and pressure tracking and native sleep tracking capabilities, an FDA-approved ECG sensor, a continuously updated health monitoring system and a fall detection system that would call emergency services automatically if it sensed the wearer was not moving.

In 2020, Apple sold 196 million iPhones, it also sold 43 million Apple Watches. Wearing Apple Watches kept all your physiological data in your mobile phone and was the top fashion statement for the year. However, Apple does not have all the solutions and has had its share of failures. When it launched its primary healthcare service with fanfare among its own employees, it struggled along with its health habit initiatives.

Alphabet, Google's parent company, has also invested heavily in telehealth in the last 5 years. In 2019, weeks before the pandemic, it purchased Fitbit for $2 billion, opening up new avenues for the search giant, which had already been offering several solutions through Google Fit, a customized health information platform, DeepMind, its healthcare AI initiative, and Calico and Verily, its biotech and healthcare research units. The company used its dominance in data storage, AI, analytics and search to land strategic hospital partnerships where it provided solutions solving issues with EHR interoperability and limited computing infrastructure along with its fitness and preventive healthcare and predictive analytics solution. In August 2020, it pumped in $100 million to pick up the controlling stakes in Amwell, a large telemedicine provider to 2,000 US hospitals, during its initial public offering (IPO).

Online retailer Amazon has focused largely on the retail pharmacy end with some successes and notable failures. It started its efforts with its familiar and time-tested segment of supply chain management, providing support for the medical supply distribution space using its worldwide network of warehousing and supply chain management. Unlike Apple and Alphabet, Amazon is used to the low margins and competitive environment the pharmaceutical industry offers. The Amazon Business initiative is a wholesale business-to-business marketplace for pharma among many other businesses. So, many were surprised when Haven, the healthcare venture by Amazon, Berkshire Hathaway, and J.P. Morgan Chase that aimed to provide US employees and their families with simplified, high-quality, and transparent health care at a reasonable cost, collapsed during the pandemic.

Microsoft's health play centers around its cloud platform Azure and its long-standing association with healthcare and data analytics capabilities. In 2021, it announced its association with pharmaceutical company CVS Health. Through custom built office products and its cloud solution, it aimed to make health data more agile, enabling retail employees to more easily consume the key information needed to answer common questions and solve customer needs faster. It has several other initiatives, such as Microsoft Cloud for Healthcare, Genomics, HealthBot, Next and Scribe.

In April 2021, it made a massive investment in telehealth, buying out software developer Nuance Communications for $19.7 billion. The CEO of Microsoft Satya Nadella stated, "Nuance provides the AI layer at the healthcare point of delivery and is a pioneer in the real-world application of enterprise AI."

So, whereas Apple would probably be your device choice, Google would guide your hospital choice, Amazon would help your pharmacy deliver and Microsoft would provide you the enterprise AI for the technology. If you thought Facebook was left behind, you are mistaken. The social media giant is creating a marketplace on its platform for mental health practitioners and plans to take it to the next level with the launch of the metaverse using advanced sensory equipment.

The telehealth industry, although much smaller in revenue than tech majors, is finding its feet even independent of Big Tech. At the same time, it needs a lot of investor funding or investment by tech majors to grow to a big enough size to make a mark on the trillion dollar healthcare segment. In 2020, after two decades of sustained growth, Teladoc acquired Livongo for $18.5 billion to become the biggest player in the telehealth space in the US. Founded in 2002, the pioneer in primary telehealthcare had more than 1,500 employees, a net worth of $5.7 billion and an annual revenue of $2.14 billion in 2021, which was tiny presence in the pharma and healthcare industries. Other telehealth businesses located in the US, such as MeMD, HealthTap and Doctor on Demand are much smaller in size with revenues from $50 million to $250 million.

However, there are others outside the US that are making their mark due to their reach and not their revenue. iCliniq, a Chennai-based global telehealth business from India with nearly 3,500 employees, operates virtually across 196 nations, offering various telehealth services, including virtual consultations that cover general medicine, dermatology, psychiatry, oncology and gynecology.

Of the 94 telehealth unicorns in the world, 64 are from the US and 14 from China. Not only startups, even big players like Alibaba, JD Health and Tencent are in play trying to entice 3.8 million Chinese doctors to join their health apps. Telehealth started becoming popular in China after the government permitted online players to enter the healthcare business in 2015. However, the real growth happened after the outbreak of the pandemic in 2020. More than 500,000 patients in China have availed remote health care annually ever since. Doctors charge around CNY 50, equivalent to $8, for a 15-min video consultation, which is equivalent to what they would charge for an in-person visit.

THE FUTURE OF TELEHEALTH

Telehealth has been around for five decades, but essentially on the fringes. During the pandemic, the interest in telehealth solutions leapfrogged. According to a McKinsey report in July 2021, telehealth utilization has stabilized at levels 38 times higher than before the pandemic. However, its growth has been largely confined to the US and it is uncertain whether public interest in distant cures will remain high after the pandemic. It is also true that investor interest in telehealth has spiraled to three times that of the pre-pandemic levels; however, the volumes are too minuscule to make a real dent in the healthcare business. The investment made by venture funds into telehealth, though twice the previous year (2019), was less than $15 billion during the first 6 months of 2021. This was much lower than expected after the pandemic, especially considering that the total venture capital investment in 2021 was a record $671 billion.

Healthcare expenditure in America rose by nearly 10% in 2020 and exceeded $4 trillion. That was nearly one-fifth of the US GDP. Per capita healthcare costs in the US are the highest in the world at $11,000 per person. However, the US had the highest number of Covid-19 cases and deaths during the pandemic, far larger than any other nation. Researchers say that was because of co-morbidities that were rampant, largely because of lifestyle issues. One in four US adults suffers from two chronic health conditions that could be managed efficiently by Remote Patient Monitoring (RPM) technologies that are being developed today, reducing doctor visits and payment of fees.

However, because of the low penetration of RPM, the overall cost of healthcare is high and does not reach all sections of society. Globally, the situation is equally dismal and although the spending is much lower, it is rising sharply. The 38 OECD nations with a population of 1.2 billion spend another $3 trillion on healthcare. China and India, the two most populous nations of the world with 2.7 billion people, spend another $1.5 trillion on healthcare. So, the opportunity to expand telehealth is immense in most nations and is much more than any other industry. We have recent examples of technology disrupting retail, banking, cab services and food supply completely, reducing costs and expanding services. Since the opportunity runs into trillions of dollars, we should soon witness telehealth revamping and remodeling the healthcare industry.

The healthcare market size of the major OECD economies, the US, China and India, is a mind boggling $8.5 trillion. Even if telehealth reduced 10% of the healthcare costs annually that would be $850 billion each year in these nations with a combined population of 4.2 billion. All these nations have developed digital infrastructure, mature digital payment systems and have a digitally savvy population with the capability to adopt telehealth without additional training. However, there is no real initiative to push through these changes by governments. That possibly does not happen because of an unspoken profit sharing pact between the healthcare and pharma industries with tacit support from insurers, bureaucrats, politicians and the mental conditioning of patients for centuries. A visit to the doctor and extensive testing is encouraged and takes place in more than 80% of the cases irrespective of the disease. Telehealth has been around for decades and has not been able to change things significantly. Could technology players change the situation post-pandemic?

The tech majors have already sensed the opportunity during the pandemic years and made significant inroads into the telehealth marketplace. Apple and Microsoft individually have invested more in telehealth than all the venture capitalist's post-pandemic. Although Amazon faced some reverses in Haven, it has started in-person healthcare under Amazon Care in 20 American cities. Apple is trying to send its HealthKit data from Apple Watches directly to hospitals. Epic, one of the largest health records companies, says that 100 of its large clients are using Apple HealthKits to capture data directly from home monitoring services. Google has stepped up its acquisitions and is expected to make the Android platform a telehealth hub for global phone makers like Samsung and Huawei.

There are many reasons why the tech majors could ultimately chart the future of telehealth. It is because the healthcare needs of each of the planet's 8 billion people are different. That means personalized care for each consumer and consequent monetization from a big data source. It has the potential to be the largest and most profitable service of the current decade. Nothing excites the tech industry more than access to personal data that gives unique insights into human health and behavior. Telehealth is the easiest window to that data. However, to get there, they will face major challenges from governments, politicians and activists with privacy concerns. China and a few nations will push ahead; however, many democracies might be reluctant to give up control of the physiological data on their citizens, even though it may do wonders to citizens's health.

Another rapidly expanding area that will transform human behavior is edutech, where technology is changing learning practices and education quantitively and qualitatively. With 800 million illiterate adults and 30% of the world's children unable to obtain sustained education due to multiple factors like cost, distance, facilities, time and convenience, it is another area that needs to be developed and assisted by new technologies. In the next chapter, we will see how technology is trying to disrupt education and its success and failures.

Chapter 9

Edu Tech

Remote Learning

At the beginning of the twentieth century, educators found that as students multiplied in classrooms, they could not retain what was being taught. The number of students had risen dramatically. Student–teacher ratios were going up by the day. It was becoming extremely difficult to assess if the students had understood and retained what they had learned in the classroom. So, educators started looking for alternative methods for teaching and testing students.

EDUCATION THROUGH RADIO AND TELEVISION

During the First World War, the US Army was looking to increase the efficiency of the recruitment process and move away from the time-consuming written and oral examination system. Dr. Robert Yerkes, then the president of the American Psychological Association, persuaded the army to conduct an intelligence and aptitude test based on multiple-choice questions. Although the efficiency of the multiple-choice testing was clearly found to be inadequate by the army, it was a faster testing option and remains the most popular way of testing knowledge retention.

In 1925, Ohio-based educator Sidney Presser created the world's first mechanical teaching machine that not only assessed but instantly rewarded students who answered multiple-choice questions correctly. It had a typewriter-like drum body to which a sheet of questions was attached, and the user could choose one of the four keys to register their chosen answer. Inside the drum were located sliding fins that positioned the correct answers and a candy reward tube with a reward dial and pointer. The machine was set for testing when the lever was down, and the pointer was set at eight. Now, eight correct answers in a row by a student would lead to the release of a piece of candy.

So, multiple-choice questioning and machine-based teaching and testing became the first baby steps in edutech taken 100 years ago. During the 1920s licenses were given to the Universities in Salt Lake City, Wisconsin

DOI: 10.1201/9781003409557-12

and Minnesota, US, to set up radio stations to conduct distance education. It took another three decades to mass-produce the practice of machine-based learning. In 1954, B.F. Skinner and a group of behavioral scientists and programmers were asked to design an instructional program at Harvard to enhance learning. Programs were written to teach math, kinematics, trigonometry, coordinate systems, basic French with dictation, phonetic notion, vocabulary and rudimentary grammar. Single demonstration disks in geography, anatomy and poetry were also produced. Once this was achieved, Skinner put the teaching machines to work in his classroom, where he taught natural science to test the program's efficacy.

According to the National Museum of American History, these teaching machines were hinged wooden boxes with a knob. Multiple paper disks were fitted inside, with questions and answers written along the radii of the disks. The hinged top covers had a window that revealed one problem at a time. In the front of the window were six levers, which allowed the student to set a number in a hole to answer the question. The teaching machines for Skinner's course on behaviorism were installed in a "self-instruction room" in the basement of the Server Hall. These machines provided added value as they tested the retention power of the student. At the end of the session, 62% of the students said that it had resulted in easy understanding and better learning. Admissions jumped by 70% the next year, and teaching machines were soon used for all subjects.

A decade later, the BBC used television for education in schools. In 1969, the British government established the Open University (OU) in partnership with the BBC to develop multimedia university programs specifically integrated with courses related to university education. In the first 40 years, before internet education took root, 2 million Britons had enrolled in and benefited from the OU. The OU was popular with individuals who did not go to school or enroll, because it was free high-quality education provided at home through their television. It made learning much more accessible to all citizens and anyone who just lived there and watched it, not just school students.

In 1983, India used its indigenously launched INSAT satellite to deliver locally produced educational television programs in regional languages for students aged from 5 to 11years old across six states through local community centers and schools. It now uses dedicated Edusat satellites and television to provide free distance education to 15 million of the poorest students in a dozen regional languages spread across 22 states and in difficult geographies.

EDUTECH IN THE DIGITAL ERA—BRINGING QUALITATIVE CHANGES

The 1990s saw the arrival of the internet and digital technologies. Computer-based learning courses and learning management system (LMS) software flooded global markets. The biggest users and providers of edutech were the governments of every nation. Radio, television and the internet helped provide scalability to cover billions of poor people who had never been exposed to formal education. Only one in four people in China and India were educated in the 1990s, and literacy rates were pretty low in most locations. Thirty years later, they are at the forefront of research, accounting for 47% of the 1.1 million students that go to US universities annually, providing a huge quantitative boost to successful international researchers.

But let us first see what digital age learning provided and how it was qualitatively different from the conventional learning of the past. What were the changes that transformed education so radically and so rapidly? We know that the tools and technology of the digital era helped create millions of additional students—a massive quantitative change, but what was it qualitatively that really enticed students and quickly helped the spread of education?

Education in the twenty-first century faced the same learning retention challenge as before; however, it had become more interactive and open to student feedback with the arrival of emails and digital polls. Also, as internet learning avenues expanded, there was a spate of highly successful Ivy League dropouts, such as Bill Gates, Matt Damon, James Park and Mark Zuckerberg, who challenged the age-old concept that college education was needed for success. Self-education became an established way to acquire knowledge and succeed in life, and most of it was free, convenient and extremely effective.

You could learn inside and outside classrooms, at all times of the day or night. Google search, YouTube and Wikipedia ruled the roost and audio and video mediums became popular in assisting self-study. MIT and Harvard started providing freemium (free + premium) online coaching. You no longer needed a college degree to be knowledgeable. In addition, a large number of those who graduated from renowned institutions proved failures in the workplace. So, when educators asked students how to increase retention in the digital era, they found an entirely different answer. They were told that education should be relevant to the student's needs. Also, it should be interesting and entertaining. All that was surely not going to be easy.

Students were not keen to learn structured, grammar-based languages, preferring the vocabulary spoken on the streets. They shied away from algebra and formula-based math, which they believed had nothing to do with how things worked. The contemporary axiomatic approach prevalent in classrooms was supposedly based on enforcing an attitude that "when we do mathematics, we don't need to know what the things we are working with are. We only need to know what the rules are." That meant those axioms were important, and it was unnecessary to understand the concepts or context to do the calculations. The modern student of the digital era, who was used to interactive learning and had more options than their predecessors, would not have any of that.

Changing how mathematics was taught in primary schools was the first big fight in the digital age. It is still not over and is a work in progress. Rote learning to memorize mathematics had been prevalent for centuries. The baby boomers who went to school in the 1960s could tell you that 19×17 would be 323 in seconds, all from memory. However, memorization was supposed to be less intellectual as it was due to repetitive learning of math tables or periodic tables by students of math and science. It was due to what is disparagingly called "cramming or mugging up" without understanding.

Around 50 years ago, the practice was discontinued in British schools after the Plowden Report was presented to the Central Advisory Council for Education. Intelligent learning grounded in context and adaptable to activities, actions and other circumstances started replacing habit learning modes of recall, recognize and remember. So, several new methods were suggested, including the four-step traditional method. Here, the first two digits of 19×17 were multiplied, and two zeros were added to get 100 as the first step. This was added to the multiplication of the last two numbers, which was 63. Then, this was added to the cross multiplication of both numbers with an addition of zero, giving two additional numbers 70 and 90. All four numbers were then added to give 323. Although adopted across schools, this method was not quick or simple like rote learning, which stayed on and remained popular because the alternatives were ineffective and not fast enough.

All that started to change with edutech in the digital era. There were many alternate learning methods that students could choose and try out. There were multiple choices, not just two. Fun learning had entered the arena. Even Vedic Mathematics from India, which had arrived thousands of years ago to simplify addition, subtraction, multiplication, division, squares and square roots, found new and enthusiastic adopters in the edutech world.

It was not only math at the primary level but the entire school curriculum that came under scrutiny. Students wanted a change, and educators wanted more students to boost their revenues. That opened a window of opportunity for edutech to try and evolve better solutions that meet academic needs and students' desire for education to be more context-driven and relevant to their needs. However, not all of the new methods have been successful.

Relevant and meaningful activities engaged students physically, mentally and emotionally. They connected them with what they knew previously and built neural connections to long-term memory cells in the brain. So, the edutech researchers started working on new teaching modules with content relevant to the students. Teaching languages based on user relevance has been an age-old practice. I go, I eat, I sleep, Mamma, Hungry, Hurt, Yes, No are taught before the student is asked to learn about the 26 letters of the alphabet. Here, relevance could be shown by identifying a used practice for a word or a group of words.

However, relevant content is a vaguely defined term in many other areas, which could mean different things to different people, especially in professional education. For example, a student who wanted to major in finance found studying business law in MBA courses irrelevant. A student of Infotech found no relevance in learning structural engineering. So, building such courses was easier said than done. Although much effort has gone in this direction, not much has been achieved. However, these are early days for edutech, and the fact that revenues are strong and the number of students is steadily increasing annually is a sign of success.

Baby boomers will tell you nobody in school during the 1960s could tell educators to make teaching interesting. Academia was a deadly serious business in those days, and it would be blasphemy to think of it as entertainment. The digital age turned everything on its head. Edutech expanded markets beyond physical classrooms and made distance learning possible. In addition, because the teacher was not physically present in virtual classrooms, edutech majors started looking for tools and aids to attract students to remote, lifeless screen learning.

Animated objects, emojis, popular cartoon characters, superheroes and glow, clap and beep boxes were used to make screen space lively. Visual three-dimensional (3D) learning entered the fray as concepts that were difficult to explain in words were easily explained visually. Such visual interpretation was also more interesting as it was imaginative, colorful and usually contextual. Even in mathematics, the retention of visual images and visual data (in 3D graphs and charts) made explanations contextual and interesting for students.

Radio and television learning had already made their mark in education in the twentieth century. The digital era, however, provided a multimedia option where text, sound, images and video could all work in parallel. Hollywood jumped in to help, and animations soon became a part of edutech. Walt Disney, Pixar, Marvel Studios and others provided popular characters and well-established themes for edutech. Animation provided charm and wit to relevant content through small and engaging story forms, apart from grabbing learners' attention. It also made storytelling interesting. It entertained young students and expanded creative possibilities to showcase relevance and context in previously dull content when making learning fun. Research shows that it will soon enter the meta world. Edutech could qualitatively improve the concepts, resulting in higher retention capability and better student learning.

HOW EDUTECH FOUND MILLIONS OF STUDENTS— QUANTITATIVE EXPLOSION

China is the world's largest edutech market, with nearly one-third of its population beneficiaries of edutech. According to a Program of International

Student Assessment survey (2018), China's edutech draws more investment than all other nations. Nearly 90% of Chinese students have an online learning support program, which is way ahead of the Organisation for Economic Co-operation and Development (OECD) average. There is huge pressure on students to qualify for a good university education where the seats are limited and competition intense. These edutech startups, through online tutoring, are known to help students to prepare for such competition.

In 2020, there were more than a 1,000 edutech startups in China and nearly 423 million users. China is the world's largest investor in machine-based personalized learning, with the highest venture capital (VC) funding support that started around a decade ago. As of December 2022, there were 36 Unicorns, with the US accounting for 15 of them. China has eight edutech unicorns, each with a more than a billion-dollar valuation, with the market leader Yuanfudao valued at $15.5 billion.

India's growing edutech market got a boost during the Covid pandemic. Offline coaching centers to prepare for competitive exams in engineering, medicine, science, business management and administrative services have always been popular in India. Like the Chinese, Indian parents are willing to spend large amounts on their children's education. So, 320 million school students took to distance learning through edutech in a big way as schools were closed for 9 months of a single year during the pandemic. Half a dozen unicorns in 2022 tasted early VC funding success and provided premium solutions to 100 million students from privileged backgrounds studying in professionally managed private English Language schools.

Market leader Byju's had a valuation of $22 billion in March 2022. Other nonfunded startups catered to students of government-run schools and taught students in regional languages in smaller cities as well. Notable among them was Rocket Learning, which helps develop core foundational concepts for children up to the age of 8 years in math and science in Hindi and Marathi languages. The startup works with 8,000 teachers and 100,000 children in four Indian states. Physicswalla, another Allahabad-based edutech startup that started as a free YouTube channel in 2016, became profitable in 2 years, teaching 6 million students science and mathematics. Most unicorns globally struggle to go through multiple rounds of funding to become a unicorn valued at $1 billion; Physicswalla raised $100 million in its maiden round of funding in 2022 to become India's 100th unicorn. The startup plans to expand its Science, Technology, Engineering and Mathematics (STEM) teaching program in nine regional languages.

The North American market, the third biggest edutech and most sophisticated, has also enjoyed robust growth and funding. Three primary markets exist that US edutech businesses cater to—unlike the Asian nations that focus primarily on school students—solutions for kindergarten to class 12, K-12 students, students pursuing higher education and the future that is augmented reality (AR), virtual reality (VR) and the gaming industry.

The San Francisco-based Lambda School provides free software engineering training in exchange for a percentage of future earnings. Full Measure Education, a Washington DC-based startup, assists students when enrolling, completing and obtaining a family-sustaining job.

Canadian startup Prodigy Learning provides fun learning in math, solved through interesting game-based learning solutions. In addition, because learners are shifting toward digital content, businesses are trying to explore how assistive technologies could help them better. There are solutions for students with physical disabilities to listen to educational content in an audio format to improve their vocabulary and encourage better interpretive reading. Similarly, there are AI-driven solutions to help assess specific learning behaviors and provide solutions that appeal to more students for academic studies and entertainment, skills testing and social media. We will look at some of these solutions and what the next-generation edutech could mean for students.

THE TOOLS AND TECH THAT MAKE EDUTECH SO DIFFERENT

Video and interactive learning are the most important tools used universally in distance learning. Video learning became popular in the digital age first through YouTube and a few other smaller players, such as Vimeo and Metacafe, more than a decade ago. At that time, only interactive communication through Skype from Microsoft and FaceTime from Apple were available. A few years later, Facebook Messenger, GoogleDuo and WhatsApp arrived and became popular for one-to-one communication or small group video calling. Then came streaming video transmission, which compressed data and made broadcasting over the internet continuous and much easier.

Interactive learning solutions flourished during the 2020 pandemic, with smart conferencing solutions like Zoom, GoogleMeet, LiveStorm, MicrosoftTeams, Google Classrooms, Webex, Zoho Meeting, GoToMeeting and Jitsi Meet flooding the marketplace. These videoconferencing facilities permitted large classrooms, multiple location participation, communication between student, teacher and peer groups, recording facilities and formatting flexibility, making virtual classrooms easy to conduct and learn from. In physical classrooms, you could not replay or archive what your teacher explained. If you were inattentive or did not understand, you just lost out. However, in virtual classrooms, you could learn from archived recordings. In addition, creating multiple study groups, extracting themes for excursions or field trips, tabulating outcomes and scoring other activities could be achieved with the virtual format. In addition, because problem-solving and testing were part of the new way of teaching, it could also be programmed to check your learning retention capacity.

Another technology that finds widespread use in virtual classrooms and gives it an edge over physical classrooms is AR/VR technology. Print books have always had the disadvantage of being two-dimensional. You cannot display a cube or show how water changes into steam and escapes from the spout of a kettle in a physical book; however, it could be achieved in the virtual format. The atomic structure that looks so daunting in a print book becomes a friendly, colorful plaything you can spin around and learn from in the virtual world. Be it physics or chemistry, botany or zoology, arts or geography, engineering or medical science, the technology of AR and VR has made things extremely simple, relatable and relevant for students and teachers. Imagine students entering the human body and internally inspecting the human anatomy wearing VR glasses without tedious and complex dissections, examining each healthy or decaying tissue, a fractured bone or a torn muscle, an abdominal tumor or a damaged kidney. Although Facebook and Microsoft may be racing to monetize social media and office space in their ideal Metaverse, medical science and education might benefit most from this innovation. We will read more about that in the next chapter on the virtual world.

The Internet of Things (IoT) and AI are technologies that edutech startups use heavily. The IoT provides smart devices like pens, highlighters and black-board screens that give feedback to the users and take their instructions. A teacher might want one or more blackboard in a virtual classroom and add, delete or archive the written material based on the participants' needs. Similarly, the use of AI and machine learning (ML) is widespread to determine how students respond to the technology tools used for training. Startups obtain actionable data from the analytics of learning retention and could change the method of teaching midterm if student performance was unsatisfactory. In addition, gamification is continuously carried out to make learning enjoyable and entertaining and the content more relatable. Walden Games, based on Henry David Thoreau's exploits from living with nature and written in 1854, was created by University of South California's Game Innovation Lab in 2018. It is a 6-hr game translating Thoreau's most famous works into a video game format with learning retention provided by entertaining Walden quotes popping up everywhere you go from the forest to the jailhouse.

In addition, educators can access deep learning (DL), a subset of machine learning, based on student responses to analyze whether the human brain is receptive to a particular course and method of teaching and counsel them during the admission process. For example, around 50 ML questions are asked before students are admitted to a data science program in most institutions. They are multiple-choice questions that check your logic, reasoning, critical thinking, and ability to ask the right questions to piece together the missing links needed for data analytics.

In addition to the previous formats, virtual learning is conducted on mobiles, tablets and laptops in conference halls with good audio and video sound systems. They permit multiple app usages like GeoGebra Classic, AutoCAD 360, Muscle and Bone Anatomy 3D, Adobe Photoshop Camera, Geo Touch, Civilisations AR and Brainly. There are also multiple platforms used like YouTube, Meta and Vimeo and social media and news channel usage that are all informative and used by students and teachers. The physical classrooms, by comparison, were extremely limited in the use of tools and technology. Most gadgets, mobiles and apps used by edutech today in virtual classrooms were not permitted in physical classrooms. Even if a few were allowed in physical classrooms, the teachers were not trained to use them and exploit their full learning potential. However, most parents and students prefer physical classrooms to edutech training universally. Why?

CAN EDUTECH THRIVE WITHOUT A PASSIONATE TEACHER?

In ancient India, a Guru was a teacher and a guide who was highly revered because they were the source of thought, knowledge and behavior that the student imbibed, from studying languages, medicine, archery or music. The student would reside at the Gurukul (the teacher's home), and the Guru would take care of their upbringing and direct their education until they could face the world. Although detached from upbringing responsibilities, a modern-day teacher passes knowledge and understanding of various subjects to their students. Most teachers also impart ethics, empathy and value systems to students globally. The concept of the teacher as not only the knowledge-giver but the spiritual guide and mentor exists in many Eastern cultures, including China, Japan, Thailand and Indonesia.

However, a teacher in the twenty-first century is not in a happy space. They are under intense pressure to perform and prove their worth every second of the day, says an American educator for three decades.

> "Even the lunch break does not give her the private space and comfort of eating by herself. There is recess duty, there is taking care of the odd child who is not feeling well, and there are several other chores that she must finish in the precious 30 minutes as she gulps down food. And every time the school bus comes to pick up the children at the end of the day, it is panic management because children keep forgetting water bottles, cardigans and going to the bathroom – that all happens at the last moment."
>
> Suzanne Kelly

Writing for *Education to the Core*, Kelly gives a vivid portrayal of "18 things that remain the same after 30 years of teaching." To cap it off, there are endless staff meetings that are hardly productive, corrections to work that inevitably goes home because time is too short and salaries that are barely enough to provide for the family. This is not a one-off rant. "Because I am teaching below class eight, it is an endless chore as you are considered the master of all general subjects," says another junior schoolteacher at a charter school in Oklahoma. Thousands of teachers worldwide feel that way and stick to the job only because they love teaching children. Some moved to edutech during the Covid-19 lockdown due to better salaries; however, the problems there were even more serious.

As local tuition centers closed down during the 2020 pandemic, droves of teachers tried out their skills at edutech, where the salaries were far better and safe work-from-home opportunities were available. However, the work atmosphere in most edutech institutions was similar to the high attrition tech industry that was extremely toxic. An MIT Sloan Management Review report indicated a sharp increase in resignations across the US after the pandemic. The research "Toxic culture is driving the great resignation" revealed five predictors of attrition after analyzing 34 million online profiles across industries. Between April and September 2021, more than 24 million American employees left their jobs, an all-time record. The research found that attrition due to toxic corporate culture was surprisingly 10.4 times higher than attrition due to low compensation.

The impact was felt most in the tech industry, where working hours stretched and working from home broke down the barriers between work and personal time. Unlike in schools, long and leisurely vacations were nonexistent in edutech. The marketing teams in edutech startups who had lured middle-class parents with high aspirations into buying very expensive annual packages had also built up sky-high expectations of miracle results from students by just joining the online courses. That did not happen. So, students returned to physical schools where real life teachers were available to teach and guide them and with whom parents could communicate, share and learn about how the student was developing. As parents did not renew the annual subscriptions with edutech businesses, the teachers at edutech were blamed and felt the brunt.

Teachers at edutech businesses complained that there was no respect for the educator, the knowledge provider says Nitin Patwardhan and Mansi Verma, reporting on "India's Edtech firms that are struggling post pandemic." They were considered just a delivery person selling a product that had to perform. Journalists reported that parents and students often complained to the marketing team if the results at the school did not improve. This marketing team was almost always under pressure to deliver and pulled up the teacher often without getting into details. If the results did not improve quickly, the teachers could lose part of their contracted payment packages or jobs. The stress on the teachers was intense with this role reversal because instead of the teachers' assessing students and interacting with parents, the parents and the marketing team were assessing the teachers in the edutech industry and telling them what needed to be done.

The July 2021 *Economist* report "South Korean tech workers are having a lousy time at work" revealed that the problem exists universally across all tech startups. The HR review of the UK in its report "Tech is toxic, say the women who work in the industry," found that when asked what puts women in technology off taking a role, a toxic culture was the most common answer (36%). According to Brain Carvalho, editor at *Forbes India*, the situation in edutech startups was similar to the Steve Jobs days at Apple when "non-performers were instantly fired, as he was supremely arrogant and didn't like to be corrected."

The atmosphere at many edutech startups is extremely tense, and the hire-and-fire culture is very dominant, unlike physical businesses like schools that are humane, secure and long-established. The introduction of zing and fizz into the teaching community where students need stable, emotionally secure and caring teachers has been extremely counterproductive. Knowledge transformation businesses need such space and freedom for the teachers, especially if young minds are to be inspired to perform. In the words of Bill Gates, "Technology is just a tool. In terms of getting the kids working together and motivating them, the teacher is most important."

However, there is an alternate school of thought which believes that if humans cannot deliver efficiently, ML and AI must be used to teach children or assist in teaching.

CAN AI AND TEACHING ROBOTS HELP?

South Korea and China have made great inroads into AI-driven automated learning systems that assist human teachers with animated robots. In 2010, South Korea started experimenting with robotic teaching assistants in classrooms to help overworked teachers easily finish their daily chores. In 2013, Daegu in South Korea tried "Engkeys," or robots with telepresence, in 8,400 kindergarten classrooms teaching English through a teacher's face displayed on the robot's screen. It helped them make up for the real time shortage of English teachers. The kids from the elementary schools were thrilled with these robotic teachers who were as tall as the kids and could move on wheels, ask questions and reply in English and even dance to music. At least three robot makers, Robotis, Roborobo and Yujin Robotics, compete in this creative space, producing several versions of teaching assistants and companions popular in many middle or high schools in South Korea, where programming and robot-building classes have been compulsory since 2017. The students use the Korean version of "Scratch," a programming language developed by MIT labs a decade ago and a $128 toolkit produced indigenously by Robotis.

In 2018, China introduced an educational robot named Keeko into 600 kindergartens. The Keeko was 60 cm tall and was priced attractively at $1,500. Keeko could interact, play and dance with the children, read stories, converse, and do mathematics. When a child answered Keeko correctly, its face would transform into heart-shaped eyes to congratulate the student. In 2020, a *Wall Street Journal* video displayed how students' concentration levels in China were being measured by an AI headband that they were made to wear in class. The brainwave-measuring sensors had three electrodes that measured the neural data from the brain. The results were immediately visible on the computer of the teacher and parents at home. China has introduced programs where students wear chips and are taught in AI-enabled classrooms that reportedly help boost students' grades and feed algorithms to curate the lessons. However, the real benefit of trying out electroencephalogram (EEG) technology, normally used by doctors in hospitals, to measure output in a classroom for fifth-grade students is highly debatable.

Although China is the biggest investor in this space today, the future of edutech might not be the mindless intrusion of AI in classrooms. The Chinese Communist Party has its own compulsion to infuse tracking and compliance tech and manage the thought processes of its young people. Facial recognition technology and thought-reading headband sensors have been developed to control the human mind, thoughts and actions. They are not equipped for classroom interactions or to guide young students well. They can be pretty stressed because of their relentless monitoring. The human mind requires breaks to digest and assimilate the knowledge we call "thinking time." It does not operate like an automated, transactional machine that can function with ceaseless repeatability without breaks. The development of AI in the education sector is much slower than in other fields, such as security, finance or customer service, say experts in edutech in China. The Korean school model looks more appropriate as robots, and AI could be used as teaching assistants to manage workloads and acute instructor shortages through remote educators using distance learning.

The teacher's role when inspiring students and providing unorthodox but highly successful teaching methods predates the edutech era and is best displayed in two movies of the eighties. *Dead Poets Society*, directed by award-winning director Peter Weir, showcased a teacher who inspired students with his very unorthodox teaching method that even took students to caves and delivered life lessons that improved their individuality. *Dangerous Minds*, a television series based on the autobiography *My Posse Don't Do Homework* by retired Marine Lou Anne Johnson, is a real life story of how tough African American and Latino students in a poor Palo Alto suburb were inspired to produce excellent results by a dedicated teacher who changed their methods of teaching. In addition, there are all-time favorite movies like *To Sir with Love* and *Remember the Titans*, which go beyond classroom learning to teach values and ethics.

THE FUTURE OF EDUTECH

Startups worldwide have been active in the edutech sector; however, to get a real idea of the future of edutech, we must find out what the big boys of the tech world are doing. Microsoft, Google and AWS are among the big technology majors developing solutions in edutech. Pearson is the traditional heavyweight of the K-12 education segment, attempting to digitally transform its print market solutions. Apple also has several K-12 solutions. Several visionary startups have entered unconventional areas, like the Pittsburgh-based Duolingo and the Maryland-based 2U Inc. and made their mark among dozens of global edutech unicorns.

Microsoft Teams, a digital collaboration platform primarily for business communications, expanded its online classes to reach 100 million students by January 2021 and has been on an acquisition spree after that. It recently acquired a 15-year-old startup TakeLessons, at an undisclosed price, which offers online lessons in music and performing arts, crafts, languages, academics and test preps.

This chat-based Teams platform currently has state-of-the-art audio and video conferencing facilities, document sharing and storage. It is being readied for VR, AR, and the metaworld. The launch of the AI powered Chat GPT in November 2022 just made Microsoft's platform infinitely more interesting as it will help it compete better with Google Classroom. Microsoft's $70 billion acquisition of Activision Blizzard, one of the largest stand-alone interactive gaming platforms, in January 2022 was a major effort to ensure that it stayed ahead in Microsoft-backed games within metaworld in the next decade.

Google Classroom offers a complete package of comprehensive solutions for blended classroom learning through Google Meet, Docs, Sheets, Photos and Slides, just like Microsoft. The idea is to make the core experience of face-to-face interaction, student–teacher communication, student engagement and assessment and digital transformation easier for students and teachers. Google Classroom's data collection, document sharing, feedback interaction and class conferencing make explaining, taking notes, and assessing students and the learning program simple. By virtue of its superior search program, Google will inevitably connect to the future of any education program. Its AI monitors all classroom study materials, connecting them seamlessly to the best and most relevant global knowledge sources. It also provides classroom management tools in its G suite, which help teachers with multiple administrative assignments they must handle apart from teaching.

Soon you could find AI-driven teaching assistants instead of the robotic teaching assistants the South Korean model provides. Teachers can build their profiles and add numerous applications to improve the existing lesson plans. This helps the teachers innovate continuously instead of teaching the same text in the same way year after year. They could also create and share their lessons on "Workbench," an online STEM platform focusing on science, technology, engineering and math. These are possibly the first baby steps in organically involving every teacher when creating the future of edutech.

The AWS startup guide identifies seven trends that are going to be the hallmark of edutech in the near future: (1) big data clouds that will provide data abundance and will be mined by next-generation AI and ML; (2) innovative game-based learning solutions; (3) digital transformation in classrooms; (4) student well-being; (5) workforce upskilling; (6) AR; and (7) VR. It provides a guide map on securely developing apps and digital tools with valuable insights from global experts. Startups could apply to join AWS EdStart if they were less than 5 years old and generated less than $10 million in annual revenue. The AWS platform provides guidance, tools and funding to startups globally and has been very active in China, the US and India—the three big global markets.

Pearson Education, one of the world's largest textbook producers, has been one of the early pioneers in the field, introducing its LMS, the Pearson Learning Studio, over two decades ago. However, it decided to revamp its solutions and enter the digital space, which was growing faster than the print market, was more scalable and even more profitable. In 2006, it bought PowerSchool, an early edutech platform, from Apple and improved its enrollments to 3 million students annually; however, the effort soon started to lose steam. In 2013, under a new CEO, it decided to reorganize its solutions and offloaded PowerSchool to a private equity firm Vista Equity for $350 million. In 2019, it started a $50 million fund to invest in education technology startups, raising two rounds of funding—the Series A and B rounds. It has started to restructure again with a focus on five new divisions composed of virtual learning, higher education, English language, workforce skills, assessment and qualifications.

Duolingo, a unicorn valued at $2.4 billion, is an interesting language-learning website with a phone app and a digital language proficiency exam. Launched in 2011, it uses a freemium model with 300 million registered users that provide basic learning for free and advanced learning at a price. Providing 106 language courses in 38 languages, the app was created by a team of language scientists and AI experts and is one of the most popular globally. With innovative audiovisual content, such as podcasts, quizzes and interactive storytelling, its website had 56 million active users in 2020 and clocked $200 million in revenue.

The language learning space is very crowded, with the Taipei-based ITutorGroup (1998) and Berlin-based Babbel (2007) among the earliest players. The Taiwanese unicorn offers students and business professionals personalized learning courses. With an employee strength of 1,600 across four locations and annual revenues of $235 million, it is the largest language study center outside the US. Babbel offers 15 European languages to students with beginner, intermediate and advanced grammar and phonetics courses. Valued at nearly €1 billion, the 15-year-old startup with an employee strength of 650 clocked €147 million in revenues in 2020. Hong Kong-based Italki (2009) and Beijing-based Palfish (2015) are other big players in the space, with revenues exceeding $100 million and an employee base of 500 servicing more than 5 million active users each. Over 1,000 startups, big and small, exist in the language learning space, mostly catering to students and workers wanting to study or work overseas.

2U is a Maryland-based edutech company that collaborates with "not for profit" universities and colleges to provide online courses with cloud-based software as a service platform, edutech infrastructure, courseware design and funding. It aggregates the traditional knowledge base of over 500 educational institutions and offers undergraduate and graduate degrees, professional certificates and training to 200,000 students globally. The startup, valued at $2.81 billion, chalked up revenues of $774 million in 2020.

The edutech school set up today is evolving with hybrid solutions, traditional and fully online solutions. Hybrid solutions that were in vogue during the latter part of the Covid-19 pandemic were those where students attended classes for half the week and attended classes online from home for the remaining days, as opposed to 5 days a-week classes for traditional schools. Online classrooms took over during the Covid-19 lockdowns, and a few have become extremely popular and grown independently as standalone ventures. The uncertain nature of schooling has affected the learning process and student engagement. There are other challenges too, and much catching up needs to be done globally.

Digital education has touched less than 10% of students worldwide. Although there are more than three dozen edutech unicorns today, 90% are located in just three nations: the US, China and India. Dozens of VCs fund them hoping that these populous nations, where digital transformation is the highest, will yield quick returns. Most unicorns are, however, yet to be profitable. Still, VCs are willing to invest copious amounts of money into high-gain high-risk areas like Meta and VR solutions in the edutech sector. In the next two chapters, we will explore the impact of virtual reality and venture capital on the technology world and how they promise to in change the future.

Chapter 10

Metaworld

Virtual Reality

The term metaverse was originally coined by the best-selling author of speculative cyber fiction Neil Stephenson in 1992 in his dystopian novel *Snow Crash*. It is a futurist's satire on two parallel worlds "real"—the physical—and "metaverse"—the online virtual reality (VR) world. The "real" or physical world is dominated by Orwellian, monopolistic, malevolent mega corporations headed by superefficient control freaks, and the "metaverse" or "VR" universe is even worse—besieged with crime, corruption, collusion, intrigue, insecurity and danger.

HOW REAL AND "REALITY" WORLDS WORK

In the real world, the protagonist of the book, Hiro the Pizza Deliverator, has limited ambitions and means and works at a maniacal speed taking life-threatening risks for the Mafia, who control the global pizza delivery business. They are unforgiving toward those who slack at work. In the VR world, Hiro is not here but in a computer-generated VR universe that is beamed through his goggles and pumped into his earphones, approaching Broadway, the Mecca of the metaverse. This is where shapely models jostle with muscular hunks for space, riding the choicest vehicles, buying pricey fashion wares, dancing, and jiving at flash mobs and laser shows. The street dimensions, hippest people, snazzy infrastructure and gadgetry, are all decided by the Global Multimedia Protocol Group, another monopolist. Hiro can still buy an apartment here if he invests early and wisely, although, in reality, he might be able to afford only a shared 20 ft × 30 ft pad in a shipping container.

William Gibson and Neal Stephenson's contribution to futuristic cyber fiction is similar to that of Jules Verne and Jack London to science fiction. They have a huge fan following in Silicon Valley, including Jeff Bezos, Bill Gates and Sergey Brin. In his best-selling book *Neuromancer*, written a decade before *Snow Crash*, Gibson describes his VR or futuristic cyberspace

DOI: 10.1201/9781003409557-13

as "a consensual hallucination experienced daily by billions of legitimate operators, in every nation."

Both futurists agree that this cyberspace or metaverse will be an irresistible world with software-driven immersive experiences produced by monopolistic mega-corporations. They expose the perils of the virtual world and directly ask the next generation of readers—do you want it?

However, the metaverse might not be all evil and addictive and might not lead to coercive persuasion of the masses as these top-selling fiction writers envisage. The metaverse, which we choose not to try and define yet, is much bigger and multifaceted than the VR experience of these fictional protagonists, imagined in the 1980s and 1990s before the internet era. In today's computer age, it is an amalgamation of four worlds: namely, virtual reality (VR), augmented reality (AR), mixed reality (MR) and extended reality (XR).

VR is a three-dimensional (3D), computer-generated environment that can be explored and interacted with by a user. It has no relationship to the person's location and what they do in the physical world. You wear the goggles, turn on the audio, and are transported to a different place and world that your computer wants to take you to. If you are activating the VR simulation, then every image hits your eyes, mind and senses and everything you see, hear or feel is generated by a computer graphics system. This technology was developed three decades ago when users could log in and create 3D virtual worlds or explore VR worlds created by others. A decade later, gaming majors commercialized it with highly popular games, such as the Sony PlayStation VR mega pack that included Star Wars Battlefront Rouge VR, Batman Arkham VR and the Nintendo Switch VR, Super Mario, Minecraft and the Legend of Zelda. VR games allow users to create avatars, explore, buy, and sell merchandise through virtual currencies and interact and socialize. It was, however, only in 2017 that comfortable, lightweight and snazzy stand-alone WiFi-connected headsets were available that could seamlessly download from websites and apps, social media or games consoles and produce the whole interactive and immersive effect of VR. Five years later, at Accenture's Nth floor, about which we will read later, the immersive effect of the VR world was enhanced, but the headset was gone.

However, by then, the novelty of VR had started to wear off, and another technology that had been around for decades (AR) started getting very popular. VR transported the user to an entirely fictional computer-generated world; however, AR changed your experience at the place you were. AR superimposed the computer-generated imagery onto a user's location to enhance the real time experience. In 1992, the US Airforce's Armstrong Research Lab first created an AR that enabled the overlay of sensory information onto a workspace to improve human productivity.

Adobe developed its AR toolkit for Adobe Flash in 2009. Then, Google did a beta launch of its Google Glass project in 2013, and Microsoft launched its AR reality headset HoloLens in 2015. Some of the most popular AR video games—Pokémon Go, Angry Birds AR and Jurassic World Alive— have millions of players using AR daily. In addition, AR apps are popular today in manufacturing, construction, education, games and healthcare; however, the technology is still in its early days.

MR is a blend of physical and virtual worlds. Using Microsoft HoloLens, two students at Case Western Reserve University, Ohio, US, recently studied human anatomy during the pandemic. In MR, human-initiated natural and intuitive action is mixed with computer-generated advanced 3D graphical processing to give spectacular effects. The AR filters they used on Instagram that makes every post look lively and different are MR experiences.

MR is a widely used feature of all mobile phones. It frees us from the drudgery of the fixed screen format by offering instinctual interactions with data in our living spaces and with our friends. It includes multiple inputs, such as hand and eye tracking, speech input and voice modulation, spatial sound and collaboration in a 3D environment. Here, the mobile data interacts with the AR server at the backend. It is also how online users of social media find new applications of MR every day without realizing the rapidly evolving technology input that helps them create endless innovations.

XR is the consolidation of several immersive technologies. It includes VR, AR and MR that enhance 3D visual and audio effects along with haptics— the touch sensation to enhance control and holography—used for better 3D effects and a myriad of other evolving technologies that use and enhance our natural senses and emotional response in a space where the boundary limits are not clearly defined. The geography of XR is too loosely defined today— it includes all that enhances user experience. However, it is something that experts believe will be a well-defined mainstream technology in the next 5 years. This is because XR will allow consumers to try before buying. For example, the IKEA app with XR activation, about which we will read more later, gives customers the ability to try and place the furniture items into their homes via their smartphone even before they buy the product.

Metaworld (the original term used before Facebook popularized "metaverse") promises to bring together the immersive experience of VR, AR, MR and XR technologies; however, it is too early to define what shape it will ultimately take. Every tech major has been trying to carve out their niche in space, and every business is looking forward to leveraging the technology to ramp up business volumes. Zuckerberg renaming Facebook as Meta in winter of 2021 did not make it the leader or the only player in the metaworld.

With its array of products in Mesh, Microsoft is way ahead when providing immersive experiences in the office space, where it has been a leader in products and services for years. Similarly, the metaworld could be connected and operated through handheld devices where the control lies firmly in the hands of Apple and Google's Android operating systems. Both are developing their products and, importantly, a slew of wearables and creating their areas of influence in this space. Now that we have a fair idea of the origin and architecture of the metaworld let us explore how it has evolved and is going to change the way we live.

THE METAWORLD OF THE GAMING UNIVERSE

Metaworld has been around for over two decades, carefully nurtured by thousands of game developers who provide immersive experiences to millions. The North Carolina-based Epic Games, founded in the early 1990s, is perhaps one of the early pioneers that have survived the competitive environment to stay at the top of the gaming world with a valuation of over $30 billion. In 2020, it peaked at 30 million active users daily and clocked a gross revenue of $5 billion. Epic has been churning out top-selling 3D video games from the Unreal Engine and Fortnite series for decades. It has over 5000 games in its marketplace that can be played on all major platforms like Windows, Mac, iOS, Android, Linux, PlayStation, Nintendo and Xbox. However, the founder, Tim Sweeney, quickly points out that Epic is more than video games and has applications for vehicle design, architecture, film creation and even holodecks that account for a major part of its revenue. With video games becoming saturated, its closest competitor Unity Technologies, the creator of *Pokémon Go* and Activision's *Call of Duty Mobile*, went public in September 2020 to expand its activities outside the familiar gaming universe into industries and applications in the real world.

Game developer Roblox was one of the earliest players in this space, introducing the concept in 2004. The platform has 47 million active users daily, around 10 million developers and 4,000 human moderators who set the rules of its experiences in this user-created world of games. Roblox believes that without major AR and VR acquisitions, it has successfully provided immersive experiences to its users. In its metaverse, kids play the game and buy and sell avatars they can hang out and trade goods with, go for a medieval adventure or a trip to space with a currency called Robux. Almost half of America's school children play *Roblox*, the most popular free game across 50 states. Most of its $500 million annual revenue comes from Robux sales on Apple, Google Play or Amazon, which is used in turn to pay the developer community.

Like Roblox, Epic and many others, Sandbox is focused on building an immersive world within existing gaming tech rather than investing heavily in futuristic VR and AR technologies. The game developers want to keep it simple. When Sandbox was released in 2012, the game maker was given a full creative freedom without setting a goal. Here the players created 3D games that was featured without writing code. The concept of the Sandbox was to let the children create anything they wanted with it. However, things started changing with the arrival of overseas competitions like Player's Unknown Battleground (PUBG), a multiplayer game with clear goals to win.

The world's most popular game, introduced by the South Korean gaming major, allows 100 online players to parachute onto an island, where they scavenge for arms and kill other players to win the battle royal contest. The metaverse we witness in the gaming world is largely VR and has computer graphics that are intuitive, user-generated and quite different from what we will use in the coming decade.

THE METAWORLD IN BUSINESS APPLICATIONS

The metaworld evolving today differs greatly from the world of intuitive 3D video games and VR. Accenture, the global consulting and IT services giant with over 700,000 employees from 120 countries had already been working to improve remote working facilities for its employees for the last decade. Before the pandemic, they built a Microsoft Mesh-enabled immersive virtual campus with AR, VR, MR and XR where employees from anywhere could gather for a coffee break, presentations, parties or other events. A senior managing director Jason Warnke at Accenture stated, "We started to call it the Nth Floor, this magical, mythical campus that could only be found in virtual reality."

Soon after the Covid-19 pandemic, it became indispensable for the onboarding process as 100,000 new employees were inducted annually by the consulting major. During the global lockdown, it helped when providing a wholesome experience to newcomers in a worldwide business conducted from 200 cities in 50 nations as they were taught to create their digital avatars and place them in their location and interact. Then, the senior leadership in an office would share a series of experiences that helped recruits to understand and personally connect with the Accenture culture globally, plant the seeds of professional relationships and set them up for success starting from their first projects.

Accenture is now creating digital twins for many of its physical offices from Dublin to Madrid, Bangalore to San Francisco, to create similar workplace experiences, where its employees can participate and virtually meet in the metaworld, contribute and feel like they belong to one place, regardless of where they work. A digital twin is a virtual replica of the real office, where remote workers may enter, leave, present and work without intruding on the physical setup. Apart from the video networking bonhomie, all of that helps with a massive cost-cutting exercise and new and evolved work-from-home practices.

AR used in the construction industry, combining physical and digital views, has resulted in massive operational cost savings. AR makes it possible to create 3D digital modeling directly from two-dimensional architectural and construction drawings. It allows the clients and project teams to walk through the project well before the execution begins, closely examining the layout, structure and safety aspects of the building with 3D building information modeling (BIM). This AR-driven foresight could make the building design cost-effective and the structure efficient and safe, besides preventing project delays, mistakes and cost overruns. The AR gear measures physical distances of height, width and depth accurately from 2D drawings and data to create a holistic 3D model. Being equipped with X-ray vision, it can also see through beam thickness, concrete formations and reinforcement. It permits on-site project alterations if the project team witnesses any mistake during the inspection of the 3D model or on-site.

Construction workers and project managers could view the 3D location of each of the doors, windows, electric wiring, gas, water and sewage pipes, outlets, switches, fittings, ventilation ducts, fire alarms, woodwork, painting and finishing. They could ensure the optimum functional design and a safe and secure project close-out without too much rework and repairs. In excavation and tunnel boring work, there is always a risk of machines potentially hitting gas lines or wrecking underground utilities. Augmented technology is an AR-driven mobile product that enables users to see underground objects, such as trenches or buried cables, using Google Maps and a 3D overview.

The use of AR in high-end equipment design and manufacturing has also started. Engineers at Siemens Digital Industries Software are superimposing virtual elements from computer-aided design (CAD) drawings and engineering data through headsets, mobile devices and wearables to obtain a completely immersive experience constructed from digital elements. AR helps users achieve faster upskilling by assisting in field training, stated Vineesh Kapoor, director of product management at Emerson Automation. It also helps in asset identification, which is very important in the inventory management of thousands of components that make modern-day machines.

A third use is knowledge transfer and problem-solving by experts from remote locations, who could be far away from the plant or machinery that needs troubleshooting. Finally, the AR modeling of a new component is superimposed in running machinery before manufacturing to check its optimum functioning. At Aveva, the first CAD data from multiple sources are put into a 3D modeling tool, such as Blender, an open-source toolkit to create animation and 3D modeling. It acts as an interface between raw data and AR ingestible data.

> "CAD data, for example, is often represented in a parametric way unsuitable for most real-time graphics. When meshed, it gives the right amount of detail and resolution that is easy for a phone, tablet, or AR glasses to ingest and render in real time."
>
> Nicholas Fonta of Autodesk, Inc.

The use of smart glasses, head-mounted displays, handheld devices and wearables when performing surgery in hospitals is becoming a practice for better evaluation and efficient diagnosis using augmented reality. AR in surgeries allows surgeons to visualize the patient's anatomy and the MRI and CT scan data. Medical students now wear VR headsets to practice life-saving cardiac procedures on human replicas that simulate cardiac disease and responses.

The metaworld is also making its presence felt in real time in complex surgeries with the help of AR. Using AR headsets made by Chicago-based startup Augmedics that work like a GPS navigator in front of your eyes, neurosurgeons at John Hopkins Neurosurgery Spinal Fusion Laboratory, Baltimore, US, have completed their first AR surgeries. The Xvision AR, a surgical guidance system, allows surgeons to see through skin and tissue as if they have X-ray vision and accurately navigate instruments and implants during spinal procedures.

META'S TECHNOLOGY WOES

According to McKinsey, the meta world seems well positioned to become a $5 trillion business in the coming decade. But it was not a much-bandied term before November 2021, when Mark Zuckerberg made an expansive prediction that it was the business of the future and announced that the social media giant with iconic brands like Facebook, Instagram and WhatsApp would rebrand itself as Meta. At that time, Zuckerberg's business was valued at well over $ 1 trillion, being the sixth largest global business based on market capitalization.

So, what prompted Zuckerberg to throw his weight behind rebranding three of the world's most powerful brands? Analysts say that despite having a rollicking journey in the first decade of its arrival, Facebook's reputation had nosedived, and several problems had started to slow the company down. So, it started looking around for gaming businesses for meteoric growth as games like Candy Crush and Minecraft made serious money on its platform every year. In 2014, it acquired Oculus, a 3D gaming company with VR chat, for $2 billion. By 2017, the product's popularity had slipped despite several iterations attempted by Zuckerberg and the Oculus price was lowered from $599 to $299. Even Facebook's VR chat with lower fidelity did not take off despite the 2 billion active users on the social media platform. Users say the software was not up to the mark.

An excellent VR setup with a fast PC costs around $3,000 in the US and allows you to detect the movement of your limbs and face and animate your avatar to mimic your gestures and expressions. Facebook and Oculus were nowhere close. So, after 5 years, Zuckerberg realized that he would have to spend hugely—well over $10 billion annually—to make a dent in the gaming market. By then, competitors Unity, Epic and PUBG were all planning to invest and take gaming to the next level.

However, it was not only gaming technology that was troubling the social media giant.

In June 2019, Apple told its developers that they must ensure that "Apps in the kids' category do not include third-party advertising or analytics." As targeted advertising became more invasive and public pressure to stop it grew, Apple countered it by adding new privacy features to its software that hurt the revenues of Facebook, Snapchat and other social media platforms. In 2020, Apple announced that in future iOS update 14.0 would only share the approximate and not the precise location of the iPhone user. This meant advertisers could not check how many times the user visited a particular Starbucks café or Gucci store. Advertisers protested. But more was soon to follow.

In 2021, when Apple finally unleashed the iOS update with the "Ask App Not To Track" feature, it became instantly popular and was opted for by over 60% of users. So, when Meta Chief Financial Officer David Wehner confirmed that Apple's privacy policy change would put a $10 billion dent in Meta's annual advertising revenue, he wiped $232 billion off its market cap in a single day. Google is working to improve its privacy features and is expected to put out similar restrictions for the Android platform in 1–2 years. In addition, the European Union's General Data Protection Regulation for privacy might hurt the operations and advertising revenues of the social media giant.

However, Meta has a stellar record of excellent operations and profitability. It has 1.96 billion users globally, and they are growing each quarter. So, analysts started looking at why its stock price kept dropping, and the market capitalization dropped by $500 billion just 6 months after its November 2021 announcement. Mathew Smith, writing for IEEE Spectrum, explains the shortcoming in detail, "What Zuckerberg announced is nothing new. If that VR vision is already accessible on hardware that costs as little as a mid-range Android smartphone, why aren't consumers already eager to experience it?"

Calling it a tired business model, he points out that transporting things has never been a problem.

> "It remains incredibly difficult to transport persons into your corner of the universe unless you are happy communicating with cartoons - nee digital avatars. Videogrammetry (mapping positions in three dimensions using multiple cameras) helps, but solutions that would work on a scale remain years away."
>
> Mathew Smith

Meanwhile, Meta's Reality Labs reported losses of $10 billion in 2021.

"It's not going to be until those products hit the market and scale in a meaningful way, and this market ends up being big, that this will be a big revenue or profit contributor to the business. This is laying the groundwork for what I expect to be a very exciting 2030."

Zuckerberg

In all probability, Zuckerberg, like the market that mauled his stock, realizes that he might have jumped into a futuristic technology a decade away from being mainstream.

However, Zuckerberg still has enough money, business savvy and knowledge of technology to shrug off that moment of misjudgment. This is because meta-technology is not a fad or hypothetical. When you are training or doing a one-off presentation from home to a global team, building a skyscraper, tunneling under New York City, designing an automobile, doing surgery deep inside the gastrointestinal tract or making a 3D environment for a movie, there's a clear use case. However, hanging out with friends at Hyde Park, London, UK, needs the touch and feel factor, warm vibes, smiles, tears, emotions and body language in play. None of these are possible to create or substitute with today's technology. So, Zuckerberg has to work doubly hard to make those things happen.

BELLA AND THE FASHION WORLD CHALLENGE META

With over 20 million fans on Instagram, Bella Hadid is one of the top fashion celebrities in the world. Everyone wants a bit of the beautiful Bella. So, in July 2022, the supermodel transformed herself into a cyborg with 11,111 stylized art versions that you could grab thanks to a new nonfungible token (NFT) platform CY-B3LLA. These online digital art pieces based on the supermodel's images are the latest treasure you can buy online.

The NFTs are digital assets or cybernetic collectibles on a blockchain for which you receive a digital purchase receipt. They could be art, images, videos, music, text or merchandise. Bella, a self-confessed gaming enthusiast, has been working with reBASE, a metaverse social networking site, for months to develop her real estate in the virtual 3D world. Soon after the Covid-19 pandemic, she asked ten creatives from different nations to make art from scans of her body, including images of her dressed as an animated cyborg queen avatar. That meant hard work for months.

"There were probably 200 cameras surrounding me and I stood in the middle and changed my shape, so it got all these different parts of my body, different versions of my facial expressions, fingers, toes. We wanted it to be very realistic."

Bella Hadid

After the announcement, she had a waiting list open for months for aspirants and half a million fans, who signed up to get a slice of the supermodel's personalized digital avatar for keeps. But you were mistaken if you thought you could buy Bella Hadid collectibles through an auction from the waiting list. Bella is looking to create a faithful community of like-minded people who believe in diversity and who will follow her at all locations to interact and vibe with her and be given keys to the Bella Hadid metaverse mansions that she hopes to launch in the coming year, "The CY-B3LLA NFT will be the passport that grants admission into an intimate community whose goal is to unite human connections within a new global nation that is inspired by and celebrates multiple cultures."

They will partner with her in the legacy business she hopes to build through several events globally—the first being in Tokyo. Bella has set the trend among celebrities who want to build a cozy world with fans sharing the mind, soul and intimate postures of their fashion icons in an all-immersive meta world.

Other celebrities, like Paris Hilton, have also entered the metaverse, although their presence is limited. The reality television star and hotel heiress has a virtual island on *Roblox* called the Paris World. This could be an exclusive getaway destination for Paris and her fans in times to come. The island, among other collectibles, has a digital copy of her California home and closet that you can raid or buy through Robux, the online currency of the video game. Following Paris and Bella, several other celebrity stars and fashion icons are attempting to create and popularize their avatars.

As expected, Mark Zuckerberg took to Facebook. He posted a message that read

"We're launching our Avatars Store on Facebook, Instagram, and Messenger so you can buy digital clothes to style your avatar. Digital goods will be an important way to express yourself in the metaverse and a big driver of the creative economy."

Mark Zuckerberg

The post featured his wife, Eva Chan, trying new looks from the Prada and Balenciaga collections.

Fashion icons and young designers are making an innovative change. London-based fashion designer Scarlett Yang designed the magical design of a meltable dress in 2020 from algae extract that changed texture with temperature and dissolved when it came in contact with water. The algae extract was set in 3D molds before being treated with silk cocoon protein. Then, she used the software to run through various textures and silhouettes and created a physical prototype of the onscreen design. The created gowns could shimmer, glow, and even plunge and merge into the ocean, "I'm super passionate about combining these elements of science, digital tech, and visual fashion. There's more creative freedom in the digital [realm], there's no constraints, no gravitation."

Yang dreams of designing clothes that could never be preserved. It is challenging for designers to move fluidly from virtual design to real time manufacturing with translucent and biodegradable products. However, the metaworld would create a marketplace for such innovations, especially in the early stages.

In addition, major luxury brands like Gucci, Balenciaga and Adidas have entered the metaverse with NFTs minted on the Ethereum blockchain. The latest arrival is Prada, which launched 100 NFTs in July 2022 to go with its latest "Timecapsule" apparel designed in collaboration with artist Cassius Hirst. It will be made available on the first Thursday of every month.

Fashion houses like "The Fabricant" and "Dematerialized" don't sell physical clothes but virtual designs that you can don on social media for as little as $50. You can find lilac puffer dresses floating around your body tantalizingly, high thigh-slit ensembles that shift around provocatively as you move, all overlaid as an AR filter on videos or as an art collection NFT. Dolce and Gabbana's nine-piece physical digital collection NFT was auctioned for $6 million in September 2021. Slowly and steadily, the hype and hoopla around the metaworld will build as more and more celebrities and luxury brands join the metaverse.

Mark Zuckerberg will be looking for such opportunities. He will, in all probability, create a vibrant marketplace with his cryptocurrency and NFTs, which could consolidate such events and monetize the star power behind these digital assets. In 2022, he devoted his energy to Instagram Reels, the short video format trying to displace TikTok, the Chinese market leader in this segment. Once that goal is achieved, he will empower it with multiple AR filters so that Facebook users bring a flood of original content for the metaverse to his stable. These are early days for the metaverse, and only those associated with gaming or 3D digital technology are getting involved. But as celebrities join, so will the fans, bringing in new audiences and money.

THE FUTURE OF THE METAWORLD

The future of cyberspace and the metaworld understandably draws inspiration from the writing and movies of the past. Around the time William Gibson was penning down his vision of the metaverse in the early 1980s, writer and director Steven Lisberger created *Tron*, one of Disney's first cyberfiction movies. Here Kevin, a software programmer, is abducted by malevolent software into the digital world and challenged to play 3D gladiatorial games. This movie of the pre-internet era gives a very early glimpse of immersive cyberspace, where artificial intelligence (AI) develops technology capable of digitizing and downloading the human developer into cyberspace, where AI terrorizes other software and humans.

Ernest Cline's novel *Ready Player One* and the novella *The Minority Report* by Philip K. Dick, movie featuring Tom Cruise are two recent Stephen Spielberg films, which provide immersive experiences and showcase some applications of VR, AR, MR and XR, including the use of haptic gloves to manipulate the environment seamlessly through the digital world. The future of the metaverse is VR and thematic applications of AR, MR and XR.

The shift toward AR started around 2020 when engagement rates jumped by 20%. In 2021, Microsoft received an order of $22 billion for a HoloLens AR headset with smart glasses for training and assisting vehicle operators in the US Army. Equipped with night vision and capabilities to interact using hand and voice gestures, it will enable soldiers to see holograms overlaid in their actual environments to enhance situational awareness. Red 6, a California-based startup, is testing its Airborne Tactical Augmented Reality System to simulate multi-aircraft dogfights by injecting virtual bogeys and real challenges, offering realistic combat situations to reduce training costs.

AR try-ons are the next big thing that could happen for physical retail clothing outlets. In a few years, you could go to the AR trial room of a retailer and try on a dozen dresses without changing even once. The different colors and shapes of clothes selected by you from the VR catalog available with the retailer would superimpose your actual body shape. This would create multiple AR images of you wearing various dresses you could choose from. Nike has already started using AR in their stores to help users learn about the features of the clothing and footwear on display. Other stores might soon follow with new features and enhanced capabilities. Many other AR applications are used by auto majors to showcase upholstery and interior features of cars to consumers and by interior designers to showcase innovative fittings and decor for retail showrooms. According to *Insider Intelligence*, 28% of Americans use AR once a month.

In an MR environment, the physical world blends with the 3D digital world. Unlike AR, which is widely used and has applications in multiple streams, the use of MR today is pretty limited. The MR world provides an immersive experience that can be felt through MR wearables. Several MR applications are being developed in physical classrooms and edutech, where students learn faster as they interact with virtual 3D objects.

For example, a student is being taught about our galaxy, the Milky Way or the complex structure of a diamond. Using MR, you could experience floating past a galaxy of fast-moving constellations, just like a scuba diver in the deep seas. It is easy to demonstrate the spiral galaxy of stars, dust and gases as 3D imagery to the students in the physical environment wearing MR glasses with the sun at one end of its spiral arms. You can even inspect the gas giant OGLE or other exoplanets that could be at the center of our galaxy some 25,000 light years away.

Similarly, it is simpler to explain to a school student the positioning of the four electrons on the outermost shell of each carbon atom and the covalent structure using MR. You could show that in a diamond, these electrons are shared with four other carbon atoms to form very strong bonds, resulting in a rigid tetrahedral crystal. This covalent structure and the unique arrangement of carbon atoms in a diamond tetrahedrally makes it so hard and unique, and this could be observed and even felt using MR.

Today, XR is a loosely defined concept. Hence, it is very difficult to predict the future of this technology and the industrial applications it could reinvent and unravel. However, this combination of VR, AR, MR and more technologies has started making serious inroads into architectural design, building construction and real estate development. An architect spends time and money designing and drawing building sketches and layout plans. Then, civil engineers do the structural design; electrical engineers create the lighting system and power supply, and mechanical engineers look after the other utilities, such as the lifts, gas, water and sewage pipes. After they are finished, the architect looks at the final layout again and makes alterations. Today, these are carried out in orthographic or 2D drawings giving plans and elevation views that are difficult for consumers to understand spatially. So, there is a genuine need for 3D intervention to make designs user-friendly.

Ikea Studio already uses LiDAR sensors on the iPhone to allow customers to virtually design the furniture in an entire room by capturing AR-assisted 3D interactable photos. The ability to occupy spaces digitally benefits architects, because they can view their spaces in three dimensions and enhance their design work and processes. The XR approach could provide builders and structural designers with a complete overview of the project and give the real estate agents and consumers an immersive experience when visiting the premises with their full-sized digital avatars enabled with the touch and feel experience. The same effect on a much bigger scale could help town planning, urban development and tourism industries.

To date, more than a dozen VCs have invested in the metaverse with a ticket size from $500 million to $50 million. That is bound to increase in the future. Only when that happens will we be sure the technology has truly arrived. In the next chapter, we will examine the role of VC in the growth of new technologies and how the tycoons of the world go about their business.

Chapter 11

Venture Capital

For Profit or Cause

The motivation for profit has always driven human enterprise. In ancient times, kings and wealthy merchants invested in innovations to promote artwork, textile design, embroidery, performing arts, handicrafts and cuisine. Excavations from the Liangzhu culture site, at Qianshanyang, Zhejiang Province, China, show that at around 3,000 BCE, Lady Hsi-Ling-Shih, the wife of the Yellow Emperor who is credited with introducing sericulture and inventing the loom on which silk is woven, employed hundreds of skilled artisans at her court.

In the sixteenth century, Michelangelo the sculptor, Nicola Salvi the architect, Giovanni the painter and many others combined their skills to create the magic of modern Rome. The Vatican City attracted talent from across the globe who helped build its historic churches, towers and monuments that tourists flock to see today. Each of these craftsmen was highly skilled but lacked the required capital, which was provided by powerful and wealthy patrons or the church.

Some 50 years later, Mughal Emperor Akbar patronized music and art and honored nine men known as the gems of his court in Delhi. Abul Fazal was the grand vizier, philosopher, writer and historian. Raja Todarmal, the mathematician, managed revenues and finances. Tansen was the famous musician. Birbal, the witty and razor-sharp close confidant and was the foreign minister. Faizi, the poet laureate, was the mentor of his children. Raja Man Singh, the chief of staff; Abdul Rahim Khan, the defense minister, Fakir Aziao Din, the minister of religion and Mullah Do Pyaza, the home minister, were the other members.

But it was only in the nineteenth century, Joseph A. Schumpeter made the entrepreneur the key figure "driving innovations in any business" in modern economic theory. According to him, innovations by entrepreneurs like skilled actors, craftsmen, sculptors, musicians, business people and inventors reduced the price of products, increased profits and expanded markets. These entrepreneurs brought new ideas to the fore that needed funding.

DOI: 10.1201/9781003409557-14

French silk weaver J.M. Jacquard, who built the Jacquard loom; British scientists Humphrey Davy, who invented the Davy lamp; and George Stephenson, who invented the steam locomotive, were among such entrepreneurs. During the 1930s many Broadway theater production houses needed large amounts of capital to put on lavish, spectacular and extravagant shows. Some of these made huge profits; however, a large number also failed. The funds for such creative artists were provided by wealthy people fondly described as "angels." The concept of angel investors funding high-risk entrepreneurs driving innovations was expanded by academics working in the Austrian School of Economics in entrepreneurship research, such as Israel Kirzner, Bill Wetzel and Karl Vesper.

HOW ENTREPRENEURS SEEK FUNDING

There are four pillars of the modern technology business: (1) entrepreneurs; (2) technology; (3) capital; and (4) markets. Entrepreneurs identify problem areas and create technological solutions. These solutions need large amounts of capital to develop into scalable and profitable businesses that can dominate large markets. All businesses start with an entrepreneur at the core and end with large consumer markets. Most traditional businesses, like chemical factories or steel plants, are asset-heavy and dependent on industrial technology. They are supported by conventional means of funding from banks or financial institutions. They receive finance from the project stage against a mortgage of fixed assets, inventory and receivables or both. However, computer technology businesses are not asset-heavy because they are based on intellectual capital. However, technology startups need investment to conduct market research, employ developers, create prototype solutions and form a company before a business launch. The early capital needed for such activity is usually known as the seed capital.

When it is provided by an entrepreneur, it is called bootstrapping. When it is sought externally, it is usually provided by institutions, grants, or angel investors in exchange for a small share of the equity capital. At times, the initial seed capital for the laboratory research until proof of concept is provided by an institutional grant. Then, the angel investor funds the business until it can be demonstrated in the real world.

To understand how this works, let us assume that your startup is trying to build an app to streamline and improve the efficiency of the bus network in the 32 megacities of the world with a population of over 10 million. This is a real time problem from a large market perspective and needs a scalable technology solution. In the laboratory stage, your startup conceives that a fleet of 20,000 buses will be run by competing service providers in each city. You create a laboratory model, which shows that by efficiently managing bus routes through the app, the operators could handle 25% more traffic without additional infrastructure investment. Your startup at that stage, January of year one, would show this proof of concept to an angel investor and seek seed capital. The angels would usually take a hard look at your project and talk to you in detail; however, they may or may not insist on a detailed, structured project proposal. Angel investors are keen on founders with a good team working on technological solutions for a large market. You would typically be able to sell this concept to an angel investor who provides seed capital of perhaps $20,000 to develop the business and becomes a 10% stakeholder in the company. In that case, your startup is valued at $200,000.

Now, with this seed capital, your startup gives the finishing touches to the app, then approaches the municipal authority in Jakarta, where four privately owned bus companies operate, and signs a memorandum of understanding in January of year two. Each of these bus operators uploads their traffic data onto the app. Since you have a product or service for the market that is operating and can be demonstrated, you would then approach a VC firm for "early-stage capital," so that you could take your business to the next level. By the fall of year two, you would make a revenue estimation of your business operating successfully with a 20% profit margin in Jakarta for 2 years. You could convince future investors that your business valuation should be $2 million. The VC firm then agrees to give you $300,000 for 15% of your stocks. A year later, in September of year three, your business has improved, and you break even. Then, you enlist a second VC firm, giving them 5% of your stocks for $200,000, as your valuation has jumped to $10 million. So, 70% of your firm's equity remains with you, 20% with VC firms and 10% with angel investors.

The angels normally exit with a good profit 3–5 years later; however, in many cases, they stay on. At this stage, by the end of year three, your angel investor could choose to sell off all or part of their equity at a valuation of $10 million, giving a healthy 50-fold appreciation. This is the expansion phase of the project, where more venture capitalists would happily join. However, the startup world is unpredictable; full of twists and turns that are known as "glorious uncertainties."

Just as you are planning to expand into other cities, you find that another startup funded by Goldman Sachs, Sequoia Capital, Tiger Global and some of the top VCs in Silicon Valley is opening a similar service in three megacities—New York, Shanghai and Mumbai—in January of year four and plan to roll out worldwide services in a six month time frame. The app is powered by Google Maps with far more advanced features like the immersive view that also integrates metro and bus data for all commuters to choose how they could use the various forms of public transport. You and your investors assess the deep pockets of your competitor and, instead of going for further expansion, decide to sell at a valuation of $30 million.

Since "time is money" in technology businesses, you would get this price without hard bargaining, if your valuation is right, as your deep-pocketed competitor has bigger goals and is looking for a worldwide rollout without competition from small local firms. The VCs who invested with you would make a healthy profit quickly. You become a serial entrepreneur looking for a second business with $21 million in your pocket in just 3 years and your investors are happy to make a quick, profitable exit. Please note this is the best-case scenario.

Angel investors, who have been around since the 1970s are a publicity-shy wealthy community of around 3 million people who have invested an estimated $30 billion in over 100,000 startups globally. Unlike venture capitalists, who are usually professionals managing money for large funds, angel investors are lone wolves with an average investment of $25,000 in each enterprise. Exceptions also exist—like British entrepreneur Alex Chesterman, American businessman Alexis Kerry Ohanian, William Bao Bean of China and Ratan Tata of India, who have invested over $50 million each in multiple startups.

In addition, some angels invest as a collective, like the Sand Hill Angels, Band of Angels and Indian Angels Network, which operate with more than 100 angel investors. It is difficult to track the investment pattern carried out by this elusive community; however, if you do so, you will find that not all investment is aimed toward high profits. Some of it has been made to help entrepreneurs develop core technologies or applications. Much of it has been to back efforts that they believe could bring about change. Most of the early investments in clean energy have come from this community, who are ready to put their money into causes they feel could improve sustainable living on the planet. We will discuss this aspect in detail later. Now, we need to delve into how the VC industry operates.

HOW VC FUNDS OPERATE

A VC business is managed by professionals, not fund owners. The VC firms are structured corporate houses with money and influence and have a completely different approach from early-stage evangelists. Angel investors fund small sums, and VC firms are far bigger and are manned by experts and professionals who fund and frequently assume a hands-on role, taking up positions on the company's board. They do not usually invest their capital as angels do but rather invest funds obtained from private equity funds, investment banks, corporates, pensions and gratuity funds.

For example, one of the world's largest VC funds (GV) is funded by Google. The fund was set up in 2009 and finances 300 active companies, including Uber, Slack, Medium and GitLab, with $8 billion in 2022. Bessemer Ventures, Insight Partners, Index Ventures and European funds are the other hugely successful funds, along with Sequoia Capital, the oldest and the most famous VC firm set up 50 years ago, in 1972. Sequoia has been an early investor in umbrella companies like Google, Apple, PayPal, Instagram, Zoom, Airbnb, WhatsApp and even FTX, the crypto derivative exchange that collapsed in November 2022.

The top five VC firms have managed to exit in approximately 20% of the ventures they have invested in, which shows that investment is not an easy business. Only a few investments reach a 20-times valuation within 5 years. They are well-known startups that have become globally successful. However, venture capital firms spend most of their time and energy with startup companies that could achieve a 5–10 times value addition within a 3–5-year period. If promoters, founders of the startup, cannot provide profitable exits within that limited time frame, the VC firms slowly take control of the company and then sell their stakes at the best market price.

Venture funds have two types of partners—general and limited partners (LPs). The general partners take the day-to-day investment decisions and manage the startup business, working with them to achieve the business goals. The LPs invest in VC firms the capital from investment banks, pension funds, corporates and hedge funds. The LPs bring in the capital to be invested and decide the broad investment strategy of VC firms. For example, they decide if VC firms should invest in developed or emerging markets and whether they will fund the semiconductor business or the e-commerce or telehealth sectors. They pursue profits, not specific causes. VC firms pay management fees from 2% to 2.5% for capital commitment along with carried interest and a healthy share in the profits, which could work out as an approximately 80:20 profit sharing between the limited and general partners.

However, venture capital is not high-risk capital. It plays a very minor role in funding basic research or innovation. VCs do not provide seed capital like angel investors. They are quick to invest when you have commercialized your project, such as the Jakarta Bus traffic management app. According to *Harvard Business Review*, "venture money plays an important role in the next stage of the innovation life cycle—the period in a company's life when it begins to commercialize its innovation."

They claim that 80% of the money invested by venture capitalists goes into building the infrastructure when growing technology businesses, funding expenses like manufacturing, marketing and sales. In short, they provide capital for fixed assets, and working capital like a banker does in a conventional business.

They do not provide any seed capital and will invest with early-stage capital if and when the startup can commercialize it early and generate revenue. They essentially fund the expansion stage of the project and exit before the startup enters the later stages when valuations start to mellow out. VC firms usually like to exit a startup once it reaches a sufficient size and gains the financial strength to be sold to a corporation or raise equity from an investment banker or the public. However, exceptions exist where VCs invest in the entire life cycle of a business, from seed capital to post-IPO.

By funding only the expansion phase of the project, when the valuation of a startup increases the most, VCs attempt to maximize profits. Therefore, VC funds are very high-cost capital for the entrepreneur, equivalent to over 50% compound interest on a loan that cannot be prepaid. Therefore, entrepreneurs need to be careful when receiving finance from venture funds because they are prohibitively expensive and remove substantial equity stakes from the founders. In addition, the time given by venture capitalists to advise startups is less than 2 hr/week. That is why a popular television reality show on investor finance, which has been running for more than a decade on the ABC and Sony Networks, is named Shark Tank. The entrepreneurs are small fish who are often treated with little respect and given deals with atrocious terms by the funding "sharks." Of the 50,000 startups that pitch to the sharks, less than 100 are aired on TV, and just a few dozen get funding. Despite this, venture capital is in high demand. Why?

The widely prevailing view is that thousands of entrepreneurs go for VC funding because no one else funds innovation on a large scale. Government and institutional support are limited and not large enough to take any business to maturity, where they could get equity from the public. VC is the only funding available to technology entrepreneurs during the expansion phase of the business. There are other viewpoints. Nobody can deny that venture capital gives wings to execution, and it is the speed of growth that makes innovation disruptive. The capability to pump in adequate capital to grow a business to maturity despite initial cash burn is unique to VC funding. We will see how it helps to propel innovation quickly and why it has become globally dominant in less than a decade.

We spoke to a few entrepreneurs from the Indian Institute of Technology (IIT) alumni network and found a different viewpoint too. Many of these otherwise geeky engineering students covet venture capital because, although it is not easily available, it takes you to the pinnacle. It gives a 1 in 1,000 chance of becoming an Elon Musk or a Mark Zuckerberg. This could merely be a starry-eyed dream of a youngster, but it propels youth toward entrepreneurship. Of the 100 or so unicorns that India has produced in the last decade, 73 have more than one founder who studied at the IIT. Moreover, top Chief Executive Officers (CEOs), such as Sundar Pichai of Google, Parag Agarwal of Twitter and Arvind Krishna of IBM, are all IIT alumni. The startups put talent in the driver's seat very early on. It is this stardom that entrepreneurs covet and which makes them flock to shark VCs in droves.

This glamour of intellectual capital is a global phenomenon bred in Menlo Park and the corridors of Harvard and Stanford. However, European startups are more conservative than their US or Asian counterparts when using VC funds as later-stage capital. They cater mostly to developed markets and are starkly different in their approach. We will look at some successful and unsuccessful startups funded at different stages by VCs from these three regions to understand how VC capital works differently worldwide.

BUILDING ROCK STAR BUSINESSES WITH VC FUNDING

In 2001, Jesper Buch, a Danish Military Academy and Export Institute graduate, along with five entrepreneurs, founded Just Eat, an online food delivery startup, from a basement in Kolding—a small Danish town with a population of less than 600,000 people. By 2004, it was profitable and headquartered in London, with operations in Denmark, Iceland, the Netherlands, Sweden and Ireland. Five years later, Just Eat operated in ten countries and was connected to 15,000 restaurants. In 2010, Jesper Buch retired, selling part of his stake to Index Ventures, a VC firm, for $10.5 million to become an author, investor and serial entrepreneur. In 2011, Just Eat had revenues of $500 million, and Buch sold his remaining stake to two leading US VC funds, Greylock Partners and Redwood Ventures.

At around the same time, Niklas Östberg, a Master of Industrial Engineering and Management from the Royal Institute of Technology Stockholm, and three cofounders started another online food delivery service Delivery Hero headquartered in Berlin. Delivery Hero went for VC funding of €25 million in 2012 and expanded operations quickly to Australia, Asia and Europe simultaneously. By 2017, Delivery Hero had availed itself of multiple rounds of VC funding and expanded operations to 50 countries with revenues of over € 500 million. By June, it raised nearly €1 billion from a public listing on the Frankfurt Stock Exchange at a valuation of €3.5 billion. Just Eat, which started in 2001 and went public in 2014, was valued at €5.5 billion in 2017. Delivery Hero scaled up its business in just 6 years using VC finance early, and Just Eat let the revenues grow and then opted for VC finance after a decade. It took 16 years for Just Eat to scale up operations and go public despite having the first-mover advantage.

However not all VC fundings see easy exit and successes. In 2009, Michal Borkowski, a corporate finance graduate from the Warsaw School of Economics, Krakow, Poland, launched Brainly, a collaborative platform for online learning, with three other entrepreneurs. Brainly quickly became a safe and trusted study-centric online community where you could study and solve problems with friends worldwide 24/7 and have experts and tutors to guide you. In 2012, it raised $500,000 as seed capital from VC firm Point Nine Capital and went through six rounds of funding to raise nearly $150 million by 2017. Headquartered in New York, the niche online learning platform was used by 350 million users in over 30 countries during its peak and was reported to be one of the largest peer-to-peer learning platforms globally. However, Brainly has yet to demonstrate its revenue potential as an edutech startup, "In some countries like Poland and Russia, more than 80% of students are on Brainly. In the US it is 15-20%, however, and in India just 10%. "There is lots more room to grow," stated Borkowski

So, you will find many renowned startups that have been in business for a decade with VC funds but without quick monetization. Not everything that appears promising and gets early VC funding succeeds. They will ultimately be bought by a rival or be simply closed down with losses to the venture fund.

French startup BlaBlaCar is another unique European business that has found early VC investment. Frederic Mazzella, a Stanford Computer Science postgraduate, and three other founders set up this unique business headquartered in Paris in 2006. Small European nations, good motorable roads, high gas costs, a secure environment and high tourist traffic made this cross-continent carpooling business an instant success. The company owns no vehicles or fixed assets but earns around 20% broker commission on each co-sharing trip arranged through its website. The carpool that operated across a dozen European nations was named after the driver's talkativeness. The less chatty ones were rated Bla, the chattier drivers were BlaBla and BlaBlaBla was for those who just could not stop talking. Being profitable from the outset, the company received funding in 2009 and 2010 from angel investors before Accel Partners invested EUR 7.5 million in 2012 and Index Ventures and Insight Ventures invested $300 million in 2014. By 2019, BlaBlaCar had expanded into 22 countries booking more than 50 million travelers annually. Its revenues were 70% higher than the previous year, and it introduced the BlaBlaBus service in France and Russia, its two biggest markets. Unfortunately, the pandemic then struck, followed by lockdowns and the Russia–Ukraine war, plunging the French unicorn into losses and postponing its long-awaited IPO.

However, the startup scene in the US is more dynamic, largely because of the large pool of entrepreneurs emerging from US institutions and the market size. In 2007, two industrial engineers from Rhode Island School of Design and Harvard graduate Nathan Blecharzik founded Airbnb, an online home and apartment sharing concept with bed and breakfast. Homeowners on the Airbnb site could find tourists by paying a modest commission of 15%. However, since they could not get funding immediately, they resorted to bootstrapping, initially selling "AirBed and Breakfast" cereal boxes during the 2008 US Presidential elections to raise $30,000. In January 2009, they received $20,000 and training at Y Combinator, a startup incubator, and by April 2009 landed a $600,000 seed funding deal from Sequoia Capital. Then, they received multiple funding rounds and, despite stiff resistance from the US hotel industry, expanded worldwide to become a household name in just 5 years. Airbnb's revenues grew by 80% to $1.65 billion in 2016, when it became profitable. After recovering strongly from the lockdown phase of the Covid-19 pandemic, Airbnb raised $3.5 billion in its December 2020 IPO and opened at $146 on the NASDAQ stock exchange, far above its IPO price of $68. The market valuation of the startup exceeded $100 billion within 15 years of incorporation.

In 2009, two serial entrepreneurs, Garret Camp (founder of StumbleUpon) and Travis Kalanick (founder of Red Swoosh), with a record of creating successfully funded startups, launched Uber, one of the most successful and disruptive businesses of the decade. Like BlaBlaCar, Uber started as a cab rental service in San Francisco without owning a cab or having the license to run a taxicab company. Within 2 years, Uber secured an $11 million investment from VC firm Benchmark against 20% equity. By 2016, it had secured multiple funding rounds and had operations in 30 countries generating revenues of $6.5 billion. However, Kalanick was forced to step down in 2016, facing charges of a toxic culture. In May 2019, Uber successfully launched its IPO, garnering $8 billion at a share price of $45, offering 180 million shares at a valuation of $75 billion. Since then, it has had a rollercoaster ride, with its stock price wildly fluctuating between $38 and $26, even as it expanded operations worldwide. By 2022, Uber became profitable, with operations in more than 70 countries and 10,000 cities, clocking over 90 million rides per month and generating revenue exceeding $25 billion annually.

It is venture capital that hunts the geeky talent at Stanford and not the other way around, says the University Entrepreneurship Report of CB Insights, which shows that Stanford and Harvard graduates get three times the funding of any other university student in the US. In April 2011, Stanford classmates Thomas Evan Spiegel, Bobby Murphy and Reggie Brown launched a mobile-to-mobile multimedia messaging app prototype called Picaboo, later renamed Snapchat. By the end of 2012, it had 1 million active users daily, and the founders dropped out of college to pursue the project full-time. Snapchat received multiple rounds of VC funding every year until 2017, when it raised $3.4 billion in an IPO at an offer price of $17. That year Spiegel married Australian model and businesswoman Miranda Kerr, whom he had been dating since 2015, and entered the coveted celebrity couples circle of Los Angeles and Hollywood. As of 2021, Snapchat had 330 million daily active users worldwide and annual revenues of $4.2 billion, with Spiegel refusing to sell out to bigger players like Facebook.

The startup scene is extremely vibrant in China, with more than 300 unicorns—nearly half as many as in the US. The world's most valuable startup, the social media giant ByteDance, valued at over $280 billion in 2022, owns TikTok, the popular short format video platform. The ByteDance IPO, one of the most anticipated events of 2022, was once again postponed as new variants of Covid hit the Chinese economy along with zero-tolerance lockdowns. The founders of TikTok were college friends Zhang Yiming and Liang Rubo at Nankai University, China. In 2012, they first launched two social media platforms, "Neihan Duanzi," the joke, memes and humorous videos platform, and "Tautiao," the content platform for headline news.

The quick success of both apps made it possible for them to attract VC capital. The startup was backed by funding heavyweights, such as Sequoia Capital, KKR, SoftBank Group, General Atlantic and HillHouse Capital. In Sept 2016, they launched the English version of TikTok, which became an instant hit. Five years later, in September 2021, it had 1 billion monthly active users making it the world's most popular short video format with early mover advantage. Reels was launched by Instagram only in 2020 to bring the short video format and audience to Facebook.

Didi Chuxing is the Chinese version of Uber, with over 500 million users and millions of cabs and drivers registered as service providers. It provides app-based transportation services for hire, such as taxis, luxury and private cars, bikes and shared rides and financing, leasing, sales, insurance, fleet operation, maintenance, electric vehicle charging and electric vehicle co-development. In 2012, Cheng Wei, a chemical technologist from Beijing University, China, with 9 years of selling experience at Alibaba, started a cab hiring service, "Didi Dache," which means "Beep, Beep, Call a Taxi" in Chinese. He hired Jean Liu, a managing director at Goldman Sachs Asia, two years later as his COO. Aggressive fundraising by the duo from Tencent, Temasek and private investors enabled them to merge with or buy off rivals like Kuadi Didi, backed by Alibaba, and Uber China, backed by Baidu, and create one of the fastest-growing startups in China. In 2017, SoftBank invested $6 billion, and Didi moved to invest in other cab hiring services in Latin America, Australia and Japan. In June 2021, it raised $4.4 billion from its IPO at NYSE at a valuation of $70 billion.

India is the third largest startup market, with over 100 unicorns and a vibrant marketplace. In 2007, two Delhi IIT engineering graduates, Sachin and Binny Bansal, who had worked for a few years at Amazon US, launched Flipkart, one of India's early indigenous e-commerce platforms, in Bengaluru, with a capital of around $80,000. In the third quarter of 2009, Flipkart received its first funding of $400,000 from Accel Partners for 20% of its equity. By December, it had attracted Tiger Global, which pumped in $2 million at an astounding valuation of $44 million. Before Amazon entered India in 2013, Flipkart had become an online e-commerce giant with over 50% market share. When Walmart picked up 77% of the stake in May 2018 at $16 billion, India was the fastest-growing e-commerce market globally; according to Forester Research, Flipkart held 32% of the market share, and Amazon held 31%. Both founders exited, selling their stakes as billionaires, and Flipkart became a Walmart company worth $37 billion. It planned a US listing at NYSE when the Russia–Ukraine war disrupted global commerce and supply chains.

India's large market, despite being intensely competitive, attracts all global brands. Cosmetics and fashion are no exception. Many large players like L'Oréal, Garnier, Unilever, P&G and Johnson & Johnson are already there, along with half a dozen large Indian brands. So, when 50-year-old

Falguni Nayar, a managing director with Kotak Mahindra Bank and mother of two, quit her 20-year banking career to start an online beauty and e-commerce platform in 2012, many eyebrows were raised. However, the mother and her digital native children realized that big multinational brands had ignored the new-age consumers who primarily shopped online. The presence of beauty products in e-commerce portals like Amazon, Snapdeal and Flipkart was not extensive, and Nykka brought 4,000 beauty brands (Indian and international) under its portal. In addition, apart from conventional advertising, it used more than 3,000 social influencers to market its products. In 2015, Nykka received funding of $9.5 million from TVS capital in addition to $3.4 million from HNW angel investors. It ramped up online sales and broke even within 5 years of launch, after which it started attracting VC funding and opened physical stores across India. By 2019, its annual revenues had exceeded $200 million, and it had opened over 40 physical stores across India. Its IPO was oversubscribed 80 times in 2021, giving it a valuation exceeding $13 billion. VC firm Lighthouse Advisors' investment grew by 23 times, Steadview Capital's rose by 13 times, and TPG Growth by 7 times, and they all made partial exits, having invested in Nykka just 4 years previously. Nayar's success has helped many female-led startups in fashion and healthcare, like MyGlamm, Sugar Cosmetics and MamaEarth to be funded by VCs and become profitable unicorns.

VC IN SUSTAINABILITY

Venture capital is for profit, not cause. However, if your cause is profitable for investors and matches their ideology, they will go for it. If we go back to the Copenhagen Climate Talks in 2008, we notice that the impact of solar and wind energy was minimal before then. At that time, the fossil fuel lobby that used to sponsor such climate conferences was dictating the agenda. As a result, the European nations were largely funding carbon credits, not renewable energy. The US was simply not interested in the talks.

The Kyoto Protocol failed because it funded carbon reduction instead of backing renewable energy. So, all subsidies and carbon credits were cornered by the polluters (i.e., fossil fuel-driven energy companies) who promised to reduce carbon but did nothing for more than two decades. The first climate conference was held in 1979, and the Kyoto Protocol was signed in 1997. No move was made to subsidize renewable energy during these years. The US quit the Kyoto Talks in 2001, and it was in 2008 that several nations realized that fossil fuels had to be replaced and not just reduced.

Subsidies had to be given to renewable energy startups and not to fossil fuel polluters to reduce their carbon footprint. Laws needed to be changed to permit renewable energy units to be connected to the electricity grid. Once that happened, the results were visible. Solar capacities jumped fivefold in 2008 to 3,416 megawatts (MW). The early leaders in renewable energy at that time were Germany, Spain, Japan, China and the US. It was mostly government funding that helped renewable growth, but some corporates in Europe, like Bosch, Unilever, Danone and IKEA, also chipped in. By 2013, solar capacities had doubled to 6,943 MW (enough to power New York City), and private investors started investing in further development. In wind energy Germany and Spain led the rest of the world with 23,900 MW and 16,700 MW installed capacities in 2008, accounting for 60% of the total EU capacity and 35% of the global capacity. Both nations accounted for 50% of the installed European Union wind capacities in 2021.

As global support grew to favor renewables, small groups of angel investors in Europe started funding them. Among them is Friedrich Nueman, a German venture partner at Swedish fund VC Norrsken, who has independently invested from €25,000 to €50,000 in over a dozen sustainability startups. In addition, the British entrepreneur of Mind Tools fame James Manketelow has turned into an angel investor funding at least 10 startups, with amounts from £25,000 to £50,000 for sustainability and circular economy projects. German startup Volt Storage, which is developing battery technology for day and night renewable energy storage, has received two rounds of funding of €11 million and €12 million from investors Korys, EIT InnoEnergy, Bayern Kapital, SOSV, Energie 360 and Business Angels. US energy giant Cummins known worldwide for its diesel generators has now invested €24 million for its C Series funding, a serious expression of interest by any industry major in renewable energy.

Jinko Solar, a solar panel manufacturing company headquartered in Shanghai, China, started making silicon wafers in Jiangxi and Zhejiang Provinces, China, in 2006. It was backed by Cayman Island-based Chinese investors and soon expanded into vertically integrated solar product value chains with over 400 products, including silicon wafers, solar cells, solar modules and recycled products. Very little is known about its founder Xiande Li who graduated in economics from Shanghai University of Finance and Economics, China, and built one of the largest solar power companies exporting to many parts of the US, Europe and Asia in 4 years. After a failed attempt to list in February 2010, it successfully had its IPO at NYSE in May 2010, backed by Credit Suisse. It has not looked back, and 10 years later, it reported a revenue of $5.38 billion and operating profits of $273 million in 2020, with a market cap of $3 billion.

In 1985, Stanford Professor Richard Swanson took a sabbatical to commercialize solar technology with improved energy efficiency. He created a manufacturing facility to make silicon wafers under the name SunPower and was funded by Robert Lorenzini, who took over as Chairman. Lorenzini had earlier sold Siltech Corp, a silicon crystal-making unit, to Mitsubishi Metals and cofounded VC firm Band of Angels. By 1989, SunPower had generated revenues of $600,000 and by 1996, over $6 million. However, following several ups and downs in the global photovoltaic market and stiff competition from China and Germany, the founders sold their controlling stake to French oil major TotalEnergy for $1.37 billion in 2011. Ten years later, the company reported revenues of $1.32 billion and operating losses of $27.5 million, still unable to break even after 35 years.

New York-based Energy Impact Partners, founded in 2015, is a $1 billion fund that has invested in a dozen cleantech projects and exited eight of them successfully. Boston-based Clean Energy Venture Group, Chicago-based Energy Foundry, Seattle-based E8 Angels Fund and Chicago-based Energize Ventures are other smaller funds available for green energy. In September 2021, Bill Gates, along with seven anchor partners including American Airlines, ArcelorMittal, Bank of America, The BlackRock Foundation, Boston Consulting Group, General Motors and Microsoft Technologies, founded the Breakthrough Energy Catalyst, a $1 billion fund in Seattle, to invest in critical decarbonizing technologies. The Catalyst will start initially by funding projects in four technology areas: direct air capture, green hydrogen, long-duration energy storage and sustainable aviation fuel.

THE FUTURE OF VENTURE CAPITAL

The Covid-19 pandemic hurt many industries, and the demand for venture capital was expected to decline. However, VC deals hit record highs because more innovation was needed to sustain these industries through difficult times. In the US, VCs invested 14% more capital than in 2019 and $130 billion was made in deals during 2020. Half of this was raised in 318 mega-rounds of over $100 million, showing that risk appetite had surprisingly increased during the period. VC funding worldwide was up by 4% and exceeded the $330 billion mark in 2020. In 2021, Crunchbase reported an unprecedented 90% growth in VC investment worldwide to exceed $640 billion.

However, exits took longer, and VC funds remained locked in for 8 years on average during the latter part of the current decade. Because exits became drawn out in 2022, VCs were reluctant to fund startups unless the product stage was complete. And as VCs started shifting focus to funding the late-stage technology startups that were close to maturity and required larger funding, a void was created in the early-stage funding, leading to new instruments and several alternative methods being adopted.

One of the existing methods of sourcing startup capital that has become popular of late is crowdfunding. Previously, this was used to raise funds for an event or a charitable cause. It started more than 200 years ago, and even the base of the Statue of Liberty was crowdfunded by 160,000 donors in 1885. Over $30 billion of fundraising has occurred through crowdsourcing in 2010–2020, which could increase in the current decade. This resulted from tech and commercially savvy users with greater risk appetites wanting to find ways to make super-profits from the startup environment by bypassing IPOs. Some well-known crowdfunding platforms for startups are

SeedInvest and StartEngine in the US, Indiegogo in China and FundedByMe in Stockholm.

To reduce the exit period, some LPs from VC firms, the people responsible for funding, are now directly investing in the startups that show potential. This helps them take direct control of operations and better understand the business risks of future investments. Sometimes, interested industries that have participated in the early stages make a direct investment at the later stage, making it easier for future takeovers. We have seen investments along similar lines made by Total Energy in Sun Power and Cummins in VoltStorage. VC firm Blume Ventures reported recently that some Japanese LPs are interested in investing in certain portfolios directly. Post 2020 as funding avenues expand, we might see this new funding avenue becoming more extensive.

Venture capital used to fund startups is here to stay, but in the future, it will be targeted toward large markets to spread the risks. Most VC firms are focused on the US, China and India, which produce millions of entrepreneurs at a fast rate. These are large markets, ideal for scalable growth. The major institutions investing, such as investment banks, pension funds and insurance companies, will look at high-interest rates in the US. They will also be looking to reduce the exit period from 8 to 6 years. To do this, they will have to cut the flab, such as reducing the organization's layers, co-invest with VCs or investing directly in startups. This will increase costs as they must develop in-house talent spotting and skill development as a core activity to find and train young entrepreneurs. The volumes will also rise. Today, 90% of skill-building work happens at the early funding stage when the scaling up occurs. So, there will have to be many AI applications to screen and test entrepreneurs of the future. In addition, new opportunities and threats will appear in the near future that will make risk management for all new technology businesses imperative.

We will look at some of these risks, threats and opportunities in the next section of the book. For example, the threat of an increasingly fractured world with wars, digital disruptions, and fierce competition to protect supply chains, to stay in business and stay ahead. We will also explore some surprising developments due to risks throwing up fresh challenges and opening new vistas and opportunities.

Part III

A Decade of Uncertainty

Chapter 12

The Great Digital Meltdown

A Fractured World

The world that we knew, and had started believing in, has suddenly changed since the start of this decade of uncertainty. First came the pandemic, then the Ukraine war, and now we could witness economic turmoil, debt-related meltdowns, trade and energy wars, and supply chain disruptions. Half a century ago, we were a world of 4 billion people. Today we are 8 billion, occupying virtually the same space and environment we had in the 1970s. Global GDP has grown 20-fold in this period, as has consumption and disparity. However, life in the future might be a little different; this could be the decade of change for the 8 billion people. We may be at an inflection point due to the conflicts that have occurred in the past five decades and those that are peaking now. We are suddenly moving from globalization to localization, from decades of trust and tolerance to a decade of mistrust and hostility. We find that wars have changed form and are now being fought simultaneously and globally in the virtual space.

WARS THAT ARE FOUGHT IN THE DIGITAL SPACE

There are multiple types of wars being fought in the digital space today. The most easily understood is the information war, communication, or propaganda war. It focuses on twisting the narrative. This war has been going on for centuries; however, it took on a different dimension with the arrival of the internet. The Gulf War of 1990–1991, fought by a 35-nation coalition of unlikely allies, including NATO nations and OPEC powerhouses, is believed to be the first modern information war. The clouds of suspicion raised in the media about Iraq possessing nuclear weapons, anthrax, and nerve gas that provided an excuse for the US-led coalition troops to enter Iraq in 2003 were part of a strategic information warfare plan to isolate and overthrow the Iraqi despot Saddam Hussein. This information warfare modus operandi was later refined to cause rebellions against long-entrenched dictators like Ben Ali of Tunisia, Hosni Mubarak of Egypt, Mummar Gaddafi of

DOI: 10.1201/9781003409557-16

Libya and Ali Abdul Saleh of Yemen during the Arab Springs from 2009 to 2013 to boost the power of democratic activists in the Middle East.

Similarly, China has been conducting information warfare against India for decades, especially in the urban pockets of West Bengal and Andhra Pradesh and the tribal belts of central and southern India, supporting armed leftist uprisings against democratically elected state governments. China conducts similar information warfare against South Korea, Taiwan, and other states it considers potential adversaries. Taiwanese President Tsai Ing-wen described the Chinese information assault against Taiwan as a cognitive warfare tactic. The Russian invasion of Ukraine and the Chinese threats to occupy Taiwan have increased this information warfare by both the Western powers who support democracy and the communists. However, this is a very small part of the big picture looming on the horizon.

Information warfare is a subset of digital warfare that is much more intrusive, disruptive, and widespread. Digital wars twist the narrative; they also include nonphysical cyberattacks on the generation, transmission, processing, storage, and usage of data that delete, alter, compromise, delay, confuse, or destroy the opponent's decision-making capability. It is what the traditional military planners have always sought in conventional warfare—similar to a secret passage under a well-guarded fortress that can breach its defenses significantly and fatally. It is like a stealth bomb—a low-cost, precision entry vehicle with highly destructive potential placed right in the heart of the enemy territory. Digital wars are conducted by activist and terrorist groups and the intelligence wings of conventional militaries. A few are developed as dormant cells that sleep for years and are activated at critical junctures to obtain maximum impact. Some only gather information and might never be discovered.

Importantly, digital wars threaten the ability of traditional defense forces to plant themselves between the population and enemies of the state, therefore, causing the loss of a safe sanctuary. Apart from life-threatening territorial intrusions and the potential destruction of and damage to assets, they create a perception of acute vulnerability. They aim to create a loss of confidence in the ability of the state to protect its citizens. The impact of such a perception could be much stronger than any loss of physical territory because, as military planners say, wars are won first in the mind and then on the battlefield. In addition, the impact of technology in all spheres of life has ensured that digital wars are being fought not just against a prepared military, but also against the people and practices of the enemy state.

SEVEN WORLDWIDE WARS OF THE FUTURE

With over half a dozen nations armed to the teeth with nuclear weapons and state-of-the-art delivery systems, a third world war in the form of a nuclear confrontation looks like a surprisingly remote possibility. Instead, we see several modern wars growing in scale and immensity, intending to dominate economically, politically and physically. These wars are happening because of a shift in the world order. They have acquired a digital dimension that camouflages their true intent and, sometimes, embroils multiple nations.

Fifty years ago, the top ten economic powers of the world were largely in the western hemisphere, with the US leading and accounting for over one-third of the global GDP, followed by the USSR, with China positioned ninth. By 2020, China had leapfrogged into second place, with Japan third, India sixth and South Korea tenth. This shift in economic power has resulted in jostling on various fronts by all nations. There has been "fair play" and "foul play." There are seven ongoing global fights, threatening the global economies, which seem likely to continue, and these are what we will focus on in this chapter to show how this will result in a digital meltdown. They could finally determine which nations move ahead and which nations fall behind.

The Debt War and Digital Intrusion

According to the International Monetary Fund, China will become the world's largest economy this decade. This momentous growth was achieved due to immense hard work, planning and shrewd strategy as China became the factory of the world and unleashed the debt war worldwide. China has a positive trade balance with more than100 nations and has extended massive bilateral debt to most nations that cannot easily be repaid. Although the US and the European Union (EU) account for the largest imports and debt worldwide, the poorer and mineral-rich nations of Africa and South America are most dependent on China's debt financing and are firmly in its stranglehold.

During the last 20 years, China has extended loans of $150 billion, primarily for infrastructure projects, to 32 African nations that most cannot repay. Among these resource-rich nations are Angola (oil), Burundi (gold), Botswana (diamond), Congo (copper, cobalt, oil and coltan), Ghana (oil, timber and gold), Kenya (Mombasa Port), Nigeria (oil and gas), Madagascar (rare earth elements REE) and Zambia (copper). This debt is extended in exchange for concessional mining rights (the license to mining contracts) given to Chinese companies. China also builds infrastructure projects in these nations, such as roads, railways, water supply and housing construction projects to make it easier for mines and businesses to operate. China's low-cost manufacturing hub is fed by this unending stream of raw materials it sources and processes from Africa and South America.

Even before the Covid-19 pandemic, 18 of these 32 African nations negotiated the repayment of bilateral loans, which meant agreeing to more restrictive terms against longer payments. Kenya, the largest borrower, could easily lose Mombasa Port just like Sri Lanka lost control of the Hambantota

Port to China if it defaults on any installment of its $60 billion debt to China's Exim Bank, says Kenya's auditor general. A similar situation exists in nations with low incomes but resource-rich states of South America.

China has exploited rare earth elements (REE), platinum group metals (PGM) and radioactive materials along with high-value metals like niobium, beryllium, tantalum, thorium, mica, gold, cobalt, nickel, chromite, molybdenum and zinc from the region as its trade with Latin American nations multiplied and the debt piled up. Corrupt autocrats and political regimes make it easy for China to gain unusually favorable terms for mining contracts. The money trap is, however, not only laid out for Africa but even for strong, vibrant democracies like Germany, China's largest trading partner in Europe. In a deft move to buy into EU assets, Chinese shipping group COSCO obtained permission from the German government to acquire a 25% stake in Hamburg Port in October 2022 during the Russia–Ukraine war.

On top of the economic consequences, Chinese debt and infrastructure has also led to a completely wired and fully compromised African electronic and telecommunication network. The French newspaper *Le Monde* first reported that the African Union (AU) headquarters in Ethiopia—built and donated by China—sent confidential data to China on the sly. Every night between midnight and 02:00 a.m., when the AU offices were deserted, the servers showed a surge in data transfers sending all the daily data to servers in Shanghai, China. This happened for 5 years before it was accidentally detected in January 2017. Following this, engineers from Ethiopia and Algeria replaced the entire information and communication technologies (ICT) infrastructure and the telecommunication equipment of the AU offices. China denied the allegations. Although new equipment was brought in, the news was kept under wraps in Ethiopia lest it creates a diplomatic controversy between the benefactor China and the African state, which was getting a good low-cost infrastructure deal. However, the entire communications of AU are now encrypted and do not pass through the state-owned operator Ethio Telecom, possibly because it has its complete telecom infrastructure wired by China.

In Africa and Asia, planned cyberattacks on critical infrastructure are becoming commonplace, usually carried out by political opponents and rebel groups. Many are by pro-China groups with sophisticated malware and intrusion devices. There are nearly half a dozen coup attempts every year in Africa. In nations where security services face limited oversight, full control over digital monitoring and surveillance gives China the power to easily undermine the security of political leaders and coordinate attempts to seize power for leaders favoring them. By the end of 2020, there were more than 495 million mobile subscribers in sub-Saharan Africa, catering to 46% of the region's population, largely led by Huawei and ZTE as the telecom equipment suppliers and China's Exim Bank as the project financier.

The East African fiber ring connects to SEACOM and PEACE submarine cables and runs from Kenya through Uganda, Rwanda, Burundi, Tanzania, Zambia and Malawi. Therefore, there is no getting away from Chinese telecommunications and its network if you are in Africa.

Contagion Wars go Digital

Meanwhile, a different digital war was developing across continental Europe, even as the African wars escalated. Soon after the disintegration of the 15-nation Soviet Union, ethnic wars broke out across Europe. The first conflict was between Bosnia, Slovenia, Croatia, Herzegovina, Montenegro and Serbia that was also the first proxy war between NATO and the Russians. All six nations were part of erstwhile Yugoslavia, which broke up soon after Slovenia and Croatia claimed independence in 1991. By 1995, NATO forces started bombing Bosnian Serbs in the capital Sarajevo and by 1999 massive air attacks by NATO forced a treaty. Soon after NATO started expanding membership and pushing eastwards. After Poland, Czech Republic and Hungary were inducted in 1999, Bulgaria, Estonia, Latvia, Lithuania, Romania, Slovakia and Slovenia were admitted in 2004. This was followed by contagion wars (ethnic, civil and intrastate rivalries) in Georgia, Chechnya, Albania, Kosovo, Crimea and finally, Ukraine in 2014 and 2022. Contagion wars will, in all probability, expand worldwide across Europe, Africa, Asia Pacific and the Middle East and be digitally and physically fought.

The first global digital attack was executed by Russian hackers on the small Baltic nation of Estonia, a country of 1.4 million people, in 2007. The cyberattack was preceded by street protests and violence by ethnic Russians over the moving of a Russian war memorial statue, following which 100 people were injured and one person was killed, with 1,300 people arrested. The Distributed Denial of Service (DDoS) cyberattack, conducted from multiple locations simultaneously on Estonia, shut down the websites of the Parliament and the presidency and all government offices, three of the country's largest news networks and two of its biggest banks for 3 weeks before they could be restored.

The Stuxnet attack on Iran's nuclear installation that closed down its centrifuges and oil and gas installations in 2009 was possibly the first digital attack that crippled the critical services of the Islamic State. Stuxnet was reportedly designed in the US with the active involvement of Israeli cyber experts. Both Iran and Iraq has been under repeated attacks from hackers backed by the US ever since.

Months later, in December 2009, the first Ghostnet attacks were conducted against Tibetan exile centers in Delhi, London and New York. Ghostnet conducts hostile information warfare for China against the embassies of over two dozen nations regularly. However, not only the US, Russia and China conduct digital warfare. In 2012, the rebel group Boko Haram, trained and supported by Al Qaeda activists, hacked into the database of the Nigerian secret service to show that the government was losing control. Many activists and terrorist groups worldwide routinely conduct such activities to undermine elected governments.

Contagion wars are rife across Africa and the Middle East. China has pockets of influence across the continents. China either backs the ruling government or the key rebel group that opposes it. "The thing I think I'm most worried about is this military base on the Atlantic coast, and where they have the most traction, for that today is in Equatorial Guinea," says General Townsend, Commander of the US Africa Command. China has colonized, wired, and virtually occupied the continent without putting soldiers on the ground. In total, 43 African nations have signed up for their Belt and Road Initiative. Ethiopian Prime Minister Abiy Ahmed pulled off a stunning victory in a conflict with the US-backed Tigray Peoples Liberation Front in 2021 with the support of the China-backed leftist government of Eritrea and with drone support from Iran and Turkey. China reportedly masterminded the entire operation with information and logistic support, looking to push out US interests from the strategically important Horn of Africa.

An October 2022 report by Booz Allen Hamilton highlighted 13 case studies of Chinese state-sponsored cyberattacks from Africa over the last decade. To ensure that other powers do not enter Africa, the Sino–African cybersecurity cooperation has emerged as a key component of China's new strategic alliance with Africa, coordinating the ICT infrastructure of 40 nations. It is a Chinese initiative to bring Africa under its digital jurisdiction. China wants African commerce to be conducted through the Belt and Road Initiative, which China will build and operate. It wants shipping lanes controlled through its blue water navy with ports that China runs in Djibouti, Kenya, Equatorial Guinea and worldwide. China is succeeding. No wonder the 54 nations that backed China's Hong Kong policy in the October 2020 voting at the United Nations General Assembly belonged largely to the African continent and easily outnumbered the 39 nations voicing concern backed by the Western Block.

Trade Wars and Digital Manipulations

China has been practicing extremely astute export policies for the last 30 years. It has a completely different model than Japan's, which also built its economy as an export powerhouse two decades before China. China exported from its mainland and through Chinese-funded joint ventures from over two dozen nations flooding the world with Chinese goods. They helped ensure that China's export books remain healthy today and its factory workers stay fully employed. Nobody realized or objected. The Western nations enjoyed a massive supply of affordable Chinese products, and the African and South American nations were content with China helping with their infrastructure and mining projects. However, the debt was mounting up dangerously, and their leaders were compromised.

Things turned on their head in 2016 when Donald Trump became the US president, backed by the American middle class, the blue-collar workers and the agricultural workforce of the midwestern states. Trump realized that when the Chinese were selling aggressively, they were taking away American jobs. In 2018, Trump slapped tariffs and other trade barriers on China, citing unfair trade practices and violations of intellectual property rights. At that time, the trade between the two largest economies was $550 billion annually. Trump's actions started a nationalistic trade war with protectionist barriers raised between two of the largest economies. The president identified other economies exporting goods to the US, which was much more than they were importing and soon placed similar restrictions on them. Soon every nation was looking at how to stop imports. Trade wars became vicious worldwide. The era of globalization ended abruptly. Although unprepared, nations started thinking of localization.

Trump's actions were in response to China's hostile trade policy. Modern-day trade wars are open to state-of-the-art digital manipulation, an innovative armory in the hands of aggressive and savvy exporters like China. Innovative digital techniques have rendered trade laws written in the last few decades toothless. The originating country could be anywhere on the globe. They could easily be camouflaged today. Digital labeling and transfers are the future of trade from the source to sale, manufacturing to delivery and investment to payment receipts. For example, Chinese mobile phone manufacturing units are being set up all over the globe. Vivo, Oppo, Xiaomi, Real Me, One Plus, Huawei and Gionee in India and Tecno, iTel, Infinix, InJoo, Huawei and Gionee in Nigeria have set up large manufacturing units in those countries. They assemble Chinese phones that are largely imported with local parts accounting for just around 5% to 15% . Three-quarters of the domestic market across India and Nigeria has been captured by such locally assembled Chinese phones beating competition from Samsung and Apple largely because they are cheap and bring in new features rapidly and in multiple variants. Chinese assembly factories take root globally, even in countries like India where they are involved in hacking and spreading malware. This occurs largely due to cheap phones, political corruption and the promise of low-paid jobs by populist politicians to the voters. They also receive cash incentives to re-export from countries like India or Nigeria. This helps China hide the products' origin because, under the World Trade Organization (WTO) Treaty, they would qualify as products exported from India or Nigeria.

It is not only mobile phones but everything from textiles to agricultural machinery, electrical equipment and packaged food that China exports worldwide to Europe and the US, billed under similar re-export schemes. Of the $1.3 trillion Chinese exports of smartphones, computers, telecoms, electrical machinery and manufactured goods, almost one-third goes to countries for re-export. This is all enabled through a huge network of artificial intelligence (AI)-driven market intelligence that places products made in China, in Chinese factories elsewhere or through Chinese joint ventures in markets worldwide to the top demand centers.

Geoffrey Garrett, a former dean of Wharton School, explains the concept beautifully in an article in the *Wharton Magazine* entitled "The 'Trade War' is Really About the Future of Innovation." He rightly observes that a digital trade war was being mounted quietly, and the digital economy was largely immune to traditional trade sanctions.

> "Though the US is far ahead in developing technologies, China's ability to adopt and adapt American technology at a massive scale at warp speed is unbelievable. If the definition of innovation is turning ideas into outcomes, China is already an innovation economy."
>
> Geoffrey Garrett

He points out that the US Trade Representative report, based on which the new tariffs were levied under Trump's rule, was titled "China's Acts, Policies, and Practices Related to Technology Transfer, Intellectual Property, and Innovation." It had nothing to do with steel or soy or the protection of manufacturing or agricultural jobs in America. The WTO is long dead and buried because neither the US nor China is ready to accept its rulings in their own country. However, both nations threaten others with WTO provisions. If China made the WTO toothless with digital manipulation, Donald Trump put the final nail in the coffin of the WTO when he invoked the provision of Section 301 of the 1974 US Trade Act. It allowed the president to take any actions he saw fit against "acts, policies or practices that are unreasonable or discriminatory and that burden or restrict US Commerce."

Virus Wars and Digital Propulsion

We have seen how Covid-19 affected the economy in 2020 but not how it could have been used to disrupt and subjugate economic activity. Perhaps a deep dive is worthwhile. First, let's take a look at viral diseases that have plagued humans and animals for centuries. Four types of diseases have been controlled or eliminated, such as smallpox (which killed over 300 million people worldwide), poliomyelitis (which affected millions of children globally), yellow fever (which raged across the Americas), and measles (which wreaked havoc largely in Asia and Africa). Half a dozen others, including HIV, Ebola, hantavirus, Covid-19, Zika, dengue, swine, bird, and horse flu, have not been fully controlled. Virology and genome research are some of the hottest topics today in the world's top universities. The debate about biological wars started after the spread of the severe acute respiratory syndrome or SARS virus, which had been researched for over a decade at the Wuhan virology lab. Although without evidence, many still believe that the Covid-19 pandemic was a premeditated attack by China on the Western economies for economic gain. China itself is paranoid about being on the receiving end of such attacks, and until the end of 2022, followed a hard-line lockdown policy to guard itself against them.

The virus research prompted a hard look at synthetic biology that may soon transform how we grow crops, what we eat, and how we produce nutrients, clothing and medicine. Rapid advances in genetic engineering and synthetic biology have brought about new-generation biological agents that could be used for the unprecedented benefit or harm of humanity. There are two dozen conventional biological agents—including anthrax, Ebola, and typhus in addition to an unknown number of genetically engineered agents.

Stanford biophysicist Steven Block believes that "black biology" today could be genetically produced and used for terror. He says "genetic maps of deadly viruses, bacteria and other microorganisms already are widely available in the public domain. Legitimate researchers are now in the process of mapping the genomes of more than 100 other microbes. Where are the biological scientists willing to go on the record about bio-weapons?"— warning that bioterrorism could be the weapon of the next decade. This was because so much critical research, which should have been confidential and in classified documents, is now in the public domain. The internet has given wings to virus wars.

Terrorists use terror to espouse their cause and ideology. Often they do not even know the people they kill. This is because they don't kill people because they hate them as individuals but rather because they hate their community or ideology. Terror attacks are planned publicity events. They aim to commit criminal acts of violence that spread fear, apprehension and dread among the general public. The internet facilitates the rapid propulsion of distress news and chaos classified as "breaking news." Hence, terrorists often search for soft targets in a population unprepared for such attacks. The easy availability of synthetic biology and genetic engineering research enables disgruntled microbiologists today, using very little capital and infrastructure, to secretly and rapidly attack food, water supply and healthcare chains. A terror unit could distribute this information digitally and set up lone-wolf researchers in enemy nations to execute attacks from within.

Energy Wars and Digital Blackouts

The Ukraine conflict resulted from a three-decade game of thrones following the dismantling of the Soviet Union. The Soviet Union collapsed due to a crumbling economy and the immense cost of maintaining arms parity with the US. The new Russian leadership focused on infrastructure development and building the economy with special emphasis on tapping its virtually unlimited oil and gas resources. After the Cold War ended, Russia developed strong ties with Germany, France and several EU nations that began to depend on cheap gas and oil supplies from the East.

The €4 billion financing of the Nord Stream 1 pipeline by Gazprom and EU stakeholders was largely undertaken by 26 international banks to supply gas from Russia to Germany via a 1,500 km pipeline under the Baltic Sea. Operating since 2011, it provided German users with low-cost Russian gas. This success was followed by Nord Stream 2, scheduled to go on stream when the Ukraine conflict broke out. Because the Western Block hit Russia with economic sanctions, Russia closed its pipelines for natural gas just before Europe's winter set in. This caused energy prices to soar across Europe in 2022. OPEC did not help and refused to increase oil and gas supplies.

Meanwhile, Russia diverted large parts of its supplies to the large eastern economies, including China and India. It has constructed a 3,000 km gas pipeline from Siberia to Shanghai, supplying Beijing, and several other provinces in Eastern China, which started trial runs in October 2022. However, you would be mistaken if you thought Russia would hitch itself to a one-horse pony. Talks were underway with Turkey to make it into a gas hub using piped gas from Russia and the Arab nations to create an OPEC plus consortium. EU nations have also been proactive. They have filled up their tanks to ensure they are not left cold and dry during the winter. So, the energy wars will continue for the next decade with two separate supply chains feeding the Western and the developing and communist blocks. These blocks and many other neutral nations will also be drawing from OPEC oil supplies. Besides maneuvering oil and gas supplies, digital attacks on energy producers are being mounted in this all-out energy war.

The cyberattacks on German wind turbine makers Enercon and Nordex and their satellite control systems soon after the Ukraine invasion were possibly the first all-out attempts to disrupt the energy services in an European nation as a threat and a warning to stop their support to Ukraine. The Centre of Strategic and International Studies reported a series of cyberattacks on other European energy infrastructure by Russia-based hacker groups in July and August 2022. It started with a DDoS attack on a Lithuanian state-owned energy provider by Killnet, a Russian hacker group, followed by attacks on Greece's natural gas distributor that caused a complete systems outage and service disruption. This was followed by an attack on Ukraine's energy provider to force them to hand over the operation of nuclear installations to Russia. In August 2022, Russian hackers breached the servers of an Italian energy provider GSE, suspending access to its website for 1 week. However, it is not only Russian hackers who are involved in this cyber war on digital assets of its European adversaries.

Soon after the clash between Indian and Chinese troops in the Himalayan valley at Galwan in Ladakh, in June 2020, 24 of the 101 servers of the J&K Power Board were hacked, and their data was deleted by Chinese hackers. According to the *NYT*, about a dozen Indian power assets were attacked by the Chinese state-backed hacker group Red Echo, including the Load Dispatch centers in Delhi and Telangana and the northeastern, eastern and western grids. Recorded Future, a Somerville, Massachusetts based internet security researcher says, "Chinese malware was flowing into the control systems that manage electric supply across India and even closed down the Mumbai metro and the stock market while power supply was disrupted for 20 million households."

The attack on electricity distribution centers across India was carried out to force Indian troops to back off from the Line of Control at Galwan. Thus, energy wars of the future will always have a digital angle as electricity blackouts lead to economic losses and demonstrate the loss of control by the state to the powerful aggressor.

Currency Wars and Confronting the Dollar Digitally

As Russia invaded Ukraine, the Western Block slapped sanctions on Russia, hoping to isolate and force it to retreat. However, Russia had been preparing for this since it took over Crimea. Some sanctions were first applied when Russia invaded southeastern Ukraine in 2014 and effectively took control of the Baltic Sea operations. Soon after, Russia started its currency exchange system that today permits it to trade with the banks of nearly 70 nations, which does not use the Society for Worldwide Interbank Financial Trade (SWIFT) mechanism. This is its homegrown System for the Transfer of Financial Messages (STFM). In September 2022, Russia joined the Chinese Cross-Border Interbank Payment System (CIPS), adding another 100-plus nations to its trading list. In addition, many of its longtime trading partners, like India, the United Arab Emirates, Saudi Arabia and Israel, refused to join the US sanctions and continued to trade with Russia.

The US was aware that sanctions would have a limited effect on Russia. Therefore, they put together a Plan B to ensure its supply chain was intact and Russia and its supporters were hurt. Consumer prices had been rising for more 1 year following the Covid-19 pandemic, and inflation in the US had reached 8% even before the Russian invasion of Ukraine when interest rates remained close to zero. However, after the war commenced, US interest rates started climbing and reached 3.25% in the following 6 months, the highest since 2009. This surprise move was reportedly made to curb rising inflation. Still, many analysts feel that the Federal Reserve's continual interest rate hike was an "investment pullback" decision by the US that would hurt the liquidity of global supply chains, which drew their economic strength from the $6.5 trillion American investment made annually worldwide.

The interest rate rise ensured investment returned from emerging economies to America and the sharp increase in the greenback, says the East Asia Forum, an Australia-based public policy forum, "Thirty-eight emerging economies are now in danger of a debt crisis or are currently experiencing one. At least 25 developing economies spend over 20 percent of government income on servicing foreign public debt."

However, the policy meant that Americans could buy more imported goods for the money spent, reducing their cost of living. With arms sales increasing due to war clouds gathering in Europe and the Asia Pacific region, the US economy had the inherent economic muscle to ensure higher consumer goods imports from a position of strength. Besides arm suppliers, the US oil companies were making huge profits. A strong US dollar and investment that flowed back to the US hurt Russia and China. They helped build confidence among Americans that the US was the only economic superpower still controlling global investment policies. As a result, other currencies continued to slide, from the yen (JPY) to the rupee (INR), the yuan (CNY) to the euro (€), as the central banks in various nations pumped in billions to protect their local currency from volatility. The dollar's hegemony has put most nations' currencies on the back foot, including the British pound and euro, and it has no challenger in the near future. Only a stable, internationally accepted digital currency could reduce its impact in the long run, and currently, that looks unlikely.

It is important to mention that many nations, including China, Japan, India and the US, plan to launch their digital currencies by 2025 "Many countries around the world, including China, are wary of US financial sanctions," says G. Bin Zhao, Senior Economist at PwC China. "This provides a historic window for China to promote yuan internationalization as the US weaponizes the dollar," he says, adding that the e-CNY provides a shortcut. The US sanctions against Russia have forced several such shortcuts. However, they are all bilateral, and Russia's trade with China, India and the Gulf states is largely in multiple local currencies.

China wants to create an alternative internationally accepted digital currency and have the first-mover advantage as the USD and the euro are still more than 2 years away from their digitized avatar. It will be the secure currency for Russia, Iran, North Korea and several others facing international sanctions from US and its multiple trading partners. Also it will be easily accessible to the remote geographies of Africa and South America, where no banks can use SWIFT codes or access the USD or the euro. However, China's record of regular devaluations to boost exports and continued currency manipulations has led to a loss of trust, a reason why it may not be easily accepted.

Supply Chain Wars and Hacking Disruptions

Today, supply chain disruptions go far beyond oil and gas. They start from food grains as Russia and Ukraine supply nearly one-third of the world's wheat, barley, corn and soy and two-thirds of its sunflower oil. The first 6 months of the Ukraine war saw 20 million tons of wheat landlocked in Europe's breadbasket as the Russian Navy blockaded and bombarded the Black Sea ports. Hundreds of grain silos were destroyed in the southeastern parts of Ukraine. After a belated treaty in Turkey, exports were allowed but halted soon after. As a result, the price of wheat, barley and vegetable oils jumped by over 40% globally, and those of sugar, milk, meat and fish rose by double digits. Russia and the West disrupted global supply chains in an all-out war. The Russian fertilizer supply was also severely hit due to Western sanctions and the withdrawal of SWIFT payments for Russian exporters. Russia is a major supplier of potassium and phosphate used to make NPK and DAP fertilizers. It also produces 10% of the ammonia needed to produce urea. The prices of nutrients shot up globally with supply disruption and reduced fertilizer consumption. That will hit 2023's agricultural output and possibly beyond. A 2022 Cambridge University report says that automatic crop sprayers, drones employed for pesticide and fumigation services, robotic harvesters, and AI-driven automated farm equipment could easily be hacked to disrupt food chains and farm services.

However, not only the food and fertilizer supply chains were hit hard. Basic metal, automobile and semiconductor supply chains were also crippled. Neon gas, a by-product of steel production in Ukraine, was first hit when Russia captured Crimea in 2014. However, the more recent attack by Russia on the plants of Ingas and Cryoin, two of the world's largest facilities for semiconductor-grade neon (critical for lasers used to make chips), has hit semiconductor production globally. The sanctions on trade with Russia also created a major crisis in the supply of palladium, nickel, copper, aluminum and steel that will directly hurt automobile and semiconductor production, along with many other industries.

According to a Forbes report, Sid Snitkin, a VP of ARC Advisory Group, says that the supply chain of software is even more vulnerable.

> "When I was younger, I did programming. Every line of code for an application would be written by me or a colleague. Now an application is written by folks that grab a piece of code from here or a piece from there. Hackers attack small suppliers. They embed malware in the code. Then when an IT professional gets a message to update that part of the software, the software is contaminated. It is almost impossible to check whether all these small pieces of code are clean."
>
> Sid Snitkin

A 2018 CNBC report pointed out that an iPhone from the US software giant Apple was assembled in the plant of the Taiwanese manufacturer Foxconn in Zhengzhou, China, and had raw materials and components from 43 nations. Today, we know that the US and Taiwan are at loggerheads with China, but with Turkey, Israel, the UK, Ukraine, Russia, Japan and South Korea being part of the global team, each has its agenda in global geopolitics, doctoring could be multidimensional. Any nation or group of compromised employees could embed malware in the hardware of chips or components being built by them. These could be undetected in the assemblies at the time of testing and could be activated 2 years later. Later in this chapter, we will explain how this fear of contaminated hardware and software is real. How it is causing the digital meltdown and could ultimately create a fractured supply chain with unprecedented digital waste worldwide.

A FRACTURED WORLD AND DIGITAL MELTDOWNS

As the US–China digital and trade war escalated, the trust deficit between both nations grew. In May 2022, Bloomberg reported that the Chinese government had instructed its central agencies to replace 50 million personal computers of foreign origin supplied to the government by 2024. The plan was to eliminate using critical digital equipment from overseas to operate its most sensitive plants. Domestic PC maker Lenovo supplies around 41.8% of China's personal computers, followed by Dell at 12.5%, HP at 9.2%, Asus at 5.5% and Acer at 5.2%. China's PC shipments increased by 10% in 2021 to 57 million units. China has always had a policy of using home-made digital products, such as personal computers, phones, servers, and network equipment, wherever possible; however, the current demand is believed to be the outcome of the Chinese government's increasing concerns about information security and faith in foreign hardware. The decision will benefit Chinese computer and server manufacturers Lenovo, Huawei, BOE Technology, Inspur, Kingsoft, Quanta Shanghai, Standard Software, and others.

However, under the new rules, certain agencies could continue to buy foreign equipment and technology, especially those that China does not manufacture. That is where the US trade laws are becoming tighter, and export restrictions are being implemented. Semiconductors power most digital equipment. They are a key area of US dominance, with Intel, Qualcomm, Nvidia and AMD holding the cards. The chip industry leaders are largely from the US, Taiwan, Japan and South Korea. Huawei is the only Chinese semiconductor maker among the top ten, and they still do not have the technology for high-end chips.

In the first week of October 2022, the Biden administration placed further restrictions on exporting high-tech equipment to China, including those having advanced computing, supercomputing and semiconductor capabilities. The interim rule required new licenses when exporting certain chips and components. It served notice to US citizens who support the development or production of integrated circuits at Chinese semiconductor fabrication facilities. Soon after, the Dutch chipmaker ASML, one of the world's high-tech semiconductor toolmakers, told US employees to stop conducting business with Chinese customers. The Dutch firm is the only manufacturer of extreme ultraviolet lithographic machines used by the most advanced chip makers in the world. The order restricting US citizens from supporting Chinese chipmakers caused all semiconductor scrips like SMIC, NAURA and Hua Hong Semiconductors to plunge by 10% on the Shanghai Stock Exchange. The decision could have an immense impact because most semiconductor designers who work in China are reportedly US citizens.

The digital meltdown is due to voluntary replacement of equipment as well as cyberwars. Both will continue to grow. China will stop sourcing digital equipment from the US voluntarily or because it is not permitted by the US administration, and the reverse will also happen. Semiconductors are key when producing smartphones, computers, automobiles, industrial equipment, robots, aircraft, satellites, missiles and all equipment that needs technology. The US is the world leader in designing and developing semiconductors; however, it only manufactures 10% of the semiconductors at home today. The manufacturing heavyweights are Taiwanese chip makers TSMC and Media Tek, Samsung of Korea and the biggest manufacturing hub is in mainland China. Around 30% of the world's semiconductor chips are produced in China, and Covid-19 lockdowns have hammered the global supply chain. In addition, because production units cannot move quickly, the world will continue to depend on Chinese manufacturing in the near future to avoid price shocks despite the threat of digital confrontations.

We are already witnessing price volatility as China's semiconductor output dropped by 4.2% in the first quarter of 2022. Chip production in China is expected to be 3% lower than the production of 2021, and a 9% increase in global demand is expected. China imports $150 billion of semiconductors annually and is heavily dependent on global suppliers. However, the global supply chain heavily depends on China's output for almost all manufactured products. The supply and demand gap has grown to more than 10%, leading to a sharp price increase. The effect of the Biden administration's ban on the exports of high-tech CPUs, GPUs, semiconductors, electronic design automation software and AI-driven units to China will result in another 10% shortfall.

The US plan is to limit China's supercomputer and semiconductor manufacturing advances; so that it will not gain military superiority or facilitate the Russian arms industry acquiring advanced semiconductors. However, China could hit back in more ways than one. China is expected to retaliate by restricting the REE supply chain to the semiconductor industry, which may hurt US production capabilities as China controls more than three-quarters of the global rare earth production and processing market. Before the 1980s, the US used to be a world leader in the extracting and processing REE, but they willingly conceded the position to China due to environmental concerns.

Over the past two decades, China has mined and processed a dozen REEs like neodymium, lanthanum, didymium, cerium, gallium, erbium, indium, tantalum and many others. The difficult task of mining, extracting and washing is followed by extremely complex intermediate processing centers for benefaction and separation. This infrastructure of chemical processing units for 17 REEs worth billions of US dollars has been developed by China. The metallurgic process is so complicated that it needs years to achieve an industry acceptance level. So, any quick movement of production facilities is highly unlikely. REEs are critical to mobile phones, supercomputers, electric vehicles, renewable energy, catalysts, permanent magnets, and aircraft and missile systems. If China slows down the supply of REEs to the US or global markets, our fractured world could see a 20% shortage of chips in the short term unless there is massive investment in fresh mining projects or we quickly move to recycle. Only new mining and recycling could enhance the supply of REEs and PMGs and neutralize China's stranglehold on the global raw material supply chain of semiconductors.

DIGITAL WARS MAY ADD TO DIGITAL MELTDOWNS

Apart from ruptures in the supply chain, an all-out digital war looks probable and could cause a massive digital meltdown. Digital wars are not new. They have been happening on a limited basis since the 1970s. Although Russia has attacked Poland, Latvia and Lithuania before, Ukraine has long been known as the favored playground of Russian hackers. This is where they try out and perfect new cyberattack strategies and techniques. The BlackEnergy malware, introduced in 2007, disrupted and shut out 80,000 consumers from their electricity supply for several hours in Ukraine in 2015. A year later, another Russian malware, Industroyer, caused a blackout in many parts of Kyiv, followed by shorter-duration attacks across several power stations. Petya and NotPetya, the malware infecting popular accounting software used in Ukraine and Europe from 2017 to 2021, inflicted damage estimated to cost around $10 billion on thousands of computer systems that had to be replaced.

The tests for all-out digital warfare in Ukraine were completed well before the February 2022 invasion. The military infrastructure and communication networks were identified and sabotaged; therefore, Ukraine's defense installations were left without information or logistics support. This was followed by the all-out attack on Viasat users across Europe just

1 day before the Russian invasion of Ukraine, which disrupted commercial and news networks. Microsoft President Brad Smith says, "the cyber aspects of the current war extend far beyond Ukraine and reflect the unique nature of cyberspace." According to Microsoft, Russian hackers attacked 128 organizations in 42 countries outside Ukraine. They included Denmark, Finland, Norway and Sweden, and the US and Eastern European nations like Poland, Lithuania and Latvia. So, whereas the physical war was local and limited to Ukraine, the digital war was global against all supporters of Ukraine. However, the attacks were not only by Russian cyber terrorists or their supporters. Russia claimed that it was attacked multiple times by European and US hacker activists, and the attacks came from varied global locations.

Various players have been assigned different roles in cyber warfare since the 1990s. They start with the "information warfare team" that includes media houses, PR agencies, social activists, actors and performers, social media influencers and trolls followed by the spin doctors and techies who propagate fake news and deep fakes. Finally, hubs of cyber attackers in various global locations possess different skills. They work in teams and launch coordinated DDoS attacks that are impossible to track and stop. Not all are anonymous guerrilla attacks. There are frontal attacks on national assets made by nations that want to stamp their unilateral dominance and create panic and chaos. In February 2022, Russia launched cyberattacks across Europe, warning all NATO allies against sending arms to Ukraine. Google's Threat Analysis Group reported that they were supported by the Chinese hackers Mustang Panda, who carried out phishing attacks using malicious attached files with names such as "Situation at the EU borders with Ukraine.zip."

However, it is not Russia that US defense analyst Dr. Andrew Erickson fears most in the case of an all-out war in the digital space that may happen this decade. The real danger comes from China, which has been preparing for "informationist warfare" since 2015. This concept was proposed in 2004 and updated in 2019 by a Defense White Paper released by China's Central Military Commission and is now being perfected for field execution under President Xi Jinping. "Informationized warfare" has six domains, including three new: (1) cyber; (2) space; (3) electromagnetics, and three traditional: (4) land; (5) air; and (6) water. The key idea of "informationized warfare" is to destroy the communications network of the enemy before attacking them with conventional weapons.

Cyber, space, satellite and electronic defense need an advanced version of weapons management platforms to engage in defensive and manage offensive counterattacks. China Maritime Studies Institute CMSI, a think tank of the US Naval War College, highlights China's move toward "intelligentized warfare," focusing on AI's full-spectrum exploitation. This will include a weapons platform supporting land, air, and seaborne missiles, bots, autonomous weapons and coordinated applications through AI- backed by big data from cloud servers.

According to the CMSI, this multiple theater warfare will be fully operational to give China "great power status" by 2049. There is a growing trend toward conducting warfare with long-range precision, intelligent, stealthy, unmanned weaponry, and equipment primarily driven by AI and big data. Although, this would be prohibitively expensive. However, we need to understand that such defense white papers are, at times, so ambitious that they rarely translate into reality. There can be no better proof of such failures than Ronald Reagan's now-abandoned Strategic Defense Initiative, popularly known as Star Wars. What is important to understand is that stealth and technology will be used in tomorrow's wars, and the key weaponization will be through microchips or semiconductors.

There is some initial evidence of what is already being achieved by stealth. In November 2016, news reports from a British daily newspaper alleged that the breakdown of the $4.4 billion high-tech 610-ft navy destroyer USS Zumwalt in the Panama Canal on 16 November was due to a failure in its propulsion system, allegedly engineered by a faulty Chinese semiconductor. The British Navy's state-of-the-art HMS Duncan, a sophisticated Type 45 Air Defense Destroyer equipped with Harpoon missiles, had also developed the same propulsion failure several times. In addition, it stalled during NATO maritime war games due to faulty chips provided by the same supplier. The US Navy did not confirm the reports of sabotage, because it could never be fully determined whether Chinese chips were faulty by design or simply due to defective low-quality wiring that would have failed anyway due to a surge in electromagnetic pulse waves.

In October 2018, Bloomberg reported that Chinese hackers used a tiny chip similar to a pencil tip to infiltrate the motherboards and servers of 30 US companies, including Apple and Amazon. Supplied to Super Micro Computers, a trusted US hardware supplier in California, the Chinese microchips were built to give unrestricted access to data from the US servers to the People's Liberation Army. They could steal data, alter operations and disrupt the US supply chain.

Such intrusions led the US Congress to introduce the Chips and Science Act in August 2022. They pushed a $52.7 billion investment package in domestic semiconductor and technology manufacturing that aimed to fulfill three main objectives. First, reduce the likelihood that a global semiconductor shortage would disrupt the US supply chain. Second, ensure that its semiconductor and STEM research and production facilities are boosted and create domestic jobs. Third, protect semiconductors and key science and technologies from being sabotaged during manufacturing or their application in the real world. This would set the stage for many world nations to revisit their semiconductor and technology supply chains.

There are three prime reasons why digital waste recycling is the next technological milestone. We have studied the shortages in semiconductors and REEs and the high cost of ramping up supplies from the existing suppliers, especially as China controls three-quarters of the REE and the PGM supply chain. We are fast reaching a point where recycling digital waste would perhaps be easier than mining PGM or REEs anew. The US would have to invest trillions of US dollars in mining, processing and manufacturing to replace the Chinese supply chain.

It is becoming clear that the US and China would find it unsafe to use semiconductors that were made outside its jurisdiction for military, communication, healthcare or key supply chain operations. They have started to melt down parts of their digital supply chains and rebuild them with in-house products or those made by their trusted allies. This meltdown would add to the existing digital waste. The third source of high digital waste would be in the case of continued digital wars worldwide. This is already happening and could easily grow in this decade of uncertainty with the global fault lines expanding. The physical wars are happening today in Europe and Asia. China and Russia both realize that the only way to hurt the geographically distant US is through cyberattacks. So the intensity of cyberattacks on US assets is increasing and is the third cause that may lead to the rise of digital waste. In the next chapter of this book, we will explore the technology behind waste recycling and how industries and science laboratories worldwide have started to plant the green shoots of a circular economy.

Chapter 13

The Circular Economy

Recycling the Meltdown

These are difficult times in a decade of uncertainty. Human resilience in difficult times has often brought about innovative responses to challenges. We can already see deep concern among the younger generation about how we are using our planet's resources and managing resources and waste. However, recycling is no longer only a social concern but also a viable and profitable business proposition. This is because of supply chain shortages. The shortage of rare earth elements (REE), platinum group metals (PGM), semiconductors and components will perhaps necessitate recycling waste—particularly digital waste—to attain higher productivity in a competitive scenario. We are seeing quite a few green shoots of change ushering in a circular economy— one that recycles waste and consumes few new resources. Industries and science labs are bringing about the efficient management and recycling of waste on a scalable level. Although few, they are already reducing the environmental pollution. We consider this a unique opportunity for every industry to manage 'resources' efficiently. According to Dr. Veena Sahajwalla, a contemporary thinker, scientist and engineer at the University of New South Wales Australia (UNSW), "everything you throw away is a resource."

The opportunity is colossal since humans are throwing away 2 billion tons of municipal solid waste each year, of which 400 million tons is hazardous. Apart from municipal solid waste, we have food, biodegradable, industrial, plastic, commercial, digital, radioactive, chemical, and sewage waste. One-third of the total solid waste is generated by 16% of the world's population in high-income nations. According to the World Bank, recycling is low in developed nations, and 93% of municipal waste is dumped in low-income countries and 2% in high-income economies.

However, the economics of waste management changed when China, which had been importing large amounts of waste to recycle, banned the import of many types of imported municipal and plastic waste in 2017. This meant nations would be forced to manage their waste independently and invest in recycling. Soon after, the trade war between the US and China and the Russia–Ukraine war led to severe supply chain shortages.

DOI: 10.1201/9781003409557-17

Dumping waste was no longer profitable if you were a consumer economy. New mining and processing were expensive and time-consuming as supply chain shortages loomed. So, recycling might get a fresh look from investors looking for profits. That could happen in the near future as environmentally friendly recycling is just getting going. It is a science that has been a great business for centuries, but one that has never been so clean and green and has never been fully exploited.

RECYCLING WASTE, AN AGE-OLD BUSINESS

The origin of recycling waste or metal scrap goes back once again to ancient Egypt over 3,000 years ago, when the tombs of pharaohs that overflowed with gold, ivory and priceless jewelry were periodically robbed. Grave robbers existed in all levels of society, from royalty to priests, nobles to serfs. There was a high price to pay if they were caught carrying this out because if caught, the tomb robbers would be executed. The 108 ft.-high Colossus of Rhodes, a monumental statue depicting the Greek sun god Helios, was reportedly built in 280 BCE from metal scrap. It was built after the Island of Rhodes had successfully thwarted a year-long attack by a powerful Macedonian king. The statue, one of the seven wonders of the ancient world, survived for more than half a century before it collapsed during an earthquake in 226 BCE.

When Alexander the Great invaded Egypt in the third century, the Greek philosophers combined their experience with Egyptian science that explored the mysteries of nature. It was initially named Khemia in Greek before being named Al Khemia or Alchemy. Cleopatra, the queen of Alexandria, was one of the famous female alchemists of the third century, along with Mary the Jewess. Both are said to have discovered several of the distillation, sublimation and filtration processes required for metal formation, including creating the alembic used for fermentation. The Europeans and Arabs developed the science of alchemy after that. The Europeans perfected the distillation process to make acids and alcohol, and the Arabs used science to make perfumes. Alchemy also had two basic, although far-fetched, objectives: (1) to turn base metals into gold using the proverbial touchstone; and (2) to create a magic potion for immortality called the elixir of life. The alchemists were searching for the touchstone— possibly a very powerful electromagnet that would rearrange the atomic structure of base metals and turn them into gold. They were also looking for a brew that would ensure the cells of the human body did not die but were rejuvenated.

The science of metallurgy and medicine during that period and even earlier was also practiced in India and China independently. A series of monolithic columns of Mauryan Emperor Ashoka weighing 50 tons each and measuring around 50 ft. high were erected at Buddhist monasteries across the Indian subcontinent during his reign from 268 BCE to 232 BCE. Approximately 20 of these intricately carved pillars, built with an unknown metal alloy that does not decay or rust, can still be found with written edicts of dharma (citizens' duties) of the Mauryan empire engraved in Brahmi script. In medicine, the Indian and Chinese focused on plants, minerals, and inner and outer elixir traditions. They used the well-developed medicinal science of "Ayurveda" and the "Huangdi neijing" for cures based on herbal and metaphysical healing. Although they espoused youthful living, they were not looking for the magic potions of immortality associated with the early alchemists of Europe. Both were focused on using natural herbs as medicine and not on the chemical-based formulations that created magical new products.

During the seventeenth century, Henning Brand, the German alchemist, started distilling the urine of beer drinkers (which had a distinctive golden tinge), thinking that he could find gold dust in urine. After distilling over 5,000 liters of urine, he obtained a white luminescent flammable powder that was phosphorus. This was later used to make matchsticks, a chemical fertilizer and plant nutrients.

Recycling made headway during the Middle Ages in Europe with the popularity of bronze and brass, which were copper alloys but much cheaper. Bronze casting received a boost from the seventh to twelfth centuries from Charlemagne and other rulers who encouraged building monumental bronze statues, portals, church bells, ornamental pedestals and decorative doors. Casting factories bought copper scrap from households and turned it into valuable, ornate castings that can still be seen in cathedrals and castles today.

The Jews, traditionally savers, started the scrap trading business in America. The Jewish Museum of Maryland traces the origin of scrapyards in the US some 200 years ago. It displays exhibits of poor immigrants from the south and east of Europe with little capital and knowledge of English buying and reselling household scrap using push carts or sacks. They set up small businesses in far-flung towns, ports and transportation hubs and started recycling metal scrap and waste cloth. By 1920, there were 150,000 scrap dealers in the US, and many had become millionaires owning large foundries and a fleet of trucks.

Today's popular fashion of faded and ripped jeans draws inspiration from old clothes handed down from one buyer to another at street-side junk sales across America. Recycling was a necessity long before it became a fashion. In the 1940s popular jazz music icon Fats Waller recorded one of the first sheet music lyrics, "Get some cash for your trash", to pitch for the reuse of waste in a society that was fast embracing a "buy more, throw more" culture. The History Channel TV shows *American Pickers*, *Forged in Fire* and *Lost in Transmission* are classics showing real time recycling success by some of the most tireless entrepreneurs.

Junk sales are still very popular across India, and you can find the scrap dealer or "Kabadiwala" visiting homes every weekend. Newspapers selling at INR 10/kg allow you to recover one-quarter of your buying price from junk sales. Plastics, glass, steel utensils, rubber, umbrellas, calculators, books, mobiles and laptops all find their way to the markets through the "Kabadiwala." The recycling market is big because a lot of poor people live in populous nations. The rich man's scrap is usually the poor man's prize. The "Kabadiwala" is the canny middleman who finds the right buyers for throwaway items and profits from the trade.

BUILDING A MODERN CIRCULAR ECONOMY

Despite the long history of recycling, would the world be able to cope if a massive response were needed following a rapid digital meltdown? That is a situation of rising digital waste that we could quickly reach in the case of a digital war or out of an indigenization drive due to security concerns. Let's turn back to the science labs of the world to learn about the current-day research into toxic electronic waste. The French Alternative Energies Alliance for Research in Circular Economy and Atomic Energy (CEA) and the Singapore CEA Alliance for Research in Circular Economy (SCARCE) of Nanyang Technology University (NTU) Singapore were launched in 2018 with Professors Madhavi Srinivasan and Jean-Christophe P. Gabriel heading their laboratories.

The NTU team had already devised a process to recycle lithium-ion batteries efficiently, producing 1 ton of recycled batteries from 28 ton of waste batteries. This was much cheaper than the mining process, where 750 ton of lithium chloride had to be processed to produce one lithium-ion battery. Surprisingly, the process does not use toxic acids but orange peel, a fully biodegradable fruit extract, for recycling.

> "Current industrial recycling processes of e-waste are energy-intensive and emit harmful pollutants and liquid waste, pointing to an urgent need for eco-friendly methods as the amount of e-waste grows. Our team has demonstrated that it is possible to do so with biodegradable substances."
>
> Professor Madhavi

Managing electronic waste is complicated stuff. This is because there are a large number of components, and they are varied. Recycling automobile, textile or construction waste is much easier. For example, you could get millions of tires, tons of steel sheets, bales of polyester fiber or truckloads of broken glass to recycle separately without too much effort. But, in 1 foot³ of electronic waste, there is a mixture of cables, metals, resistances, capacitors, chips and motherboards— over100 metals, polymers and ceramics that are tedious to segregate and process. The conventional method is to separate, sort, grind the mix and finally separate the polymers or plastics by incineration and then the metals by iterative chemical synthesis. The process is toxic and energy-intensive. On top of this, it is inefficient and time-consuming.

One new way to process e-waste is to dismantle all the components and sort and grind all the e-waste. After that, the composite mixture is dissolved in a solution of nitric acid to form a homogeneous solution, which is sent to the chemistry lab. Then, it is mixed with an organic solvent, like kerosine, in an extraction column, and multiple extractions are carried out to separate, analyze and identify the material. Normally it would take months to complete the hundreds of extractions and processing methods to separate each element.

At the SCARCE lab in NTU, Singapore, they reduced the time and cost of developing new extractions by miniaturizing sample sizes. The processing of microfluidic samples was automated, and because of the microscopic sample size, hundreds of specimens were analyzed in days instead of months. This made sample extraction from mixed wastes much more efficient and nontoxic than the traditional methods of incineration and separation. The idea for such a process dates back to the days of alchemy when magic brews and metal alloys were created to make gold and silver out of base metals.

Similarly, Chinese researchers have made huge strides in recycling PGM. They have perfected various methods of hydrometallurgical, biological and physical separation processes for the efficient extraction of PGM from waste catalysts that are hazardous and difficult to process. The waste catalyst from automobile and industrial exhausts is homogenized and pretreated with multiple acids and alkaline reagents. After that, the PGM concentrate and solution are separately processed and purified. Johnson Matthey, a leading British player in automotive catalysts and fuel cells, started a plant in Jiangsu Province, China, in October 2022 to recycle the PGM content from membrane electrode assemblies (MEA). MEA are a key component in an automotive fuel cell from Unilia, a Canadian fuel cell stack technology provider that collects PGM from transport vehicles. China is the biggest PGM market and a large source of stack emissions—emissions from exhausts. Therefore, it is an ideal place to check out a secondary supply of PGMs that is expected to grow from 3% to 5% annually.

UNSW'S NEW-AGE "WASTE TO RESOURCE"

Modern-day waste management no longer depends on classical sorting, burning and chemical separation processes. The chemistry learned at school today differs from that learned 50 years ago. The old school of learning taught us that the chemical and physical properties of materials defined whether they were metals, polymers, plastics or ceramics. Chemical compositions were unique, and they were responsible for definitive physical properties. For example, metals were hard, ductile, opaque, highly conductive and reflective, and polymers were soft, ductile insulators that were transparent or translucent. Ceramics were equally distinctive, hard but brittle, and insulators. They had specific chemical compositions and physical properties as different as chalk and cheese.

Modern-day science states materials are defined by structural symmetries. This means you don't have to focus on chemical properties but on the electronic structure of a material to understand its behavior. The fundamental building block of all materials is the atom. Atomic interactions result in bonds that define the atom's electronic structure and the properties of materials. They are responsible for the condensed phases of matter such as liquids, glasses, crystals, liquid crystals and quasicrystals that comprise materials and are available in three stages, such as solid, liquid and gas.

Scientists who started studying the structures of materials found many similarities and dissimilarities in the atomic bonding in various materials they looked at. They found imperfections in ideal structures that could be organized to form new materials and uses. They found that silicon oxide could exist as quartz, a heavier crystalline compound and silica, a lighter noncrystalline, amorphous substance, because of different atomic bonding. Thus, it was not the chemical composition of silicon oxide but the electronic structure that defined the physical properties and use of that material. Scientists also started looking at the atomic structure of waste and thinking about how it could be treated as a substitute resource and reduce our carbon footprint. Multiple efforts are being made worldwide; therefore, tackling mountains of electronic waste is no longer just a dream.

One such pioneering thinker and scientist in this field is Dr. Veena Sahajwalla, the daughter of a civil engineer father and a doctor mother from India. Born and brought up in a part of the populous Mumbai, where many small-scale industries were located, and a lot of scrap, waste and repairing occurred, she was fascinated as a young adult by the recycling in those crowded by-lanes.

"I would walk past these factories day-in and day-out and see all this waste, and I thought: this is what I want to do," says the engineer-turned-scientist. She went on to study metallurgical engineering at IIT Kanpur. She completed her material engineering postgraduate degree in Vancouver, Canada and a doctorate from the University of Michigan, US, before moving to Australia, where she works as the Director of Sustainable Materials at UNSW, Sydney.

During her studies in the US, she started researching the properties of carbon-bearing materials like coal, coke, graphite, plastic and rubber. She attempted to find similarities and dissimilarities in their chemical, physical and atomic structures. Initially, she started injecting polymers from plastic waste, like shampoo and detergent bottles, into the steel-making process. The Japanese industry giant Nippon Steel had already been experimenting with infusing plastic waste and cutting waste tires to boost carbon and hydrogen in coke oven furnaces.

The steel industry was highly energy-intensive and had a very high carbon footprint. Electric arc furnaces needed coke, which had a 97% carbon content. Neither plastic nor rubber had half that carbon content. So, according to the science of the time, waste plastics or rubber could not substitute coke. However, Sahajwalla kept experimenting in the UNSW lab for 3 years and found that shredded rubber tires worked as a partial replacement for coal and coke in electric furnaces.

One Steel, the largest Australian steel maker, was also on the lookout for substitutes for coke. They teamed up with UNSW to use Sahajwalla's patented technology. They started using old rubber tires with the polymer injection technology (PIT) process and prevented 1.6 million rubber tires from going to landfills by 2013. Conventionally, coke is used to heat and produce a slag-like blanket of molten cover over liquid steel to maintain a high temperature for a longer period. The shredded tires used as a coke substitute boosted the slag's volume and foaming properties, improving energy efficiency by 3% and reducing the carbon footprint by one-sixth. It was an extremely environmentally friendly solution, because instead of using freshly-mined coke, it used waste tires from landfills.

In 2015, as a journalist, I had the opportunity to interview Dr. Sahajwalla when she visited India as a speaker at a steel industry conference. Dressed in black jeans and a top with stiletto boots, she looked more like a rock star than a typical scientist with sloppy clothes and heavy glasses. When her presentation began, I realized that she was a gritty shop-floor engineer-cum-scientist who could just make things happen. A hands-on expert who would not only think and recreate matter but could walk through the landfills, pick the waste she wanted to use, grind and weld with aplomb, pass it through a furnace and produce things that even industry veterans could never think up.

Frankly, like most others at the conference, I had never heard of the PIT or green steel that One Steel had produced with UNSW technology for nearly 3 years. The idea that waste tires could replace coke in steel-making in an electric arc furnace seemed pretty bizarre then. India was importing shiploads of coke from Australia, despite producing around 8% of the world's automobile tires, almost all of which went to landfills after use. The attendees' curiosity focused on the cost of the furnace and the technology and whether it would be feasible for India.

I was surprised when Dr. Sahajwalla said that no special furnace was needed and that the technology was affordable and could be licensed. She explained how she began experimenting with rubbish and how waste needed to be treated as a resource.

"Old tires are not the only things you can use in a car. Batteries, switchboards, air conditioners, starter motors, glove compartments, dashboards, seats, foam, glass, aluminum, and steel are all recyclable. But then again, sorting and segregation are both very time-consuming and expensive.

But then it is not only the rubber from the landfills that could help produce steel. Everything you throw away is a resource."

Dr. Sahajwalla

For the next 10 min, she was almost speaking aloud to herself, excitedly explaining things that I did not understand then but had the good sense to record on my mobile phone.

"For example, you can extract metal out of a packet of potato chips, you can make your house or a road from broken glass, you can extract copper, tin, nickel, or lithium from your mobile phone or laptop, you can create smart filaments for 3D printing out of plastic waste. We have to just think of things at an elemental level and find out how to reduce finished and used products back to the elements they were originally made of. That way we would not have to mine for new resources – and every piece of garbage would be a priceless resource and even the scrap dealer, *Kabadiwala* would be able to earn a decent living."

Dr. Sahajwalla

Was this Harry Potter speaking?

It took me 5 years and a lot of reading to understand what she said in those few minutes that day. At that time, UNSW had only produced green steel. As the years passed, more of her innovations came to light. Five years later, UNSW licensed the technology to make floor tiles using a combination of broken glass and used garments to Mirvac, a construction industry giant in Australia. "We have never seen anything like what Veena has been doing," Mirvac CEO and managing director Susan Lloyd-Hurwitz says. "It is really pioneering. We were just blown away." In 2021, Mirvac designed and displayed an apartment entirely built from industrial waste at Sydney Olympic Park. It featured floor and wall tiles, kitchen fittings, lighting fixtures, furniture and artwork, using waste glass and textiles to revolutionize sustainable home construction and transform waste into a valuable resource.

However, Sahajwalla was not satisfied with licensing her technology to industry giants. UNSW is now building small micro factories to achieve waste recycling locally across Australia and the rest of the world.

"The micro factories can use e-waste like computer circuit boards to make metal alloys such as copper and tin, while glass and plastic from e-devices can be converted into micro materials used in industrial-grade ceramics and plastic filaments for 3D printing. Our e-waste (micro-factory) and another under development for other consumer waste types offer a cost-effective solution to one of the greatest environmental challenges of our age, while delivering new job opportunities to our cities but importantly to our rural and regional areas, too."

Dr. Sahajwalla

USING PLASTIC WASTE AS A RESOURCE

One of the largest and most complex sources of modern waste is plastic. Some 150 years ago, the growing popularity of billiards caused the mass slaughter of Asian elephants for ivory, which provided the best billiard balls. So, a New York firm offered $10,000 to anyone who could find an alternative material. That material was plastic, discovered by John Wesley Hyatt in 1869. When plastic arrived, advertisement billboards declared it a savior of humankind, because it was a substitute for ivory, wood, cloth, metal and even glass in many applications. This would prevent the consumption of natural products, like wood, cotton and animal skin, and avoid great environmental damage. However, things changed rapidly in the next 100 years, with the extensive use of plastics leading to unimaginably high levels of plastic production and substantially lower costs. During the Second World War, plastic production in the US rose by 300% and kept rising, even after the war. Rachel Carson's 1962 book *Silent Spring* first exposed the dangers of chemical pesticides. Soon, people started witnessing the explosion of plastic waste as consumers went into a "buy more, throw more" spree where everything was disposable. The products were mostly packaged with or made from plastic. More studies condemning the irresponsible use of plastic arrived, but the use of plastic did not slow down.

In total, 9 billion tons of plastic have been produced globally since the 1960s. Of this, 390 million tons were produced in 2021. As the use of plastic has increased, its waste has rapidly and menacingly spread on land and water. Only 10% of plastic is recycled, a little over 20% is incinerated in Waste to Energy (WTE) plants, nearly 30% ends up untreated in landfills, and the remaining 40% is left unaccounted for on streets, in open areas and water bodies worldwide. An estimated 8 million tons of plastic waste enters the ocean every year, adding to the 150 million tons of waste already dumped in the seas. As plastic is not easily biodegradable, the ocean takes from 10 to 20 years to break down plastic bags, 50 years for foam cups and 450 years for plastic bottles.

The only solution to solve the plastic waste menace is to recycle and reuse it. That has been happening recently, although the pace of reuse needs to increase especially in the US which consumes the most. The National Highway Authority in India has successfully laid out 700 km of plastic roads composed of from 6% to 8% of plastic waste and 92% to 94% of bitumen in India since 2018 and tested them for heavy-duty use. Using waste plastic in the wearing course of the flexible pavement increases bonding and is likely to reduce cost and increase the life of the roads. They plan to lay out 100,000 km of plastic-coated roads in the next 5 years in 11 states where trials have been completed. Sibele Cestari is a polymeric materials scientist from Brazil who has been studying waste plastic in the rotomolding process, which is ideal for making large hollow objects in building construction. "Blocks made of 25% recycled plastics have performed extremely well in mechanical tests," she says.

Automated sorting robots that could segregate plastic waste are being developed and tested by Spain, Germany, the US and Japan. In Hong Kong, cost-effective robots clean and segregate trash from waterways quickly and economically.

Asian nations are working on using plastic debris and waste to manufacture cement in furnaces of 1,450°C. A Norwegian project to use waste plastics in the cement industry called Ocean Plastic Turned into an Opportunity in Circular Economy (OPTOCE) is currently underway to explore the use of waste plastic in the lime kilns of the cement industry. "We now have cement factories in China, India, Thailand, Vietnam and Myanmar taking part in the project. All of them are testing the use of plastic as a fuel," says Kåre Helge Karstensen, a senior research scientist who heads the OPTOCE project. Other projects are being discussed to break down waste plastics to the molecular level and use them with coke feed in the cement and steel industries.

WTE IS STILL NOT GREEN AND CLEAN

Although the burning of waste is one of the most popular ways to get rid of mountains of trash, it is inefficient and harmful to health. In total, 80% of municipal waste worldwide goes into landfills or is incinerated. Incinerators are major emitters of carcinogenic pollutants. They also emit tiny carbon particles that could lead to pulmonary disease, decreased lung function, asthma, cancer, heart attacks and premature death. They emit more carbon per megawatt hour of energy produced than gas, oil or coal-fired plants. In addition, they have huge running costs as the garbage brought to the incinerators to burn as fuel has to be bought and shipped daily to the plant under long-term contracts. So, most existing methods of waste incineration are not cost-effective and are pretty harmful to the environment.

A large number of WTE plants in Asia are moving to grate incinerators, where the compressed waste is placed on moving grates mounted on a feed shaft and then burned. However, fluidized bed incinerators, which are much cleaner, are also rising. In these, the waste is fired in a fluidized state, but the process needs a more uniform waste size, making it more complex and expensive to operate. Gasification plants use composite waste, including plastic and solid organic wastes, in a chemical conversion process that produces synthesized gas at a high temperature. Another way of recycling complicated toxic waste, including medical waste, is plasma gasification. Five plasma gasification plants worldwide operate in Wuhan in China, Mitaka in Japan, Pune in India, Tainan in Taiwan and a US Navy super-carrier. This is because costs are currently very high. One alternative that is also used is biomass gasification technology with syngas cleaning. This method uses advanced wet and dry electrostatic precipitation to convert waste into clean energy.

China and Japan are the Asian leaders in WTE plants, with more than 500 WTE plants each producing over10 gigawatts (GW) of energy individually. Japan also aggressively exports its WTE technology, with Hitachi Zosen, Mitsubishi Heavy Engineering, and JFE Engineering at the forefront. Japan has been putting up WTE plants across Asia in Vietnam, Indonesia and the Philippines.

Japan and the Scandinavian nations are the global WTE leaders—they burn 75% of their municipal waste. They are followed by Switzerland at 47%, the UK at 42%, France at 38%, Germany at 31% and the US at 12%. However, US plants are much bigger. In 2021, the US produced 13.6 GW of energy from 64 WTE plants, in which biomass materials accounted for 60% of the weight and 45% of the energy. Dry waste, including paper, synthetics and plastics, produced 55% of the energy. Unfortunately, most WTE plants produce high emissions and are still not a source of clean energy.

THE FUTURE OF RECYCLING: 20 YEARS LATER

Dozens of scientists and engineers are working furiously to create a new world of recycled waste. The broken global supply chains, shortage of REE, digital wars and the vast amount of digital melt will all provide opportunities for the circular economy of the next decade. Hundreds of other engineers and scientists are also working to produce energy from waste and recycling digital meltdowns. Many new initiatives are producing clean energy, some of it from renewable sources, some entirely from waste.

The key problem with recycling is choosing the right process to break down the composite waste structure from landfills without a high carbon footprint. The burning of waste that is widely prevalent today is polluting and toxic. When the microfluidic sample extraction from composite wastes, being trialed by the NTU lab, becomes a commercial practice, much more efficient and nontoxic processes than the traditional method of incineration and separation will evolve. Feedback from the industry shows that the next ten years might unravel many sustainable solutions, which could change how we manage our toxic waste. An optimum recycling process that produces fewer pollutants and effluents could be available. So, costs will reduce, and volumes will rise.

For example, we can analyze and source the types of waste needed to process aluminum and platinum. We will also have the requisite plant and machinery to extract these metals efficiently from industrial and municipal wastes. Recycling aluminum requires 5% of the energy needed to mine bauxite ore, refine it into aluminum oxide, and again refine it into aluminum metal. So, nearly one-third of the aluminum in use today is recycled from used Coke cans into automobile parts, making it the third most recyclable product after paper and steel. Nearly $5 billion worth of aluminum scrap was recycled in 2020. The recycling market is growing at a phenomenal pace of over 8% compound annual growth rate (CAGR) and is expected to touch $25 billion by 2030. It will surely outpace the global bauxite market size of around $15 billion in 2020 that grows at less than 1.8% CAGR. That would mean more recycled aluminum would be in use than the mined product and would be the way forward 20 years later.

The global metal recycling market was $217 billion in 2020 and could double by 2030 with a CAGR of 6%. However, that original estimate did not consider the long-drawn out effect of the Covid-19 pandemic returning in new variants and the Russia–Ukraine war, which could run for years. NATO's expansion across Europe has made the US alliance much stronger. It has also made Russia more insecure and hostile and move closer to China, forming a formidable communist block that is no pushover, especially as it has close allies in the mineral-rich states of Africa the Gulf nations and South America. If the digital meltdown escalated, with or without digital wars, mining requirements could jump fourfold to produce the required semiconductors, electronic components and catalytic converters, besides computers, cars and gadgets from the broken supply chains. Even if we avoid digital wars, the mining needs would have to grow sizably to meet the existing commitments made by the US and China to boost their local supply lines following the Chips Act and China's self-reliance directive. So, the next 20 years will be difficult for manufacturing and will force recycling because of this two independent supply chains meeting the global supply and demand gap.

We explored five key technologies in the first part of this book and four key applications in the second part. The technology of recycling waste, including digital waste, is perhaps the most important addition to the process of understanding and sustainably using technology. You cannot throw away your old smartphone, batteries, laptops or television sets as junk. No more. They are all resources and must have multiple digital marketplaces for recycled goods and warehouses to store, segregate, and process units to turn them back into raw materials or energy for reuse.

In the next 20 years, we may well see that happening, especially outside the US where resource shortage haunts the citizen's most. The science of recycling waste might step out of the shadows and earn the respectability and monetary muscle it deserves as raw materials become scarce due to supply chain disruptions.

Scientists and engineers will turn landfills into resource pools that could be exploited and monetized, like any other mining resource. We must remember that any business becomes sustainable not because it is a great cause but because it turns profitable. A resource crisis that we might face in the coming days due to supply chain disruptions would be destabilizing; however, it would provide great opportunities for entrepreneurs who could profit from the recycling trade.

In the next 20 years, you could find Doraemon, Dozer and a host of cartoon and manga artists performing imaginative storytelling across the massive landfills we created, just like Astroboy and Captain Nemo did decades ago when going around the world. They will connect with modern-day scientists and engineers and produce games, movies and animation films for startups who cleaned up the earth and built multimillion dollar businesses from scrap. That will inspire the next generation, brought up on stories of a clean, sustainable world, to create a circular economy and turn things around for the better. Profits, not activism, deliver solutions that are technology-driven and making technology and consumer waste sustainable and profitable is the next big barrier to cross.

Afterword

Conclusion

Burning waste to turn it into energy is a temporary measure and not sustainable in the long run. It must change into a pollution-free solution in the near future. Like waste management, renewable energy today is at an inflection point. It is just where computers were around 50 years ago. In 1965, Gordon Moore, the founder of Intel, made an interesting observation. The number of transistors in integral circuits doubled every 18 months to two years without increasing costs. This meant the computational power was doubling at the same cost. This observation of exponentially accelerating technology at the same cost, later termed Moore's Law, was not only unique at that time. It defied the odds and kept repeating itself for the next 50 years. It led to data prices nosediving and, consequently, to data usage skyrocketing.

Energy, like technology, is an enabler, giving wings to industries and commerce to multiply and reach scalable levels quickly. The lower the cost, the more the usage and benefits for humanity. Today, renewable energy produced globally doubles every couple of years, with the cost remaining constant. This is because, the cost of renewable energy, which was three times the cost of thermal energy produced by coal power plants just 5 years ago, had dropped sharply before this decade started in 2020. It made renewable energy in certain areas as cheap as energy from fossil fuels like coal. This is just the beginning. Power producers are grappling with the problem of how to price power from the grid when gridless renewable energy is popular and available with near-zero running costs in the future. Today, the US consumes twice the energy that most European nations consume, three times that of China and five times as much as India. If renewable energy costs dipped further, Europe, China, and India would have the same opportunities as the US.

There is another reason why this decade is the tipping point. Had this book been written before 2020, only nine positive, gung-ho technologies would have been covered in Part I and II of the book because the decade of uncertainty had not started. Now, we have a more holistic template that

DOI: 10.1201/9781003409557-18

will be needed for future living. However, this is neither a complete list nor a complete solution without the energy sector. This book barely skims the surface of a mighty ocean. We hope this will lead to more research and books on new technologies and future living. We have already started working on our next technology book for future collaboration with an expert in an industry undergoing a supply chain crisis—and soon plan to write a third book on future of living with renewable energy and the evolution of the circular economy.

Photovoltaic cells that today account for the phenomenal growth of the solar industry are like the diodes and transistors of yesteryear. In our book on new energy, we will explore how science is looking at the possibilities beyond photovoltaic cells; from wind to hydrogen to mirrors, how scientists and engineers are relentlessly pushing boundaries and trying to find the energy sector's equivalent of semiconductors; how over half a dozen variants of renewable energy sources are being developed to meet the needs of the future world; how sustainability will become profitable despite the pushback from the fossil fuel industry besides volatility and recession. This will need a lot of research and probing because, like the technology industry, the energy industry is moving rapidly, changing and growing exponentially, which is often difficult to track and document. Until then, au revoir.

Bibliography

1   The Internet of Things: All Things Interactive

Blum, A., & Baraka, C. (2022). With 1.4 billion inhabitants Africa is the least connected continent. Retrieved from https://restofworld.org/2022/google-meta-underwater-cables/

Gabriel, P. (2019). Decades after Reagan's Star Wars Trump calls missile defenses. Retrieved from https://www.science.org/content/article/decades-after-reagan-s-star-wars-trump-calls-missile-defenses-would-blast-warheads-sky

Gasparini, A. (2021). Stanford's NIAC fellows are working to bring Sci fi concepts to real space exploration. Retrieved from https://news.stanford.edu/2021/05/03/bringing-sci-fi-concepts-real-space-exploration/

Grijpink, F., Ménard, A., Sigurdsson, H., & Vucevic, N. (2018). The road to 5G the inevitable growth of infrastructure cost. Retrieved from https://www.mckinsey.com/industries/technology-media-and-telecommunications/our-insights/the-road-to-5g-the-inevitable-growth-of-infrastructure-cost

GSMA. (2019). Mass deployments of IoT solutions transforming China, says GSMA. Retrieved from https://www.businesswire.com/news/home/20190626005572/en/Mass-Deployments-of-IoT-Solutions-Transforming-China-Says-GSMA

Gurkan, A. (2019). The internet of things will bring the internet's business model into the rest of the world. Retrieved from https://www.economist.com/technology-quarterly/2019/09/12/the-internet-of-things-will-bring-the-internets-business-model-into-the-rest-of-the-world?gclid=Cj0KCQiAt66eBhCnARIsAKf3ZNEtw81gEzavWCHiKVYnvSvPHZkWI3yScCtW7gN0OOSwbwFMklxdK20aArpdEALw_wcB&gclsrc=aw.ds

Pearson, N. O. (2020). Did a Chinese hack kill Canada's greatest tech company. Retrieved from https://www.bloomberg.com/news/features/2020-07-01/did-china-steal-canada-s-edge-in-5g-from-nortel

Silica, A. (2018). Interview with IoT inventor Kevin Ashton, IoT is driven by users. Retrieved from https://www.avnet.com/wps/portal/silica/resources/article/interview-with-iot-inventor-kevin-ashton-iot-is-driven-by-the-users/

Strawn, G. (2003). A brief history of NSF and the internet. Retrieved from https://www.nsf.gov/news/news_summ.jsp?cntn_id=103050

Sumits, A. (2015). History and future of the internet traffic. Retrieved from https://blogs.cisco.com/sp/the-history-and-future-of-internet-traffic

2   Artificial Intelligence: Adding to Our Three Pounds

Carew, J. M. (2020). Prescriptive analytics in healthcare finds use amidst pandemic. Retrieved from https://www.techtarget.com/searchbusinessanalytics/feature/Presc riptive-analytics-in-healthcare-finds-use-amidst-pandemic

Carlson, N. (2010). The full story of how Facebook was founded. Retrieved from https://www.businessinsider.com/how-facebook-was-founded-2010-3?IR=T#we-can-talk-about-that-after-i-get-all-the-basic-functionality-up-tomorrow-night-1

Constine, J. (2013). Compassion researcher helps Facebook App get emotional with animated stickers. Retrieved from https://techcrunch.com/2013/04/26/facebook-animated-stickers/

Dagle, B. (2021). Data centres around the world: A quick look. Retrieved from https://www.usitc.gov/publications/332/executive_briefings/ebot_data_centers_a round_the_world.pdf

GPT 3. (2020). A robot wrote this entire article, does that scare you human. Retrieved from https://www.theguardian.com/commentisfree/2020/sep/08/robot-wrote-this-article-gpt-3

Malik, A. (2022). Amazon's new physical retail analytics service gives brands shopper data and product and as performance. Retrieved from https://techcrunch.com/2022/06/29/amazons-physical-retail-analytics-service-gives-brands-shopper-data-ad-product-performance/

Marr, B. (2015). Big data in big oil. How Shell uses analytics to drive business. Retrieved from https://www.forbes.com/sites/bernardmarr/2015/05/26/big-data-in-big-oil-how-shell-uses-analytics-to-drive-business-success/?sh=42d87017229e

Morgan, B. (2018). How Amazon has reorganised around artificial intelligence and machine learning. Retrieved from https://www.forbes.com/sites/blakemorgan/2018/07/16/how-amazon-has-re-organized-around-artificial-intelligence-and-machine-learning/?sh=7d1bda73618b

Smith., B. (2021). Orwell 1984 could happen in 2024. Retrieved from https://www.bbc.com/news/technology-57122120

Thompson, C. (2014). Computers will be like humans by 2029: Google's Ray Kurzweil. Retrieved from https://www.cnbc.com/2014/06/11/computers-will-be-like-humans-by-2029-googles-ray-kurzweil.html

3   Robots: The Machines Learn

Amenemhet. *Clepsydra of Karnak* (Sculpture) Retrieved from https://egypt-museum.com/clepsydra-of-karnak/

Greenemeier, L. (2016). GPS and the world's first space war. Retrieved from https://www.scientificamerican.com/article/gps-and-the-world-s-first-space-war/

Ito, J. (2018).Why Westerners fear robots and Japanese do not. https://www.wired.com/story/ideas-joi-ito-robot-overlords/

Kageyema, Y. (2021). Smart robots do all the work at Nissan's 'intelligent' plant. Retrieved from https://apnews.com/article/technology-business-japan-84a67e727 3b32a15a9e6ee1502b57d86

Nikkei. (2017). Fujitsu relies robots that discerns emotions. Retrieved from, https://asia.nikkei.com/Business/Fujitsu-readies-robot-that-discerns-emotions-pref erences

Saige, C. (2017). Asimov's laws won't stop robots from harming humans so we have developed a better solution. Retrieved from https://www.scientificamerican.com/article/asimovs-laws-wont-stop-robots-from-harming-humans-so-weve-developed-a-better-solution/

Sandoval, E. B. (2020). Social robots show promise for future pandemics. Retrieved from https://newsroom.unsw.edu.au/news/art-architecture-design/social-storiesrobots-show-promise-future-pandemics

Schomberg, H. (1988). For the first time a chess computer outwits a grandmaster in a tournament. Retrieved from https://www.nytimes.com/1988/09/26/nyregion/for-first-time-a-chess-computer-outwits-grandmaster-in-tournament.html

Tsuneoka, C. (2020). This Japanese engineer created the robots that make your car. Retrieved from https://www.wsj.com/articles/this-japanese-engineer-created-the-robots-that-make-your-cars-11602856803

Westmaas, R. (2019). We may finally come to know how the pyramids were built. Retrieved from https://www.discovery.com/exploration/how-the-pyramids-were-built

4   Blockchain: Keeping Track

Brue, M. (2021). Blockchain beyond bitcoin transforming fintech healthcare and more. Retrieved from https://www.forbes.com/sites/moorinsights/2021/01/15/blockchain-beyond-bitcoin-transforming-fintech-healthcare-and-more/?sh=39fabec667

Copeland, J. (2012). Alan Turing, the code breaker who saved millions of lives. Retrieved from https://www.bbc.com/news/technology-18419691

Darda, M. (2021). How the Internet of contracts will define a new era of business. Retrieved from https://www.outlookindia.com/website/story/business-news-how-the-internet-of-contracts-will-define-a-new-era-of-business/405026

Department of Justice (2017). AlphaBay the largest dark market shut down. Retrieved from https://www.justice.gov/opa/pr/alphabay-largest-online-dark-market-shut-down

Kastner, E. (2017). History of the dark net. Retrieved from https://www.soscanhelp.com/blog/history-of-the-dark-web

MI News Network. (2019). 7 major blockchain technology developments in maritime industry. Retrieved from https://www.marineinsight.com/know-more/7-major-blockchain-technology-developments-in-maritime-industry-in-2018/

Morey, J. (2021). The future of blockchain in healthcare. Retrieved from https://www.forbes.com/sites/forbestechcouncil/2021/10/25/the-future-of-blockchain-in-healthcare/?sh=1a5e7036541f

Pollock, L. (2011). How a Pentagon program and a hacker assisted a revolution. Retrieved from https://www.popsci.com/technology/article/2011-07/how-pentagon-program-and-hacker-assisted-revolution/

Rapier, G. (2017). From Yelp reviews to mango shipments IBM CEO on how blockchain will change the world. Retrieved from https://www.businessinsider.in/finance/from-yelp-reviews-to-mango-shipments-ibms-ceo-on-how-blockchain-will-change-the-world/articleshow/59257222.cms

Roxburgh, A. (2016). A short history of darknet markets and impact disruptions along the way. Retrieved from https://ndarc.med.unsw.edu.au/blog/short-history-darknet-markets-and-impact-disruptions-along-way

5   Cryptocurrencies: Beyond Tracking

Bloomberg, E. O. (2021). Nigeria becomes first African nation to roll out digital money. Retrieved from https://www.aljazeera.com/economy/2021/10/25/nigeria-becomes-first-african-nation-to-roll-out-digital-money

Del Castillo, M. (2021). Corporate America cashes in on Bitcoin mania. Retrieved from https://www.forbes.com/sites/michaeldelcastillo/2021/02/02/forbes-blockchain-50-corporate-america-cashes-in-on-bitcoin-mania/?sh=7be826636e01

Guttierez, M. (2022). Crypto is banned in China and 8 other countries. Retrieved from https://fortune.com/2022/01/04/crypto-banned-china-other-countries/

Iwamato, K. (2022). Cambodia's digital currency reaches nearly half the population. Retrieved from https://asia.nikkei.com/Business/Finance/Cambodia-s-digital-currency-reaches-nearly-half-the-population

Revill, J., & Wilson, T. (2022). Switzerland tests digital currency with top investment banks. Retrieved from https://www.reuters.com/technology/switzerland-tests-digital-currency-payments-with-top-investment-banks-2022-01-13/

Schmidt, J., & Powel, F. (2022). Why does Bitcoin use so much energy. Retrieved from https://www.forbes.com/advisor/investing/cryptocurrency/bitcoins-energy-usage-explained/

Shaxson, N. (2019). Tackling global tax havens. Retrieved from https://www.imf.org/en/Publications/fandd/issues/2019/09/tackling-global-tax-havens-shaxon

Sigalos, M. (2021). Bitcoin mining difficulty drops after hash rate collapse in China. Retrieved from https://www.cnbc.com/2021/07/03/bitcoin-mining-difficulty-drops-after-hashrate-collapse-in-china-.html

Stevens, R. (2022). Can you still mine bitcoin and other crypto from home. Retrieved from https://www.coindesk.com/learn/can-you-still-mine-bitcoin-and-other-crypto-from-home/

Tiwari, M. (2021). Only 2 million bitcoins left to be mined, here is what happens when it runs out of supply. Retrieved from https://www.indiatoday.in/technology/features/story/only-2-million-bitcoins-left-to-be-mined-here-is-what-happens-it-runs-out-of-supply-1894586-2021-12-31

6   Cyber and Financial Crimes: Ruling the High Seas

BBC. (2021). Coronavirus: The world in lockdown, in maps and charts. Retrieved from https://www.bbc.com/news/world-52103747

BBC. (2021). Why the Wuhan Coronavirus lab leak theory is being taken seriously. Retrieved from https://www.bbc.com/news/world-asia-china-57268111

Carmiel, D. (2022). 5 trends shaping the future of cybercrime threat intelligence. Retrieved from https://www.forbes.com/sites/forbestechcouncil/2022/12/19/5-trends-shaping-the-future-of-cybercrime-threat-intelligence/?sh=1f2d815730a6

Duggan, H., & Glade, M. (2020). Financial crime increases in global crisis. Retrieved from https://www.fticonsulting.com/-/media/files/emea--files/insights/articles/2020/may/financial-crime-increases-global-crisis-covid-19.pdf?rev=4ecc0 4e2e3a842ae8d24125d02342703&hash=DD99C466802C23480E677F682 A9172AB

Europol. (2020). Covid 19 sparks upward trend in cybercrime. Retrieved from https://www.europol.europa.eu/media-press/newsroom/news/covid-19-sparks-upward-trend-in-cybercrime

Fearn, N. (2021). Why some jobseekers have turned to cyber crime during the pandemic. Retrieved from https://www.computerweekly.com/feature/Why-some-job seekers-have-turned-to-cyber-crime-during-the-pandemic

ILO. (2020). 81 million jobs lost as Covid 19 creates turmoil in Asia Pacific labour market. Retrieved from https://www.ilo.org/asia/media-centre/news/WCMS_763 819/lang--en/index.htm

Jones, D. (2022). Ransomware attacks, payouts soared worldwide in 2021. Retrieved from https://www.cybersecuritydive.com/news/ransomware-attacks-payouts-2021/622784/

Sheng, E. (2020). Cybercrime ramps up amid coronavirus chaos costing companies billions. Retrieved from https://www.cnbc.com/2020/07/29/cybercrime-ramps-up-amid-coronavirus-chaos-costing-companies-billions.html

Whitaker, Z., & Page, C. (2022). Meet the cybercriminals of 2022. Retrieved from https://techcrunch.com/2022/12/30/meet-the-cybercriminals-2022/

7   Digital Transformation: Will it Cut or Grow Jobs?

Benioff, M. (2018). What is digital transformation. Retrieved from https://www.sal esforce.com/in/products/platform/what-is-digital-transformation/

Brics Business Magazine (2019). Through the digital barrier. Retrieved from https://www.bricsmagazine.com/en/articles/through-the-digital-barrier-025a408e-ead8-4e91-a06f-10406f95d32f

Chime, V. (2022). Covid 19 and the acceleration of digital transformation in Nigeria. Retrieved from https://guardian.ng/opinion/covid-19-and-acceleration-of-digital-transformation-in-nigeria/

Eloksari, E. A. (2020). Indonesian internet users hit 196 million, still concentrated in Java. Retrieved from https://www.thejakartapost.com/news/2020/11/11/indones ian-internet-users-hit-196-million-still-concentrated-in-java-apjii-survey.html.

Kitani, K. (2019). The $900 billion reason why GE, Ford and P&G digital transformation program failed last year. Retrieved from https://www.cnbc.com/2019/10/30/heres-why-ge-fords-digital-transformation-programs-failed-last-year.html

McKinsey. (2020). How Covid 19 has pushed companies over the technology tipping point and transformed business forever. Retrieved from https://www.mckinsey.com/business-functions/strategy-and-corporate-finance/our-insights/how-covid-19-has-pushed-companies-over-the-technology-tipping-point-and-transformed-business-forever

Morgan, B. (2019). 30 companies that failed at digital transformation that we can learn from. Retrieved from https://www.forbes.com/sites/blakemorgan/2019/09/30/companies-that-failed-at-digital-transformation-and-what-we-can-learn-from-them/?sh=71aa208a603c

Roy, M. (2021). Top 6 reasons why digital transformation failures happen. Retrieved from https://www.techtarget.com/searchcio/tip/Top-6-reasons-why-digital-transformation-failures-happen

Tabrizi, B., & Lam, E. (2019). Digital transformation is not about tech. Retrieved from https://hbr.org/2019/03/digital-transformation-is-not-about-technology

Thomas, L. (2020). Nike's online business is booming, digital is here to stay. Retrieved from https://www.cnbc.com/2020/09/23/nikes-ceo-says-digital-is-here-to-stay-e-com-business-fuels-sales.html

8   Telehealth: Distant Cure

Apollo Healthcare. (2019). The benefits of telehealth in rural health care. Retrieved fromhttps://www.apollotelehealth.com/the-benefits-of-telemedicine-in-rural-areas/

Bestnenny, O., Gilbert, G., Harris, A., & Rost, J. (2021). Telehealth a quarter trillion dollar post Covid 19 reality. Retrieved from https://www.mckinsey.com/industries/healthcare/our-insights/telehealth-a-quarter-trillion-dollar-post-covid-19-reality

Bose, A. (2022). Apple leads the global wearables market. Retrieved from https://timesofindia.indiatimes.com/gadgets-news/apple-leads-the-global-wearables-market-here-how-samsung-and-others-performed/articleshow/92108520.cms

Drenik, G. (2022). The future of telehealth in a post pandemic world. Retrieved from https://www.forbes.com/sites/garydrenik/2022/06/02/the-future-of-telehealth-in-a-post-pandemic-world/

Fortune Business Insight. (2020). 2020–2027, Telemedicine market report. Retrieved from https://www.fortunebusinessinsights.com/industry-reports/telemedicine-market-101067

Kruglyak, I. (2023). 20 examples of wearables and IoT disrupting healthcare. Retrieved from https://www.avenga.com/magazine/wearables-iot-healthcare/

Novak, M. (2012). Telemedicine predicted in 1925. Retrieved from https://www.smithsonianmag.com/history/telemedicine-predicted-in-1925-124140942/

Schroer, A. (2022). 10 examples of wearable technology in healthcare and medical devices. Retrieved from https://builtin.com/healthcare-technology/wearable-technology-in-healthcare

Sucich, K. (2020). The growth of telehealth and how analytics can support it. Retrieved from https://www.dimins.com/blog/2020/03/25/analytics-support-telehealth/

Varshney, R. (2021). The growing role of artificial intelligence in telehealth. Retrieved from https://www.medtechintelligence.com/column/the-growing-role-of-artificial-intelligence-in-telehealth/

9   Edu Tech: Remote Learning

AFP. (2018). Robot teacher Keeko invades Chinese kindergartens. Retrieved from https://www.ndtv.com/world-news/robot-teacher-keeko-invades-chinese-kindergartens-1908138

Anand, S. (2022). India's Edtech startups regroup as pandemic bonanza fizzles. Retrieved from https://www.livemint.com/companies/start-ups/indias-edtech-startups-regroup-as-pandemic-bonanza-fizzles-11662895983297.html

Geromel, R. (2019). Why is China leader in edtech. Retrieved from https://www.for
bes.com/sites/ricardogeromel/2019/04/05/why-is-china-the-worlds-leader-in-edt
ech/?sh=2ffbbcd85756

History of BBC. (1957). BBC Television for Schools. Retrieved from https://www.
bbc.com/historyofthebbc/anniversaries/september/bbc-television-for-schools/

Hollander, S. (2013). When a teacher is 2 ft tall. Retrieved from https://www.wsj.
com/articles/SB10001424127887323820304578410730962208740

Kelly, S. (2021). 18 things that remain the same after 30 years of teaching. Retrieved
from   https://educationtothecore.com/2021/04/18-things-that-remain-the-same-
after-30-years-of-teaching/

National Museum of American History. (2020) Skinner Teaching Machine. Retrieved
from https://americanhistory.si.edu/collections/search/object/nmah_690062

Petch, L. A. (2022). Is there a place for rote learning multiplication tables in
English primary schools. Retrieved from https://www.herts.ac.uk/link/volume-
2,-issue-1/is-there-a-place-for-rote-learning-multiplication-tables-in-english-prim
ary-schools

Spence, R. (2022). Edtechs honeymoon might be over but expect a second boom.
Retrieved   from   https://techcrunch.com/2022/10/04/edtechs-honeymoon-might-
be-over-but-expect-a-second-boom/

Wan, T. (2021). A record year amid pandemic, US Edtech raises $2.2 billion in
2021. Retrieved from https://www.edsurge.com/news/2021-01-13-a-record-year-
amid-a-pandemic-us-edtech-raises-2-2-billion-in-2020

10   Metaworld: Virtual Reality

Antin, D. (2020). 10 sci fi stories that inspire the pioneers of met averse. Retrieved
from   https://medium.com/predict/10-sci-fi-stories-that-inspire-pioneers-of-the-
metaverse-66fd811be218

Associated Press. (2021). Missing the moment: Will virtual reality ever take off.
Retrieved from https://lifestyle.livemint.com/smart-living/innovation/missing-the-
moment-will-virtual-reality-ever-take-off-111622578705026.html

Bradshaw, T. (2022). Can augmented reality really take of where VR has failed.
Retrieved   from.   https://www.ft.com/content/83f54137-3374-48f6-a4ee-7a52b
aa422a7

Frank, A. (2022). Bella Hadid arrives in the metaverse with a new line of NFT.
Retrieved from https://www.vogue.com/article/bella-hadid-nft-metaverse-interview

O'flaherty, K. (2021). Apples Stunning iOs 14 privacy move a game changer.
Retrieved from https://www.forbes.com/sites/kateoflahertyuk/2021/01/31/apples-
stunning-ios-14-privacy-move-a-game-changer-for-all-iphone-users/?sh=6ada2
fff7e8d

Novet, J. (2021). Microsoft wins contract to make modified hololens for US army.
Retrieved   from   https://www.cnbc.com/2021/03/31/microsoft-wins-contract-to-
make-modified-hololens-for-us-army.html

Porter, M. E. (2017). Why every organization needs an augmented reality strategy.
Retrieved from https://hbr.org/2017/11/why-every-organization-needs-an-augmen
ted-reality-strategy

Silberling, A. (2022). Meta says it's metverse lost another $3 billion.... But the 2030 looks promising. Retrieved from https://techcrunch.com/2022/04/27/meta-facebook-q1-2022-earnings/

Silverling, A. (2021). Apple's privacy changes show the power it holds over other industries. Retrieved from https://www.cnbc.com/2021/11/13/apples-privacy-changes-show-the-power-it-holds-over-other-industries.html

Whittaker, Z. (2022). Apple restricts adds and third party trackers for iPhone. Retrieved from https://techcrunch.com/2019/06/03/apple-kid-apps-trackers/

11   Venture Capital: For Profit or Cause

CBINSIGHTS. (2019). 50 European unicorns ranked by valuation. Retrieved from https://www.cbinsights.com/research/european-unicorns-valuation/

Dillet. R. (2021). BlaBla car raises $115 million to build all in one travel app. Retrieved from https://techcrunch.com/2021/04/20/blablacar-raises-115-million-to-build-all-in-one-travel-app/ https://www.investopedia.com/best-crowdfunding-platforms-5079933

Lee, J. L. (2021). Venture capital hits record high in US despite 2020 pandemic. Retrieved from https://www.reuters.com/article/us-venture-capital-data-idUSKBN29D0IR

Marquee Equity. (2021). The future of venture capital. Retrieved from https://marquee-equity.com/blog/future-of-venture-capital/

Nelson, E., & Satariano, A.(2022). European green energy firms often fall short of financing. Retrieved from https://www.nytimes.com/2022/04/18/business/europe-green-energy-investors.html

Reuters. (2010). Chinese solar company shelves IPO. Retrieved from https://www.reuters.com/article/us-jinkosolar-ipo-idUSTRE61A04T20100211

Sahay, P. (2017) Raining dollars: Why limited partners are investing directly in Indian startups. Retrieved from https://www.moneycontrol.com/news/business/startup/raining-dollars-why-limited-partners-are-investing-directly-in-indian-startups-2441487.html

Start up stalky. (2021). Top 10 startups in Europe. Retrieved from https://startuptalky.com/startups-in-europe/

Tiwari, S. (2021). How Nykka captured the online beauty market in India even before its IPO. Retrieved from https://www.moneycontrol.com/news/trends/features/storyboard-how-nykaa-captured-the-online-beauty-market-in-india-even-before-its-ipo-7656381.html

Voltstorage. (2021). Storage systems for energy transition. Retrieved from, https://voltstorage.com/en/investment-2022/

12   The Great Digital Meltdown: A Fractured World

Bashuk, B. (2022).War tearing trade apart, hitting logistics, prices and supply. Retrieved from https://www.bloomberg.com/news/newsletters/2022-03-08/supply-chain-latest-war-s-effects-already-hurting-supply-logistics

Buchaniek, C. (2022). US consumers expect cyberattacks on uncrewed military vehicles. Retrieved from https://www.c4isrnet.com/home/2022/08/23/us-consumers-expect-cy berattacks-on-uncrewed-military-vehicles/

Burgis, T. (2016). Looting machine oligarchs, corporations, smugglers and the theft of Africa's wealth. Retrieved from https://www.amazon.com/Looting-Machine-Oligarchs-Corporations-Smugglers/dp/1610397118

Carpenter, T. G. (2022). Many predicted NATO expansion would lead to war, those warnings were ignored. Retrieved from https://www.theguardian.com/commentisfree/2022/feb/28/nato-expansion-war-russia-ukraine,

Nalawade, S. (2022).Battle cyber threats enable revops and build effective DEI strategies. Retrieved from https://www.spiceworks.com/tech/tech-general/articles/battle-cyber-threats-enable-revops-and-build-effective-dei-strategies/

Panag, H. S. (2022). China is preparing for a full spectrum AI war, India is still 15 years behind. Retrieved from https://theprint.in/opinion/china-is-preparing-for-a-full-spectrum-ai-war-india-is-still-15-years-behind/1098942/

Sanger, D. E. (2021). China appears to warn India: Push us too hard and the lights go out. Retrieved from https://www.nytimes.com/2021/02/28/us/politics/china-india-hacking-electricity.html

Stubbington. T., & Duguid, K. (2022). Soaring Dollar raises spectre of reverse currency war. Retrieved from https://www.ft.com/content/2eca224f-7923-4f9b-ba11-6c8832768edf

Taylor, C. (2019). US China trade war is unresolvable: Strategists say. Retrieved from https://www.cnbc.com/2019/12/03/us-china-trade-war-is-unresolvable-strategist-says.html

Tollefson, J. (2022). What the war in Ukraine means for energy, climate and food. Retrieved from https://www.nature.com/articles/d41586-022-00969-9

13 The Circular Economy: Recycling the Meltdown

Bearup, G. (2015). Turning trash into treasure. Retrieved from https://www.smart.unsw.edu.au/news-events/news/australian-feature-story-green-steel

Bloomberg News. (2022). China orders government state firms to dump foreign pcs. Retrieved from https://www.bloomberg.com/news/articles/2022-05-06/china-orders-government-state-firms-to-dump-foreign-pcs

Clifford, C. (2022). Hydrogen power is gaining momentum but critics say it is neither efficient nor green enough. Retrieved from https://www.cnbc.com/2022/01/06/what-is-green-hydrogen-vs-blue-hydrogen-and-why-it-matters.html

Dangwal, N. (2022). Netizens 'warn' Elon Musk as China displays mammoth 'anti-starlink' Radar SLC-18P At Zhuhai Airshow. Retrieved from https://eurasiantimes.com/netizens-warn-elon-musk-as-china-displays-mammoth-anti-starlink/#amp_tf=From%20%251%24s&aoh=16680796905145&csi=0&referrer=https%3A%2F%2Fwww.google.com

Indo Asian News Services. (2018). Mumbai born Indo Australian scientist Veena Sahajwalla develops worlds first micro factory to tack, Retrieved from https://www.ndtv.com/indians-abroad/mumbai-born-indo-australian-scientist-veena-sahajwalla-develops-worlds-first-microfactory-to-tackle--1834826 https://www.ndtv.com/indians-abroad/mumbai-born-indo-australian-scientist-veena-sahajwalla-develops-worlds-first-microfactory-to-tackle--1834826

Joshi, N. (2022). The roadblocks coming in the way of the circular economy. Retrieved from https://www.forbes.com/sites/naveenjoshi/2022/05/02/the-roadblocks-standing-in-the-way-of-the-circular-economy-dream/?sh=2776a8a84c38

Kadam, T. (2022). Blasting satellites, crippling attacks -- Russia's invasion of Ukraine has given a clear glimpse of future wars. Retrieved from https://eurasiantimes.com/russias-invasion-of-ukraine-has-given-a-clear-glimpse-of-future-wars/?amp

NTU. (2020). NTU Singapore scientists use fruit peel turn old batteries new. Retrieved from https://www.sciencecodex.com/ntu-singapore-scientists-use-fruit-peel-turn-old-batteries-new-655115

Szewczyk, C. (2022). E waste is an untapped source of rare earth materials. Retrieved from https://www.pcgamer.com/e-waste-is-an-untapped-source-of-rare-earth-materials/

UT News. (2017). Lithium-ion battery inventor introduces new technology for fast-charging, noncombustible batteries. Retrieved from https://news.utexas.edu/2017/02/28/goodenough-introduces-new-battery-technology/

Printed in the USA
CPSIA information can be obtained
at www.ICGtesting.com
LVHW020605170924
791293LV00001B/147

9 781032 529837